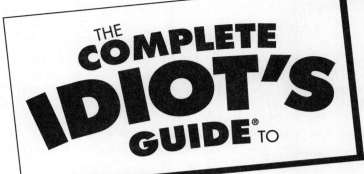

# THE COMPLETE IDIOT'S GUIDE® TO

# Recession-Proof Careers

*by Jeff Cohen*

## ALPHA

A member of Penguin Group (USA) Inc.

*For Gabriel, my little man who is quickly becoming a big boy.*

## ALPHA BOOKS

Published by the Penguin Group

Penguin Group (USA) Inc., 375 Hudson Street, New York, New York 10014, USA

Penguin Group (Canada), 90 Eglinton Avenue East, Suite 700, Toronto, Ontario M4P 2Y3, Canada (a division of Pearson Penguin Canada Inc.)

Penguin Books Ltd., 80 Strand, London WC2R 0RL, England

Penguin Ireland, 25 St. Stephen's Green, Dublin 2, Ireland (a division of Penguin Books Ltd.)

Penguin Group (Australia), 250 Camberwell Road, Camberwell, Victoria 3124, Australia (a division of Pearson Australia Group Pty. Ltd.)

Penguin Books India Pvt. Ltd., 11 Community Centre, Panchsheel Park, New Delhi—110 017, India

Penguin Group (NZ), 67 Apollo Drive, Rosedale, North Shore, Auckland 1311, New Zealand (a division of Pearson New Zealand Ltd.)

Penguin Books (South Africa) (Pty.) Ltd., 24 Sturdee Avenue, Rosebank, Johannesburg 2196, South Africa

Penguin Books Ltd., Registered Offices: 80 Strand, London WC2R 0RL, England

International Standard Book Number: 978-1-59257-971-6
Library of Congress Catalog Card Number: 2009932859

12   11   10        8   7   6   5   4   3   2   1

Interpretation of the printing code: The rightmost number of the first series of numbers is the year of the book's printing; the rightmost number of the second series of numbers is the number of the book's printing. For example, a printing code of 10-1 shows that the first printing occurred in 2010.

*Printed in the United States of America*

**Note:** This publication contains the opinions and ideas of its author. It is intended to provide helpful and informative material on the subject matter covered. It is sold with the understanding that the author and publisher are not engaged in rendering professional services in the book. If the reader requires personal assistance or advice, a competent professional should be consulted.

The author and publisher specifically disclaim any responsibility for any liability, loss, or risk, personal or otherwise, which is incurred as a consequence, directly or indirectly, of the use and application of any of the contents of this book.

Most Alpha books are available at special quantity discounts for bulk purchases for sales promotions, premiums, fundraising, or educational use. Special books, or book excerpts, can also be created to fit specific needs.

For details, write: Special Markets, Alpha Books, 375 Hudson Street, New York, NY 10014.

**Publisher:** *Marie Butler-Knight*
**Editorial Director:** *Mike Sanders*
**Senior Managing Editor:** *Billy Fields*
**Acquisitions Editor:** *Karyn Gerhard*
**Development Editor:** *Julie Coffin*
**Production Editor:** *Kayla Dugger*

**Copy Editor:** *Cate Schwenk*
**Cartoonist:** *Steve Barr*
**Cover Designer:** *Bill Thomas*
**Book Designer:** *Trina Wurst*
**Indexer:** *Tonya Heard*
**Layout:** *Chad Dressler*
**Proofreader:** *John Etchison*

# Contents at a Glance

# Contents

# Foreword

One by-product of the current financial turmoil is that hardly a day goes by without some pundit coining a new name for the upheaval. The Second Depression, Great Recession, and Nightmare on Wall Street are just a few that have been bounced around. But whatever name we finally end up with, it is certain to be a turning point in how work is organized. And while the emphasis understandably has been on the pain, economic upheaval also presents opportunities as people draw on creativity to reinvent themselves.

In the past, every broad shift in the economy has resulted in reinventing, redefining, and re-energizing the workforce. The nineteenth century's Industrial Revolution, culminating in the Great Depression, transformed an agrarian society into an industrialized one marked by a mobile workforce. Stagflation in the 1970s signaled the decline in manufacturing in the United States and the rise of a knowledge-based, service-oriented economy. Finally, the dot-com-driven 2000 recession marked the explosive growth of the Internet and globalization. Each of these periods represented inflection points in employment opportunities and saw the emergence of important industries such as aviation, petrochemicals, and aluminum in the 1930s, and IT and biotech, more recently.

Certain fields and industries present perennial growth. The graying of the U.S. population and technological innovation can be expected to produce high-paying jobs in health care and computers. Openings for dental hygienists, physical therapists, and physician assistants will jump 30 percent to meet demand, while data communications analysts and software engineers should see employment jump significantly, too. Openings in education and government are on the rise as well. Meanwhile, innovation continues at small start-ups and big companies, and federal funding for basic scientific research at universities is fostering breakthroughs in biotech, high-tech, and green technology. These innovations will spur new businesses, industries, and jobs.

But looking for a job is a bit like going on a journey and, as with any journey, it's good to have a guide. In Jeff Cohen, you have one of the best. He's successfully made the transition from a corporate job to an entrepreneurial one—reinventing himself, achieving financial security, and maintaining a balance between work and leisure time. But like all good guides, Jeff recognizes that no two paths are identical. So he's organized this guide to let you find the path best suited to your goals, gifts, and strengths, whether you are transitioning to a new career or are a new graduate just starting out.

Recessions present new challenges but also new opportunities. And it calls on both experienced workers and those first entering the workforce to develop new skills that safeguard them from the vagaries of a shifting economy and enable them to compete in a global economy. Good luck as you begin your own personal journey toward finding a recession-proof career.

—Clarke Havener, Global Sector Leader, Aerospace and Defense, Korn/Ferry International

# Introduction

Maybe you battled through the Great Depression or heard tales of struggle from grandparents. Perhaps you remember the 1970s gas lines the length of football fields. Quite possibly, the 2008 financial collapse cost you 50 percent of your 401(k) and maybe your job. At the very least, you've been around long enough to know economic cycles can inflict mayhem on your financial and career security. But do you really have to live at the mercy of economic booms and busts? What if you could go to work every day protected by a powerful shield? This body armor would repel stock market nosedives, economic meltdowns, and even layoffs. You would sleep well at night knowing your career was protected, your financial well-being intact.

Unfortunately, this career protective shield is not yet available in stores. (Although something tells me it will be an instant bestseller once it lands on shelves.) In the meantime, I'm here to offer you something nearly as powerful. Welcome to *The Complete Idiot's Guide to Recession-Proof Careers*. This book, incorporated into your career plan, has the power to fend off pink slips, recession blues, and balance sheets in the red. You'll keep your career on the rise even if the economy is sinking faster than a bottomless boat.

Now, it's quite possible you're reading this book during an economic upswing. Corporate earnings could be at record highs. The real estate market could be flourishing. Banks might be back in the black, lending money faster than your Uncle Fred. Before you put this book back on the shelf in favor of a guide to living it up while the going is good, let me ask you one question: Is it possible the good times won't last forever? You want to protect your career and hard-earned dollars just in case economic clouds rear their ugly heads.

I want to help you build a career that thrives in good times *and* bad. While the economy undulates, I want your career on a steady climb to retirement bliss. I want you so confident in your career progression that you're unfazed by economic woes. Ultimately, finding and building a recession-proof career comes down to three factors:

1. **Growth industries:** You have to work in an industry poised to grow for years to come. You can't keep your job if there are no jobs to be found. That's why this book covers careers in some of the hottest industries, including health care, education, government, and renewable energy.

2. **High performance:** Working in a high-flying industry is not enough to lock in career success. You have to master the technical competencies, leadership skills, educational requirements, and computer proficiency needed to become an indispensable high performer.

3. **Transferable skills:** Sure you want to get good at your job, but why not learn skills that make you marketable in multiple careers? If one career starts to lose its luster, you can easily transition to a new job on the rise.

How's this for a triple book-buyer guarantee? By the time you finish this book, you'll be armed with the growth industries, high-performance tips, and transferable skills required to recession proof your career. You'll be so confident in your career outlook that you'll never again wonder how you'll put food on the table if the stock market plunges.

If I do my job right, you'll know your job is safe. So let's get started before the *next* recession is upon us!

## How to Use This Book

The chapters in this book are divided into seven parts that take you on the journey toward a recession-proof career.

**Part 1, "The Recession Procession,"** covers recession-proofing basics. Similar to a freshman year 101 course, you learn the fundamentals of building a career that can withstand economic downturns. You read about trends shaping the future job market, how to maximize career stability in any job, and which skills translate best across multiple careers.

**Part 2, "Here's to Your Health,"** shows you how to be well off while caring for others' well-being. From medical assistants and registered nurses to therapists and pharmacists, you can always find work if you know how to work on a patient's mind, body, and soul.

**Part 3, "Learn to Teach,"** reviews how to make money by educating others. From pre-K and middle school teachers to substance abuse counselors and special education teachers, great career prospects will always be in reach if you can learn to teach.

**Part 4, "Climate Control,"** clarifies why green collars will earn big dollars for years to come. If you have any interest in working with wind, water, heat, air, or even the sun, then this is the part for you.

**Part 5, "Honor and Defend Your Country,"** illustrates how you can protect your career by protecting others, by working in the public sector, or by giving back to your community. You read about government, military, security, and community-service careers that are bound to grow in good times and bad.

**Part 6, "Scratch Your Career Itch with a Niche,"** explains some alternative recession-proof careers you may not have considered. From franchises and home-based businesses to careers in gaming and erotica, you can switch to a niche and solidify your career outlook.

**Part 7, "Corporate Support, at Home and Abroad,"** describes how to earn a dollar wearing a white collar. Careers in human resources, insurance, computer systems administration, and international management are all in growth mode.

## Extras

Throughout this book, keep an eye out for little extras sprinkled in the margins. These sidebars include juicy tidbits, potential pitfalls, and expert advice to help catapult you into a recession-proof career.

### Another Path

Discover transferable skills and related occupations that can improve your odds of working in a recession-proof career.

### Career Caveat

Learn to avoid the most common mistakes, blunders, and missteps that can derail even the most promising career.

### In Their Own Words

Read insightful quotations from industry experts and workers in recession-proof careers to learn from their experience.

## Acknowledgments

This book is about weathering economic ups and downs, but I also want to thank the family, friends, and colleagues who help weather life's ups and downs.

First, thank you to my wife Carol, my soul mate forever and a day. Never extinguish that fire in your belly. Your passion and zest for life embody the heartbeat of our relationship. Thank you to my son Gabriel for giving me insights into the years I can't remember from my own childhood. Your gentle spirit and inquisitive nature make my heart melt.

Thank you to my parents, Janis and Bert Cohen. Having a child has helped me appreciate all you've done to make me the man I am today. So thanks for diaper changes, catches in the cul-de-sac, homework help, holiday getaways, a college education, and a lifetime of wisdom, love, and respect. Thank you to Alice "Gram-Gram" Winitt for telling me in sixth grade I would someday be a published author.

Thank you to my older sister Alyssa for childhood memories I will cherish forever. Toothpaste tug-of-war, ankle clanking, and pew-knee-deep really should be Olympic sports. Carol and I are excited to grow old with you and Jeff #2 while watching Samantha, Rebecca, and our kids bond.

Thank you to Miriam, Victor, and Diana Mimon for debunking the "in-law" stereotype. Miriam, my "mommy #2," has treated me like "son #1" from day one. Victor is the reason I know how to turn life's obstacles into stepping-stones. Diana brings creativity, artistry, and soul into my life. Thanks also to Daniel for loving Miriam and being up for anything on a moment's notice.

Thank you to Kim Lewis and Stephen Power, two bosses who know the value and impact of incredible leadership. Thanks to Mark Levy, the man who makes compelling words bounce off the page. Thanks to Kevin Jacobson, Marc Klatzko, Brad Prutkin, and Mark Rosen. We've shared some memories best left unprinted.

Thank you to Marietta "Cupid" Cozzi for introducing me to Clarke Havener, who wrote a wonderful foreword and went above and beyond to connect me to many of the renowned experts in this book. Thank you to all of the experts who helped shape this book including Dr. Harry Greenspun, Executive Vice President and Chief Medical Officer, Perot Systems Healthcare Group; the Honorable Dr. Stephen L. Johnson, former Administrator of the United States Environmental Protection Agency; Margaret Spellings, former Secretary of Education and President of Margaret Spellings and Company; Todd Stottlemyer, former President and CEO, National Federation of Independent Business; as well as Dr. David Eidman; Lorraine Heber-Brause; Lawrence and Michael Heier; Joel Konikow; Marc Madison; Harriet Shugarman; Lawrence G. Walters; and Stephen Yagielowicz. Thanks also to the folks at Dolce Café in Ridgewood, New Jersey, and Café Life in Westwood, New Jersey, for smoothies, hot chocolates, and chicken wraps during all those hours spent writing.

Thank you to Janet Rosen and Sheree Bykofsky for believing in my talent and guiding this project from contract to completion. Thanks also to Karyn Gerhard for diving right into her new role at Penguin and helping to mold this book from day one. Thanks to Julie Coffin, Kayla Dugger, Cate Schwenk, and the rest of the Penguin Group for sharing these pages with the world.

Finally, thank you to the readers inspired by this book to take charge of your life and recession proof your career. Tell me your success stories at jeff@boldroad.com. I love to hear them!

## Trademarks

All terms mentioned in this book that are known to be or are suspected of being trademarks or service marks have been appropriately capitalized. Alpha Books and Penguin Group (USA) Inc. cannot attest to the accuracy of this information. Use of a term in this book should not be regarded as affecting the validity of any trademark or service mark.

# Part 1

# The Recession Procession

Before we dive into the more than 100 recession-proof careers covered in this book, we have to start with the basics. What, exactly, is a recession-proof career? What trends are shaping the future labor market? How do you make yourself recession proof regardless of economic conditions? These and many other fundamental questions are answered in Part 1.

We begin with Recession Proofing 101, in which we officially define a recession-proof career and help you figure out if you're working in one. Next, we cover transferable skills. These are the overlapping skill sets you can take from one job to the next if your current career flounders. From there, you learn how to build a recession-proof resumé. Here we're talking about the experience, training, computer skills, and leadership performance that build high-potential workers in any profession. Finally, you get a chance to overcome those pesky obstacles that might otherwise prevent you from finding and building a recession-proof career.

# Recession Proofing 101

## In This Chapter

- The definition of a recession-proof career
- How to know if you currently work in a recession-proof career
- The labor market trends shaping the future workplace and how those trends should shape your career choice
- An overview of how the 100+ recession-proof careers were selected for this book
- Why jobs headed offshore have not been included in this book

Before we jump into a breakdown of recession-proof jobs, we open Chapter 1 with the basic definition of a recession-proof career. Then we'll know we're speaking the same language as we dissect more than 100 recession-proof careers. From there, you take a quiz that helps you to determine whether your career is recession proof or not. Next, we review the labor market trends on the horizon, which should factor into your future career choices.

After the definition, quiz, and trends, you get a sneak preview of how the recession-proof careers in this book were selected from the thousands of professions that exist. Finally, we talk about outsourcing and how it can turn a growth industry with potential into one headed offshore. These are the careers you want to avoid to mitigate the risk of losing your position in a company cost-saving initiative. By the end of this chapter, you'll have mastered recession proofing 101 and will be ready for more advanced material.

# What Is a Recession-Proof Career?

What exactly constitutes a recession-proof career? Let's take the words one at a time. Then we'll combine them into a basic definition.

- **recession**    a general downturn in the business cycle, or a slowdown in economic activity lasting for a sustained time period.

- **proof**    a resistance to or resilience in the presence of certain trying conditions.

- **career**    a profession or field for which one trains and in which one progresses over time.

Now, let's put it all together. A recession-proof career is a profession resistant to slow-downs in economic activity. Or we could say a recession-proof career is a field that is resilient in business cycle downturns. You get the idea.

You might naturally wonder whether a book about recession-proof careers is valuable only in down cycles. After all, if the economy is flying high, who needs to worry about careers that are at risk only if the good times go bye-bye? This is where the definition of "career" comes into play. The difference between a job and a career is longevity. A given job can last anywhere from a day to a lifetime. But careers progress over many years. That means you're bound to experience good stretches and bad stretches throughout your employment years. So this book is really about finding and maintaining a career that continues upward regardless of economic conditions.

**Career Caveat**

Always remember not to make snap career decisions based on the latest economic news. A career is a long, winding marathon that needs to withstand multiple economic reports, not just the hot news of the moment. Pay attention to economic reports and understand their impact on your career, but think long term.

Let's talk a little bit more about economic cycles to understand their relationship to the labor market. We all wish the chairman of the Federal Reserve had the power and foresight to maintain a continuous upward economic cycle. Our 401(k)s would grow 20 percent every year, bonuses would be handed out freely, and salaries would increase handsomely. Unfortunately, even the brightest financial minds can't prevent economic cycles from occurring.

What do we typically see during an economic upswing? Well, businesses react positively. They build up inventories, invest in new technologies, hire more staff, and develop new products. As long as economic indicators are positive, businesses realistically expect to sell their inventories, keep employees busy, and crank out new products or services desired by insatiable consumers. However, somewhere along the line, economic indicators sour. Inventories build up, staff idles, and those new products and technologies seem like extravagant investments. Suddenly the reverse happens. Once-thriving factories get scaled back or shut down. Departments formerly in growth mode slash the workforce. Investments in research and development of new products are cut back to hold on to money.

If you've ever worked in a job during an economic downturn, you've probably experienced one of the following:

- Your boss notified employees that salaries will be frozen and no bonuses will be paid.

- Your department underwent a restructuring and some jobs were lost.

- The CEO of your company sent a memo restricting corporate travel, offsite meetings, administrative expenses, and other nonessentials.

- Your company closed two plants and consolidated work among remaining factories.

- Your department instituted a hiring freeze so open positions could not be filled.

Any of these situations spells bad news for income and job security. But some occupations are less sensitive to economic fluctuations than others. Some businesses and industries produce goods and services needed in both good times and bad. That's what this book is all about. I want to help you find a career that can weather economic storms. Why should you put blood, sweat, and tears into a career only to see it wiped away due to economic circumstances beyond your control? You'll sleep so much better at night knowing the latest government report won't sabotage an otherwise flourishing career.

# Is Your Career Recession Proof?

Now you know the basic definition of a recession-proof career. And you may have a sense of whether your career is recession proof, but let's find out for sure. The following quiz will help you determine whether your career is on the upswing or downswing. Answer the questions honestly. Then we can work together to make the career adjustments necessary to get you on track for years to come.

1. Do you currently work in the health care, education, green, government, or defense industry?

   (A) Not even close.

   (B) My industry is related to one of these industries.

   (C) Yes, I work in one of these industries.

2. Do you work in a field experiencing outsourcing?

   (A) Yes, many jobs around me have been outsourced.

   (B) There are outsourcing rumors, but it hasn't happened yet.

   (C) Outsourcing is not on the horizon for my field.

3. Has your field suffered major layoffs in previous economic downturns?

   (A) Yes, jobs are lost every time the economy sours.

   (B) There have been some layoffs, but many folks kept their jobs.

   (C) No, jobs have held steady in good times and bad.

4. Are you seeing anything online or in print indicating your field may be in trouble?

   (A) Yes, stories abound of bad times ahead for my field.

   (B) A few stories, but nothing definitive.

   (C) I haven't seen anything negative about my field.

5. Does the U.S. government show any signs of investing development dollars in your industry?

   (A) No, the government has no plans to invest in my industry.

   (B) I'm not sure whether the government is investing in my field.

   (C) Yes, billions of dollars are going toward my industry.

6. Are you in a career in which your skills could easily translate to a related field?

   (A) No, my skills are specialized and apply only in my field.

   (B) My skills could translate, but it's not a simple transition.

   (C) Yes, my skills translate well in multiple industries.

7. Do you work in an industry in which foreign competition is eroding your company's market share?

   (A) Yes, our market share has been in steady decline.

   (B) Foreign competition is a concern, but not a major one.

   (C) No, our market share has held up to foreign competition.

8. Do you work in an industry where jobs are increasingly going to lower-paid, immigrant workers?

   (A) Yes, I am seeing immigrant workers take over many jobs.

   (B) Some jobs are going to immigrant workers, but not many.

   (C) No, the immigrant population is not taking on the jobs.

9. Do you work in an industry where jobs are increasingly automated?

   (A) Yes, many of the jobs in my field are getting automated.

   (B) Some jobs are now automated, but others are not.

   (C) No, automation has not had a negative impact on job prospects.

10. How will changing demographics in the United States impact your industry?

    (A) Demographic changes will negatively impact my industry.

    (B) Demographic changes won't help or hurt my industry.

    (C) Demographic changes will positively impact my industry.

Okay, now for the results. Count how many times you chose each letter—*A*, *B*, or *C*. If you chose *A* for the majority of the questions, then your career is anything but recession proof. In fact, quick, decisive action may be necessary. Don't worry, that's exactly what this book helps you do. Just understanding your starting point is an important step in ultimately finding a recession-proof career. If you chose *B* for many of the questions, then you sit somewhere between a recession-proof and at-risk career. There are some facts in your favor, but you want to pay attention to certain other aspects to keep your career on track. Finally, if you chose *C* in most cases, then you're in great shape. You can then use this book to determine new growth areas or to identify jobs that might enhance your career path.

Now let's review some of the biggest macro- and micro-trends driving the future labor market. You'll want to stay on top of these trends because they can impact your career success more than anything.

**Another Path**

Just because your industry falters doesn't mean your skills have no future. As you find out in this book, particularly in Chapter 2, many skills are translatable across multiple industries. Working long term in a recession-proof career is as much about developing transferable skills as it is about choosing a high-growth industry.

# Labor Market Trends

We all know that nobody can predict the future with utmost certainty. Still, there are certain trends that seem fairly locked in for the next several years. I've selected five major trends that are worth noting as you consider career options. Pay attention to these trends and you'll improve your odds of finding and building a recession-proof career.

## #1: Health-Care Information Technology

The U.S. government has slated more than $19 billion to update an archaic medical records system. Industries outside of health care have been implementing cutting-edge technologies for years, but the health-care industry lags more than 10 years behind.

If you work for a company that can help the health-care industry catch up in the medical records technology department, then your career is on safe ground. Of course, you'll want to make sure you're not focused on a technology that can automate you out of a job or get outsourced. But if you're on the side of designing and implementing the systems, then you're in good shape.

**In Their Own Words** _____

Because we know that spiraling health-care costs are crushing families and businesses alike, we're taking the most meaningful steps in years toward modernizing our health-care system. It's an investment that will take the long overdue step of computerizing America's medical records to reduce the duplication and waste that costs billions of health-care dollars and medical errors that cost thousands of lives each year.

—President Barack Obama, from a speech delivered February 17, 2009, at the Denver Museum of Nature and Science, Denver, Colorado

## #2: Aging Baby Boomers

Nearly 80 million baby boomers born between 1946 and 1964 are racing toward retirement. Nearly 8,000 of these Americans per day celebrate their 60th birthday. As this population ages, demand for medical care will soar. There will be major growth in the need for home aid, hospital care, physical therapy, and drug treatments. And it's not just the boomers who will need medical attention; their parents are getting older, too, and will require extra medical assistance.

A wide range of growing medical services means tremendous employment opportunities in the health-care sector. Careers poised for growth include registered nurses, medical assistants, pharmacists, physical therapists, and counselors. Basically, anyone who works on a patient's mind, body, or soul will see major opportunities in the years ahead.

## #3: Educating Our Nation

The need to educate our youth is a constant. Furthermore, the gap between the number of people needing education and the number of educators is only growing. That means if you have the wherewithal to teach, you're in a secure spot for years to come.

Teachers of pre-K through middle school will be in high demand, but they're not the only ones. Vocational teachers, special education instructors, math and science teachers, and English as a second language teachers will also be in demand. The U.S. government is pouring billions of dollars into ensuring the next generation of adults can compete with those educated in other countries. That government backing provides a secure backdrop for a career in education.

## #4: Crime During Recessions

If only criminals and terrorists scaled back their operations during economic down-turns. In fact, the opposite often happens. Economic despair makes folks desperate, and that can make a life of crime all the more attractive. A good defense against crimi-nals is critical to our nation's long-term safety.

There are many ways to contribute to safety at a local, state, and federal level. Careers in aerospace and defense, the military, homeland security, law enforcement, security, and probation are all on the upswing. If you have a desire to keep your community or country safe, then this trend is your ticket to a recession-proof career.

## #5: Green Jobs on the Rise

Concerns about climate change, pollution, and energy resources are global. Areas ranging from renewable energy to recycling and nanotechnology are getting signifi-cant funding. Some of the brightest minds in America are looking to save the environ-ment and keep our planet healthy.

If you have a desire to wear a "green collar" to work, you can join the environmen-tal crusade and make a recession-proof living. Recession-proof opportunities exist at multiple educational levels—from environmental scientists searching for solutions to workers on the ground implementing those solutions.

# Criteria for Recession-Proof Careers

To see a snapshot of the 100+ recession-proof careers covered in this book, simply flip through the detailed Table of Contents at the beginning. You'll get a quick sense of the most durable jobs in health-care, education, government, defense, environment, business, and niche industries. I want to share some of the rationale behind how I chose these jobs for this book.

I researched in five basic categories to determine whether or not a particular career should be considered recession proof:

1. **Job growth**
   The U.S. Department of Labor publishes information on hundreds of careers. Listings include the job description, training required, and salary ranges. In the most current report, job growth is projected through 2016. So the first criterion was to make sure that the jobs included in this book are poised for expansion according to the U.S. Department of Labor projections.

2. **Labor trends**

   In magazines, websites, and industry organizations, stories abound on the careers in growth versus decline mode. After an in-depth assessment of these resources, common themes emerged. It became clear which industries and associated careers had the best shot at staying in growth mode.

3. **Expert opinions**

   To understand the marketplace, I needed more than statistics and reports. I wanted to hear from people at the top of the recession-proof industries. The careers covered in this book were vetted by top-of-the-line industry and government experts, as well as people working in the very careers described.

   The invaluable expertise of these individuals helped me to choose the careers selected for inclusion in this book. Their expertise also added tremendous industry context to round out the job-specific information included in the coming chapters.

   **Another Path**

   Choosing a career path based on expected labor trends is a great way to go. But you can also succeed if you know about a trend that is likely to reverse itself in future years. For example, you can up-skill in a down industry while you wait for it to take off again. Then when the good times come again, you'll be first in line and the most qualified to land a great job.

4. **Access and advancement**

   I wanted this book to provide recession-proof opportunities for workers with little to no education as well as for workers with advanced degrees. So whether you never earned your high school degree or studied for years to earn a Master's degree or a Ph.D., there's something for you in this book.

   I have two goals related to this category. First, I wanted to present recession-proof careers at multiple education levels. Second, I wanted to share the road to advancement, regardless of where you start. That's why most careers covered include how to move up or specialize through continued education or on-the-job learning and growing.

5. **Government investments**

   There is no question that the U.S. government has access to all the latest trends and forecasts. This information is used to make investment decisions related to our nation's infrastructure, technology, and health. The more money going to an initiative, the more you can count on stable future jobs in that area, too.

The government's investment in industries such as health care, education, the environment, and defense cannot be ignored. That's why many of the jobs included in this book fall into one of these industries.

# Outsourced Careers

Outsourcing, by definition, involves procuring goods or services through an outside supplier. You're probably familiar with outsourcing in the context of a job or department moving to India, the Philippines, or China. Why do companies choose to outsource certain aspects of their business? The reason typically comes down to one or more of these three factors:

1. Goods can be produced at a lower cost overseas.

2. Employees can be hired for less overseas.

3. U.S.-based employees can be redirected toward more complex, strategic initiatives.

The bottom line is that companies are increasingly under pressure to produce more for less. That means faster, better output at a lower price. Sometimes the equation just doesn't work for a company in the United States, so the company looks abroad to meet revenue and expense objectives. This isn't necessarily a bad thing because savings can be passed on to consumers. It just doesn't feel good when it's your job that's getting outsourced.

Some careers are in super-growth mode, but mainly in the context of outsourcing. Because they are likely to be outsourced, I have not included them in this book. What are these careers? It's important for you to know and recognize them, so let's look briefly at five careers that are certainly in growth mode, but are also certainly being outsourced. This way, you'll avoid getting tricked into believing you've found a solid career choice when the jobs may be headed offshore any day—or maybe they've already shipped out!

## #1: Customer Service Representatives

Call any bank, credit card company, or major product manufacturer and your call is likely to be rerouted overseas. Thousands of companies in the United States need trained professionals to answer customer calls; they just don't want to pay for the more expensive U.S.-based labor. That's why your call to a company's toll-free number often gets re-routed to the Far East. Training for offshore customer service representatives is so advanced, you may not even realize the person on the other line definitely doesn't live around the corner.

## #2: Technical Support Staff

Your computer displays the dreaded "blue screen" and you may be on the cusp of inadvertently wiping out your hard drive. As you contemplate the possibility of losing years of hard work to a computer glitch, you look up the technical support phone number for your computer manufacturer.

Companies are increasingly relying on offshore labor to help customers through their darkest computer moments. Of course, companies would prefer you use their online support tools before dialing the phone. However, if you need more guidance than the online support provides, that guidance will likely come from across an ocean.

## #3: Computer Programmers

For the computer novice, the art of programming appears to be more complex than arranging world peace. The reality is that many computer programs are routine and can be written by low-cost labor overseas. This means some of the programs you use may have been written by outsourced labor rather than by techie genius college kids staying up late at night. You'll see later in this book that *some* computer-based careers *are* recession proof. These include information systems managers, computer analysts, software engineers, and database administrators. However, programming jobs, particularly routine programmers, are often outsourced.

**Career Caveat**

This is not meant to be an exhaustive list of the jobs most likely to be outsourced. The main point is that if your job could be done for less, or if it could be automated, then there is a risk that it will be outsourced. Your best bet is to learn not only the basics but also the more complex skills that are less likely to be headed offshore.

## #4: Small Goods Manufacturers

There used to be a time when everything—from toys to shampoo bottles—seemed to be manufactured in the United States. Those days are long gone. Turn over your favorite product and you're likely to see "Made in China," "Made in Korea," or "Made in Anywhere but Your Backyard."

Again, there's not necessarily anything wrong with producing goods at a lower cost so that savings can be passed on to consumers. But if you were hoping to make a living manufacturing toys or shampoo bottles, you just may be out of a job.

## #5: Data Entry

Yes, I know, data entry covers a wide range of jobs and careers. Let's just say that many companies choose to outsource the basic capture, storage, and retrieval of customer and product information. What does this mean for you? Well, if you get the sense that your data entry days could be numbered, you might be right. If a company can find a quicker, cheaper way to load and store information, it's awfully tempting to go for it.

## The Least You Need to Know

- Recession-proof careers hold strong in good times and bad.
- It's important to know whether you're in a recession-proof job so you can make informed career choices.
- Pay attention to certain labor market trends driving which jobs will be hot for years to come.
- The more than 100 jobs covered in this book have the most potential to withstand economic booms and busts.
- Many computer-based and customer service jobs are headed offshore and are therefore not recession proof.

# 2

# Take This Job and Transfer It

## In This Chapter

- ◆ Skills that translate well across multiple recession-proof careers
- ◆ The most stable jobs with overlapping skill sets that can make career change easier
- ◆ The steps required to turn a career transition plan into an actual career change

Think back to the last time you moved. Do you remember packing up all your valuables, furniture, and clothing for transport to your new home? Moving your belongings to the new place made the transition easier, didn't it? You weren't starting from scratch; you simply transferred what you already owned to a new address and continued your life.

Changing careers is a lot like moving to a new home. You might change your work address, but you get to take your skills with you. The biggest misconception about career change is that you can't land a job in a new industry without direct experience. Though 15 years of experience certainly won't hurt you, transferable skills can also be your ticket to an effective career change.

In this chapter, we review the most transferable career skills. These are the skills that you can master and then use in multiple industries if one should fade during a recession. From there, we connect stable jobs that have overlapping skill sets. Here you discover how seemingly unrelated jobs in health care and education, for example, actually require many of the same skills. Finally, I present a five-step game plan for turning a career transition plan into an actual career change. By the end of this chapter, you'll understand what transferable skills are and you'll know some career change tactics that can help you find and stay in a recession-proof career for years to come.

# The Best Transferable Skills

Thanks to the U.S. Department of Labor/Employment and Training Administration (USDOL/ETA), ample data is available about transferable skills. In fact, the Occupational Information Network (O*NET)—a database sponsored by the USDOL/ETA—is one of the best resources from which to learn about the skills required to land many of the recession-proof careers covered in this book.

The following list names what I consider to be the 11 most transferable skills. I generated this list based on a thorough review of the O*NET site, discussions with human resources and recruiting experts, and my own research and expertise. Master as many of the skills on this list as you can, and you'll have an arsenal of transferable skills to take from job to job. By the way, in the appendixes of this book, you'll also find tons of resources to help you build transferable skills and improve your career prospects.

1. **Transferable Skill #1: Communication**
   Reading, writing, and speaking. These seem like skills you would master in grade school, but it can take a lifetime to become an effective communicator. You need to be able to read and digest information, write in a clear and articulate fashion, and speak clearly and professionally.

2. **Transferable Skill #2: Attention to detail**
   Disorganized people can be so hard to deal with at work. They forget about meetings, lose important paperwork, and often fail to respond to e-mail and voice-mail. Attention to detail is all about organizational skills and time management. Get the small details right and you'll hold on to big jobs.

3. **Transferable Skill #3: Work ethic**
   Everybody wants to be around hardworking people who have integrity. They say what they mean, follow through on commitments, and never try to cheat you. A strong and honest work ethic serves you well in life and on the job.

4. **Transferable Skill #4: Leadership**
   At some point in your career, you may advance to a leadership level. You must understand how to motivate people, build a following, set a vision, and bring out the best in those who report to you.

5. **Transferable Skill #5: Thinking abilities**
   From analytical skills to problem solving and decision making, how you think matters to those who hire you. Employers want to know you combine logical reasoning with an ability to think through difficult workplace challenges.

## In Their Own Words

Look at yourself in terms of skills and traits. Core business skills never lose their relevance. Financial, leadership, and communication skills are the foundation. Some traits, however, will keep you on top and in demand. Being resilient, creative, and demonstrating a positive "make it work" attitude can safeguard and even grow careers during uncertain times. These traits can also be transferred to other emerging industries.
—Lorraine Heber-Brause, Professional Development Advisor (www.foxgloveadvisors. com); from personal e-mail with the author

6. **Transferable Skill #6: Human relations**
   If you can work effectively in teams, build relationships, and earn respect from those around you, then you've mastered human relations at work. People who are difficult to work with rarely gain the trust and admiration of colleagues and supervisors.

7. **Transferable Skill #7: Sales and persuasion**
   So much of business has to do with selling your products and services. You've got to be able to persuade people to take an interest in what you have to offer. If you can stir up interest and drive sales, you'll always have a job in sales and marketing.

8. **Transferable Skill #8: Service nature**
   Making sales is only the beginning of the customer experience. Once you have a buyer, you have to manage the relationship. Sales make money, but service builds loyalty and repeat business. Learning to manage accounts and customers effectively is a worthwhile skill at any company.

9. **Transferable Skill #9: Computer proficiency**
   Some jobs require very specific computer skills, such as programming or working with highly complex software. In many cases, employers are looking for general

computer skills such as word processing, spreadsheets, presentation design, and Internet research skills. These are the computer-based skills you can likely take from job to job throughout your career.

10. **Transferable Skill #10: Creativity**
Companies would fail without new ideas. You don't have to be an artist to create a masterpiece. Developing a new product, launching a new service, and improving a process all qualify as creativity on the job. If you can break through the status quo and think outside the box, companies will clamor for your innovative mind.

11. **Transferable Skill #11: Self-motivation**
From entrepreneurs who start their own companies to everyday employees who know how to get a new initiative off the ground, self-motivated workers are highly valuable. These are the folks who can rally the troops around a new idea, build new revenue channels, and turn nothing into something.

Let's make one thing clear about transferable skills. If you hypothetically acquired all 11 skills on this list, it doesn't mean you can have any job on the planet. Most jobs require a combination of academic training and on-the-job experience in addition to these transferable skills. This section is about building transferable skills you can take from job to job. You'll still want to focus on the educational requirements and relevant work experience necessary to land a recession-proof career. But these 11 skills will serve you well as you consider changing jobs or industries.

# Stable Careers with Overlapping Skill Sets

This book covers six main recession-proof industries: health care, education, government and defense, green careers, niche jobs, and corporate roles. Let's look at the overlapping skill sets you can take from one of these industries to the next.

## Communication Skills

If you're going to work in government, you have to be able to communicate effectively. Government is all about making a case to the public and rallying support for a cause. Guess who else needs to communicate effectively? Translators need to express ideas in multiple languages. In fact, many translators support government employees meeting with diplomats from foreign countries.

# Attention to Detail

All of the jobs that support medical professionals—doctors, dentists, and veterinarians—require solid organization skills. If you want to work as a medical assistant, dental hygienist, or veterinary technologist, you have to be good with details. The medical professionals are relying on you to get the small stuff right so they can focus on the big stuff. Where else is attention to detail important? Environmental scientists and engineers need to track lots of information and keep it all straight.

Again, we're not saying you can or should jump overnight from dental work to environmental science. The point is that seemingly unconnected professions actually have more in common than you might think at first glance.

## Another Path

Don't assume you have to change careers completely to move transferable skills from one job to another. You can also stay in the same industry and make a smaller change. For example, changing from a registered nurse to a home care aid is an easier move than insurance agent to high school teacher. You'll still be moving among recession-proof careers, but the transition (i.e., the time it takes to switch) will be smoother and probably shorter.

# Thinking Abilities

School counselors and counselors in private practice require expert thinking skills. They must take in information about a student or patient, analyze the issue, and come up with recommendations to help improve the situation. Where else would thinking abilities serve you well? Community developers need to think through problems all the time. The logistical issues required to organize an entire community are endless.

# Sales and Persuasion

Sales representatives, of course, need razor-sharp persuasion skills. How else will they convince prospects to become paying customers? However, sales reps are not the only ones who persuade people. Personal appearance workers sell every day as they persuade customers to buy hair care or styling products to keep that new hair style looking like the stylist just fixed it. Convincing someone you can make him or her look better is a sales skill required to keep the personal appearance prospects coming your way.

## Service Skills

Folks who work in utilities—lighting, heating, and cooling—all provide a valuable service for their customers. Who else needs expert service skills to succeed? Both physical therapists and occupational therapists rely on service skills to keep their appointment books full of client visits. These professionals must understand client needs and develop a plan to keep them healthy and satisfied.

## Self-Motivation

Self-enrichment educators need self-starting skills. You may have expertise worth sharing, but it takes initiative to get folks interested in seeing and hearing what you have to say.

The list of transferable and overlapping skills could go on and on as we review all of the recession-proof jobs covered in this book. However, at the very least, take away this important point. If you're thinking about a career change, don't assume you're starting from scratch. Many of the skills you've spent years honing will serve you well in your new career. And that's the perfect lead-in to talk about making an actual career change happen.

# The Steps Required for a Career Change

You've already seen that transferable skills make career change possible. You now know that if your current career stagnates or disappears during a recession, you can pack up your skills and take them to a new, recession-proof career.

But how exactly do you change careers? It's not as if you can go to bed one day as a family counselor and wake up the next morning as an environmental engineer. There are some straightforward steps that can make the transition as smooth as possible. Here is my five-part, foolproof plan for changing careers. I'm going to show you how I transitioned from a consultant and marketer to a human resources specialist. Then I'll give you a chance to assess and execute your own career change game plan.

## Step 1: Industry Assessment

I'm a big believer in the fact that people naturally gravitate toward what they enjoy most. For example, you may be paid to answer customer service inquiries for a manufacturer. Your primary job is to listen to customer gripes and solve their problems.

However, you may find that you naturally enjoy building camaraderie with the callers and ultimately selling them alternative products. So you're paid to handle customer complaints but you're gravitating toward customer account management and sales.

This gravitation toward what you enjoy most is, to me, the most important first step in a career transition. If you're going to make a big change, at least make it to a career that matches your natural talents and desires. That's why I recommend beginning any career change assessment with a review of your last three or four jobs, your primary responsibility in each job, and your favorite project from each role. I'll come with you on this journey. First, let's look at my own assessment from when I was considering a career change.

## Jeff's Industry Assessment

| Job or Role | Primary Responsibility | Favorite Project |
|---|---|---|
| Business Consultant | Help clients manage travel costs | Undergraduate recruiting |
| Senior Consultant | Research and report on business travel trends | Employee satisfaction initiative |
| Marketing Manager | Develop promotions for joint venture partners | Philanthropy project |
| Account Manager | Act as primary contact for corporate clients | Career progression planning |

Let's break down my industry assessment. Then you'll get a chance to fill out your own assessment and draw some conclusions. For me, an obvious trend leaped off the page: I gravitated toward human resources projects. I hadn't noticed until I completed this exercise that a theme existed for me. Somehow, even though I was paid primarily for consulting and marketing roles, I kept volunteering for side projects on recruiting, employee satisfaction, charity, and career development.

This was quite an insight for me. Luckily, this gravitation toward human resources had some recession-proof cachet to it. You'll see in Chapter 20 why the human resources career track has recession-proof potential.

For me, the human resources theme fairly shouted that I was in the wrong career. Your insights may be just as obvious, or they may be harder to interpret. Let's find out together. I want you to fill out the same table for yourself. In the first column, list your last four job titles. In the second column, write a phrase that describes your primary responsibility in each job. Then in the third column, write your single favorite project carried out during each role. Don't worry about whether the favorite project had anything to do with your primary job. Just think back to your favorite project and record it in the last column.

## Your Industry Assessment

| Job or Role | Primary Responsibility | Favorite Project |
| --- | --- | --- |
| | | |
| | | |
| | | |
| | | |

What did you learn? Do your favorite projects match your job responsibilities, or are they completely different? Is there an industry or area that encapsulates your favorite projects? For me it was human resources. What about you? Are you working in the right industry today, or do your favorite projects indicate a change should come soon? Remember, you may be working in a non-recession-proof industry, so change could be thrust upon you anyway. If you've uncovered an industry from your favorite project analysis, read on to discover whether it's a recession-proof industry. (Or, if you're curious, you can scan the Table of Contents of this book and see if it's covered here.) Otherwise, you may inadvertently switch from one dead-end career to another. Right now, though, let's take what you just learned and uncover your desired work.

## Step 2: Desired Work Within Industry

Identifying a recession-proof industry is a great first step in making a career change. However, as with any industry, there are multiple jobs and roles. So for me, it wasn't enough just to identify human resources. What exactly drew me to the field? Step 2 helped me understand exactly the kind of work I desired within my target industry. In this next table, you'll see I've copied my favorite projects from Step 1. Then for each favorite project, I recorded what I enjoyed most about it.

## Jeff's Desired Work

| Favorite Projects | Favorite Work Within Projects |
|---|---|
| Undergraduate recruiting | Writing job descriptions; presenting at colleges |
| Employee satisfaction | Researching and writing about employee needs; presenting findings to management |
| Philanthropy project | Giving to and helping others; presenting results against goals at town hall meeting |
| Career progression | Coaching employees to develop their skills and reach their potential |

This exercise helped me narrow down what exactly draws me to human resources. Three transferable skills jump out at me: writing, public speaking, and personalized coaching. Note that these are skills applicable in multiple fields.

So what about you? What is it that you like most about your favorite projects from your last four jobs? Complete the same exercise on the following table. First, copy your favorite projects from the first table you completed. Then, next to each favorite project, record why you liked it.

## Your Desired Work

| Favorite Projects | Favorite Work Within Projects |
|---|---|
| _____ | _____ |
|  | _____ |
| _____ | _____ |
|  | _____ |
| _____ | _____ |
|  | _____ |
| _____ | _____ |
|  | _____ |

What skills jump off the page for you? Is it communication-type skills, like it was for me, or something completely different? Examples of skills you might find enjoyable include problem solving, spreadsheet analysis, working in teams, entrepreneurial ventures, creativity and artistry, organizational skills, and even leading others. This is not an exhaustive list, of course—just some ideas to get your mind moving.

The object of Step 2 is to identify exactly what you like about your favorite projects. For me, Step 2 helped me to understand what specifically drew me to human resources. I'm hoping you'll discover similar insights into your skills and your desired industry. You want to be able to say the following: "I am drawn to ABC industry because I enjoy utilizing my X, Y, and Z skills." That one sentence will be powerful as we move into Step 3 and begin to consider actual jobs you could land in your new career.

> **Career Caveat** _____
>
> Just because you love presenting doesn't mean you should automatically find a public speaking career, per se. Rather, stay open to careers in which your public speaking skills play a significant role, even though your primary responsibility might not be public speaking. For example, politicians and public servants do a lot of public speaking, as do teachers.

## Step 3: The Right Job or Role

It's time to get more specific. Now it's time to translate what you've learned about your skills into real-life jobs you could land as you consider a career change. Let's continue our journey by first looking at how I worked through Step 3. Then you'll have the chance to do the same for your own career transition.

Step 3 requires some research. I began looking on the Internet, reaching out to my network, and talking to folks working in human resources to better understand potential careers. This research uncovered three potential paths for me. I've outlined these options in the following table:

## Jobs or Roles That Meet Jeff's Chosen Criteria

| Job Title | Job Description |
| --- | --- |
| HR Talent Manager | Work in a learning and development department to write and present employee training programs |
| HR Consultant and Coach | Coach employees one-on-one to develop their skills and reach their personal potential |
| HR Process Expert | Work in an HR process area to learn compensation, benefits, compliance, and other HR disciplines |

These three jobs all offered the opportunity to bolster my human resources skills while using the writing, speaking, and coaching talents I enjoy most. At this point, I'm not concerned with whether I could land one of these jobs right away. Step 4 is all about the practical steps to landing the job. Right now, I'm only concerned with identifying the right jobs for me.

Now it's your turn. Either from your existing knowledge of the desired industry or through research, identify three potential jobs. These jobs should all be in your new desired industry and should make use of the skills you enjoy most from Step 2.

## Jobs or Roles That Meet Your Chosen Criteria

| Job Title | Job Description |
|-----------|-----------------|
| _____ | _____ |
|           | _____ |
| _____ | _____ |
|           | _____ |
| _____ | _____ |
|           | _____ |
| _____ | _____ |
|           | _____ |

Now we're making some progress! Your career change plan is coming to life. You know the recession-proof industry that's right for you, the skills you like most, and three real jobs you could shoot for in your new career. The next step is to figure out exactly what it would take to land one of these jobs. Let's roll up our sleeves and build the necessary credentials to open some recession-proof career doors.

## Step 4: Personal Profile Needed

If only you could walk into the hiring leader's office and hand over the results from Steps 1, 2, and 3. You could say, "In lieu of an interview, why don't you just give me my dream job because my career analysis indicates I'm born to do this work." Let's just say this strategy is not the best way to score your career change job. Instead, you've got to show you've developed the transferable skills and gained the educational requirements necessary to succeed. So how do you make this happen? For me, I started reading actual job descriptions from job sites to see the typical qualifications.

Researching a handful of related jobs helped me understand the personal profile necessary to get one of the jobs I desired. My results are in the following table.

## Jeff's Personal Profile Needed for the Right Job

| Profile Needed for Right Job | Do You Possess the Skill? | Steps Required to Gain or Expand Skills |
|---|---|---|
| Advanced degree or credential in human resources | No | Find good program and apply for admission |
| Real experience working in human resources | A little bit | Land more human resources projects before making the move |
| Active in writing and speaking industries | No | Join relevant writing and speaking clubs and organizations |

Ultimately, I knew that the right person for a human resources role would come to the table with three key competencies. First, the ideal candidate would have the proper academic training. Second, the ideal candidate would already have some experience working in human resources. Finally, the right person for the job would be active in writing and speaking outside of his or her daily job. The findings from Step 4 turned into my action plan for making it so. I was truly ready to jump into Step 5—turning my career transition plan into an actual career change.

### Another Path

I chose to expand my skills while still working at my old job. Another way to go would be to quit your job and enter a full-time academic program for your new career. The downside is you lose out on income while studying. The upside is that you may find the transition easier. Many companies are eager to hire fresh graduates.

So what about you? If you were to review actual job descriptions for your desired career path, what qualifications would come up over and over again? Put pen to paper one more time and fill out the same table I just shared with you. In the first column, write a skill or experience required. In the second column, indicate honestly and realistically whether you already possess that skill. Then in the third column, brainstorm at least one straightforward step you could take to close the gap and turn a "no" into a "yes" for column two.

## Your Personal Profile Needed for the Right Job

| Profile Needed for Right Job | Do You Possess the Skill? | Steps Required to Gain or Expand Skills |
|---|---|---|
| _____ | Yes or No | _____ <br> _____ |
| _____ | Yes or No | _____ <br> _____ |
| _____ | Yes or No | _____ <br> _____ |

Now you have some tangible steps to make your career change possible. It's no longer just a hypothetical transition. Right in front of you are the very steps you could take to build the resumé to actually land a new and improved recession-proof job. The question for you is whether your work will stop at Step 4 or continue to the action phase in Step 5. Let's not stop all of our positive momentum here. It's time to take the words on the page and get to work.

# Step 5: Making It So!

Here I was sitting in my consulting and marketing roles looking for an opportunity to switch to human resources. I had my action plan in hand and the desire to close the gap on my missing skills. So I took the lessons from Step 4 seriously and got down to business. Here's how I built my resumé and made the career change happen.

## Jeff's Career Change Steps

| Category | Steps Taken |
|---|---|
| Education | Found a program through the Society for Human Resources Management to learn human resources fundamentals, including staffing, compensation, and employee development |
| Experience | Continued to raise my hand for human resources projects on the side to keep building skills |
| Organizations | Joined the National Speakers Association and landed my first few speaking engagements in the career management field |

These tangible steps paid off for me. I eventually transitioned within my company from marketing and consulting to human resources. I gained valuable experience in a corporation and then used those skills when I left my job and started BoldRoad.com, a company that inspires people to take action toward working less, earning more, and living a better life.

Now it's your turn. Do what's required to gain experience (see Step 4) and write down what you plan to do to turn your career plan into an actual career change.

## Your Career Change Steps

| Category | Steps You Will Take |
| --- | --- |
| _____ | _____ |
| | _____ |
| _____ | _____ |
| | _____ |
| _____ | _____ |
| | _____ |

There you have it—a five-step, straightforward plan to change jobs and land yourself in a recession-proof career. Now get out there and make it so! I know you can make it happen.

## The Least You Need to Know

- Just because you are changing jobs doesn't mean you can't take your transferable skills with you.

- Some jobs may seem quite different on the surface, but actually have overlapping skill sets.

- If you desire to change careers and land a recession-proof job, there are tangible steps you can take to make it happen.

# Chapter 3

# What It Takes to Make Yourself Recession Proof

## In This Chapter

- Why recession-proof careers are driven by your resumé as much as by stock market fluctuations

- How to build the work experience necessary to make you indispensable at the office

- Why your education and training can get you in line for promotions and interviews

- How to establish yourself as a high performer

- Why your computer can be your best friend when learning new software and making new networking connections

Have you ever been laid off? How quickly did you make a list of the reasons you got fired that had nothing to do with you? *It's the economy. Your boss had it in for you. The company is headed in the wrong direction. You were put on the wrong projects.* Should I keep going, or did I strike a nerve? It is true that even the highest performers with the best experience and education can lose their jobs. It's more true that people with recession-proof resumés tend to outlast layoffs, restructurings, and unfair bosses.

Even though this book is about recession-proof careers, there are steps you can take to protect yourself regardless of career choice. This way, you're in good shape even if a once-promising industry falters. This chapter is really all about taking charge of your career. Why be at the mercy of stock market plunges, economic meltdowns, and mismanaged companies? Instead, put yourself in the best position to weather any economic storm.

We start this chapter with a quiz to find out how close you are to recession proofing your career. From there, we talk about the work experience, education, and training that lead to fantastic interviews and impressive promotions. Next, we talk about why high performers rarely get the pink slips. Finally, we cover how the computer is your ticket to mastering new software and making connections to last a lifetime. By the end of this chapter, your resumé will be your recession-proof best friend.

# Is Your Resumé Recession Proof?

How does your resumé stack up against the competition? Would you get the gig or get passed over? Would you get promoted or demoted? Would you get pink slipped or would you slip past pink? Let's not leave these questions to chance. Here's a quiz that can tell you exactly where you stand. These questions are geared toward folks who work at companies. However, if you are self-employed or if you own a business, you'll still be able to apply the questions to your own situation.

1. How much experience do you have in your industry?

   (A) None at all

   (B) Less than two years

   (C) Three to five years

   (D) More than five years

2. How long have you been in your current role?

   (A) Not working right now

   (B) Less than six months

   (C) Six months to two years

   (D) More than two years

3. How long have you been at your current company?

    (A) Not working right now

    (B) Less than six months

    (C) Six months to two years

    (D) More than two years

4. Do you have the certifications required for your job, company, or industry?

    (A) I'm lacking the required certifications.

    (B) I'm in the process of getting certified.

    (C) Yes, I am fully certified.

    (D) No certifications required.

5. Do you have the educational degree typically required for your job, company, or industry?

    (A) I'm lacking the education.

    (B) I'm in the process of earning the right degree.

    (C) Yes, I have all the degrees necessary.

    (D) No educational requirements for this career.

6. What rating did you get at your last performance review?

    (A) My company doesn't do performance reviews.

    (B) I received a below-average rating.

    (C) I received an average rating.

    (D) I received an above-average rating.

7. What have your bosses or other company leaders told you about your long-term potential at your company?

    (A) I've never heard anything about my potential.

    (B) I've been told my performance needs to improve.

    (C) I've been told I'm a solid contributor.

    (D) I've been told I'm a high performer with potential.

8. How well do you know the computer programs and software needed to perform your job?

    (A) Computer skills are irrelevant in my role.

    (B) I could definitely brush up on computer skills.

    (C) I'm pretty comfortable with most programs.

    (D) I consider myself an expert.

9. What role does networking play in your life?

    (A) I never attend industry events and know very few people who do my job at other companies.

    (B) I attend an industry event here and there and know a few people who could help me.

    (C) My address book is fairly full and I do my best to get to events and meet new people when my schedule permits.

    (D) I'm a busy beaver who attends lots of industry networking events, collects business cards, and stays in touch.

10. How many skills do you possess that could be easily transferred to another job in a new industry?

    (A) None of my skills are transferable.

    (B) Maybe one skill could transfer to another role.

    (C) Two or three of my skills could transfer.

    (D) Most of my skills would transfer easily.

The more times you chose answer *A*, the more you need this chapter. The more times you chose answer *D*, the more you can smile because your resumé is recession proof. Lots of *B* and *C* choices probably mean you have some good stuff as well as some holes in your resumé, in which case this chapter will help round you out. Now let's dig even deeper into each of the elements that make up a recession-proof resumé.

> **Career Caveat**
>
> Most companies, especially larger corporations, conduct semiannual or annual performance reviews. Without a review, you have no idea where you stand. Don't be afraid to ask for a review in writing. If your company has no performance review guidelines, at the very least, ask for informal feedback from your boss.

# Tell Me About Your Experience

It comes down to you and another candidate for a job. You size up the competition. What's he got that you don't? One word ... experience! It's the one word that has killed the dreams of many fresh-faced workers. "You seem great, but we're looking for someone with more experience." As soon as the hiring manager utters that phrase, your chances are lost. Your stellar grades, your semester abroad for international experience, your willingness to donate your body to science ... none of it matters if experience is the deciding factor.

I'll be the first to admit that sometimes you just *don't* have the experience to get the gig. This section is not about that situation. What we're talking about here is taking charge of your career and going after the experience necessary to get and keep the job of your dreams.

Here's a quick personal story to illuminate my point. When I worked for a corporation, I found my calling as a human resources generalist. I did not get that job the day I realized it was my corporate calling. First I gained business experience in the marketing and consulting departments. Then I gained human resources process experience, working on compensation, benefits, and talent development. Then it was time to make my move. In my human resources generalist interview, I said "Having worked in the business and human resources, I'm uniquely qualified both to understand business challenges and to lend human resources expertise to the solutions." I got that gig. The guy before me had human resources experience only. The lady after me had business experience but no human resources knowledge.

> **Another Path**
>
> Gaining experience for a job from multiple perspectives is a great way to get the gig. Imagine working in both sales and customer service. Or both finance and marketing. Or shipping and receiving. The more perspectives you understand, the more qualified you become for bigger jobs. That also means your value goes up and your layoff likelihood goes down.

I've come to realize there are five surefire strategies to get the gig every time. Consider this my five-step recession-proof experience extravaganza. Now that's a mouthful!

1. **Befriend someone in your dream job.**
   Why guess what it takes to land a great job? Make friends with someone already in the role and check his or her experience. Better yet, meet two or three people in great jobs and compare their experiences to build your own master experience plan.

2. **Read the job descriptions of your future.**
   Just because you're three promotions away from your dream job doesn't mean you can't peruse those openings. See what experience you'll need three to five years from now. Then actively choose your next job to round out your skills.

3. **Cross-pollinate your competency growth.**
   Don't just master one skill in each job; go for multiple competencies. This speeds up your cycle time to gaining experience. Learn three new skills in each of your next three jobs and that's nine skills you can take to the bank!

4. **Get on the right projects in each job.**
   There's nothing more disappointing than wasting two years in a job learning nothing new. If your job is not helping you grow, then it's not building experience. Without that continued experience, you're on a fast track to nowhere.

5. **Rewrite your resumé frequently.**
   Old buzzwords make a resumé look stale. At least twice per year, update your resumé so it's current and includes the latest key words. This will get your resumé to the top of the pile for interviews every time.

# Study! Study! Study!

Sometimes a job posting says "no graduate degree necessary." Sometimes it says "graduate degree preferred." And sometimes it says "graduate degree required." In other words, your education or lack thereof may or may not cost you the job. Let's keep this section short and sweet. Experience matters, but you can't forget the importance of academic education, certifications, and on-the-job training. Let's take these one at a time.

First, your academic background. Commit the time to get the degree you need. It might be a GED or a Ph.D., but whatever it is, you can't shortcut this one. Lack of education will shut doors in your face faster than you ever realized. Once you know where you want to be in 5, 10, or more years, get the associated education. Full-time school is no longer the only option. Part-time, evening classes, and even online distance learning are all viable options.

Depending on your career choice, a national, state, or local certification may be required. This may include an exam, supervised work hours, and even future educational requirements or retesting to keep your certification active. Certification need not scare you away from a particular recession-proof career. Consider it an obstacle that many people will not overcome. Study, ace the test, get your certification, and you've got an airtight credential to pull you to the top of the applicant pile.

Finally, let's talk about on-the-job training. We're not talking about the three to six months it takes to get good at your job. We're talking about specific training, classes, and experiences your employer requires when you first join. Take this training seriously. Your performance is part of the first impression you'll make. Hit the ground running and your employer will notice. Come up short in training and you may be landing on the street sooner than you'd like.

# Be Aware of Software

I can't tell you how many people I've interviewed over the years who claim to be proficient in a particular software program. Their first foray with the program quickly tells me I've got a novice on my hands. I understand that people don't want a lack of computer skills to cost them a job. But claiming to be something you're not certainly doesn't get you off on the right foot.

Online training programs, local classes, and bookstore manuals are everywhere. You know your career. You know the job you want. You know the training required. So put down the clicker for a few nights after work and learn what you need to know. Often, a particular program seems intimidating only until you jump in and learn a few tricks. Then you'll be claiming computer proficiency with the confidence to back it up.

# What a Performance

Have you ever seen a truly amazing performance at the theater? You're compelled to get out of your seat, clap endlessly, and shower the performer with praise. Guess what? You don't have to be a Tony award winner to put on a great performance. Here are nine steps you can take, starting today, to be a high performer.

1. **Find a mentor.**

   What's the quickest way to learn a new skill? Figure it out for yourself, or ask someone who already knows? Okay, so there's some personal satisfaction in going it alone. But the better bet is going with someone who has been there, done that. A great mentor, especially within your company, serves two important roles. First, he or she can advocate for you when times are tough. One thumbs up from a senior executive can save you from the unemployment line. Second, your mentor can be honest with you, answer your personal questions, and guide you through tough work challenges.

2. **Volunteer for opportunities.**

   When the boss needs someone for a new project, what do you do? Bury your head, avoid eye contact, and hope you don't get singled out? Or do you raise your hand, jump into action, and make a difference? Volunteering for opportunities, particularly those on your boss's radar screen, is a great way to become an essential employee. First, your boss will appreciate your willingness to go the extra mile. Second, you'll show you can handle more than just basic responsibilities. Finally, if layoffs should come, the last person your boss wants to lose is someone who's taking care of his or her pet projects.

3. **Connect with influential leaders.**

   Having a mentor who loves you and a boss who adores you is a great start. But two people may not be enough to save you when the going gets tough. You need some or all of the decision makers to value your contribution. Let's say three senior executives run your company. One is your boss, but the other two barely know you. Guess what will happen at the next round of layoffs? Your beloved boss will be outvoted by the other two. Find a way to get all the decision makers to love you. Taking on a new role and volunteering for projects are two great ways to expand your influence beyond one leader.

4. **Suggest a new project.**

   Sometimes your current job is not enough to get you noticed. Don't be afraid to identify a new revenue channel, brainstorm a new product idea, or find a way to improve customer service. Your leaders will appreciate your initiative and may put you on the team to make it happen.

5. **Be helpful and resourceful.**

   When I first started working, my boss told me to return phone calls, respond to e-mails, and be accountable. It seemed obvious at the time, but I soon found out that an awful lot of folks don't return calls, don't respond to e-mails, and rarely deliver on what they promise. It's amazing how these three seemingly simple things can set you ahead of so many people. You'll seem so much more proactive and responsible than your peers.

### Another Path

Companies run on new ideas. Without a pipeline of fresh thinking, even a well-run company may lose its steam. You can get yourself on cutting-edge, invaluable projects by starting a new business idea brainstorming group. You'll network across your company, come up with some killer ideas, and earn a label as a truly strategic, innovative employee. And that's not a bad reputation to have around the water cooler.

6. **Perform at the next level.**
   You spend hours convincing your boss you're ready for more responsibility and a bigger paycheck to match. Somehow the words fall on deaf ears and the promotion never materializes. Have you ever considered operating at the next level before you get the promotion? Think about the strategies and execution delivered at the next level. Become that person now and the new title and extra dough will follow.

7. **Demonstrate your expertise.**
   You know the old saying about a tree falling in the woods with nobody around to hear it. Well, the same holds true for expertise nobody knows about. If you're a great presenter, don't hold back. Raise your hand to deliver the sales presentation. Volunteer to speak at a conference. Let that talent out of the bag and you'll stand out from the crowd.

8. **Fill those holes.**
   Do you remember that kid from elementary school who didn't play well with others? Do you think he still struggles with teamwork, or did he find a way to collaborate effectively? We all have areas that could use some development. You can ignore them or turn them into strengths. Development areas can cost you a job; working to improve yourself shows initiative. So fill those holes in your skill set and personality. You'll be more well rounded and therefore more valuable to your company.

9. **Enjoy the ride.**
   You can be great at what you do, but if you create stress among the people around you, no one will want to work with you. If no one wants to work with you, then you just may find yourself out of a job. Do your job, and do it well, but make sure those around you see that smile and a good attitude. Positivity is contagious, so be the one who spreads the goodwill around the office.

# Networking

I'm going to share my secret theory on networking. Don't tell anyone what you read here … Wait a minute. That's contrary to the idea of networking. Okay, spread the word on this tip all you want. I'm a big believer in five power relationships.

That's right. I believe that five amazing relationships will do more for you than all of the entries in your address book combined. Why do people fill their address books with people they hardly know? Well, there's a false sense of popularity that comes from 412 Facebook friends or 823 people following you on Twitter. So you focus on building the total network rather than cultivating relationships.

**Career Caveat**

People can smell selfish networkers a mile away. Your mind-set has to be helping others, not getting what you want. If people perceive a relationship to be one-sided, it won't last. Give, give, and give some more. The more you help others, the more networking will come full circle to open doors for you.

Instead of building the address book to recapture those high school years when popularity ruled, go for five power relationships. Find five people who can mean the most to your career, your current job, your future plans, and so on. Don't beg these fine folks for help right away. Simply get to know them. Help them solve their own problems. Become a resource they can count on first. Then slowly share the story of your own dreams. You'll find these five power relationships become a cheerleading squad pushing you to success.

## The Least You Need to Know

◆ A recession-proof resumé can withstand the most extreme economic fluctuations.

◆ Solid work experience and relevant training are the two backbones of a recession-proof resumé.

◆ High performers rarely lose sleep when layoffs and restructurings are announced.

◆ Your address book can keep your career on a roll even when times are tough.

# Chapter 4

# Turning Recession-Proof Obstacles into Stepping-Stones

## In This Chapter

◆ The top reasons people don't take charge of their careers to find and keep a recession-proof job

◆ Solutions to each of the obstacles to a recession-proof career

◆ How to drown out the negativity when those you love and care about don't support the changes you need to make

Finding and keeping a recession-proof job may seem easier said than done. Maybe that little voice inside your head doesn't really believe you can pull it off. I'm a big believer in listening to the little voice, but don't let it guide you completely. So before we get to the meat of this book—the recession-proof jobs—let's do a little housekeeping. Let's get all of our fears, concerns, and worries on the table. Let's face them so we can move forward together.

In this chapter, we start with a look at why people don't take charge of their careers. I guarantee more than a few of these excuses and myths will resonate with you or someone you know. It's important to take the time to make this list together. I don't want to pretend recession-proof careers happen without having to overcome obstacles.

After we admit our fears together, we stomp them out one by one. We cover solutions to all of these obstacles to landing a recession-proof career. From there, we discuss ways to drown out the negativity associated with making changes. Trust me, the very people you rely on—your friends, family, and colleagues—may not support you 100 percent as you make some necessary changes. So we need to arm you with strategies to keep your relationships intact without giving in to the naysayers. By the end of this chapter, negativity will be squarely in your rearview mirror as we drive together toward the recession-proof career destination right for you.

# Why People Don't Take Charge of Their Careers

Let's not pretend you can snap your fingers and land in a recession-proof career. We all know there are fears and anxieties about solidifying your career prospects. Anytime you're not the boss, there's always the risk of getting fired. Let's get these fears on the table right here, right now. Without further ado, here are nine things that may be keeping you up at night as you contemplate your career prospects. Don't worry, after we list our fears, we're going to conquer each and every one of them together.

## Obstacle #1: Change Is Bad

Who wants to live in a world of change when stagnation feels so comfortable and familiar? I get it. You may like your career, you may be good at it, and you may want to stay forever. So the thought of giving up what you enjoy rubs you the wrong way, even if I'm telling you the current path may not be recession proof.

Or you may despise your career, but somehow you stay anyway because at least you know what to expect every day. There's comfort in predictability, even if it's not all that comfortable. You choose to stay in a bad situation out of fear that change might actually be worse, not better.

## Obstacle #2: Decisions Are Bad

Recession proofing is a decision, and maybe you prefer living with ambivalence. Making a choice comes with accountability. So if you never decide anything, you never have to commit to anything either.

Even if you're in a bad situation or a dead-end job, there's still a powerful pull to avoid deciding on a new career. That decision would trigger a need to get your resumé in order, a job search, interviews, and maybe even rejection. Why put all that on your plate when procrastinating is just easier?

> **Career Caveat** _____
>
> Just because you don't like change and decision making doesn't mean you won't be forced into changing and decision-making situations. Too many people back themselves into a career corner where the ultimate choices range from bad to worse. A little pain now is better than major problems down the road.

## Obstacle #3: Recessions Impact All Jobs

Recessions seem so all-encompassing. News programs report unemployment, cutbacks, and spending freezes. Watch enough TV and you'll soon believe the clouds will never lift. Maybe we're all doomed no matter what path we choose.

So if every job is destined for a pink slip, why waste your time? Why not just accept your fate like everyone else and hope for better times in the years ahead? After all, if we're all getting fired sooner or later, why bother taking charge of your career?

## Obstacle #4: You're Not Qualified

Maybe you scanned this book's Table of Contents and noticed industries such as health care, government, education, and renewable energy. None of these industries match your current job, so how in the world can you land a recession-proof career?

You made your bed when you picked the "wrong" career years ago. Of course, you wish you had been forward-thinking enough to choose a recession-proof industry. But you weren't and you didn't, so you'll never compete effectively against people already working in these industries. Oh, well.

> **Another Path** _____
>
> You don't have to go into a career search thinking about industry first. Another strategy is to build transferable skills that can serve you in multiple industries. Don't assume you have to start by choosing a field—health care, for example. Instead, you can simply build technical, leadership, and academic skills that can lead to success across industries.

# Obstacle #5: Your Bosses Have It in for You

Even if you magically land in a recession-proof career, you'll be sabotaged by your boss. Your job history shows that your outstanding performance has been underappreciated by your bosses. No matter how hard you try, you can't seem to build an effective working relationship with a boss.

Because your boss is going to kill your career no matter what job you choose, there's no reason to search for a recession-proof industry. Why put in all the extra effort to pick a solid career track when your boss will ultimately send you to the unemployment line?

# Obstacle #6: No Competitive Edge

The list here could fill up a chapter. You're too old. You're too young. You don't have the training. You're overqualified and pigeonholed. No matter whom you compete against for a job, you'll never have the edge.

Even if you find the perfect recession-proof option, you'll still get out-interviewed by someone else. These so-called career handicaps cannot be overcome; you're simply stuck with them. Sure you can make some changes. But there are certain qualities you simply can't do anything about no matter how hard you try.

# Obstacle #7: Too Technical

You've spent years mastering a super-specialized skill. Once, you thought you'd be the best in the world at what you do. Now you're finding out that this once-special skill is getting outsourced or automated by most companies.

Your resumé is all about this one skill, so you can't imagine getting a job in any other industry or specialty. No matter how much you want to reinvent yourself, your resumé speaks for itself. You're simply destined to be a casualty of outsourcing and automation.

# Obstacle #8: You Have a Resumé Gap

Maybe you took five years off to raise a family. Maybe you traveled the world for three years doing odd jobs. Perhaps you left the corporate track for four years to take care of a sick relative. Whatever the case, you have a clear gap in your resumé.

You know this gap is going to come up in interviews. You don't feel confident you can successfully explain why your career track lacks a consistent upward trajectory. This gap is going to cost you, so why bother putting yourself out there?

### Another Path

You can always work part-time or as a contractor during employment breaks to keep your skills fresh and your resumé intact. Websites such as guru.com, elance.com, and momcorps.com all match skilled workers with employers in need. It's a great way to fill those resumé gaps when circumstances take you off the traditional path.

## Obstacle #9: Trends Are Bad

You can think of many examples of trends that reversed themselves. You remember gas prices being high and then suddenly at an all-time low. You know of drugs once considered helpful that are now ruled harmful.

Because trends are bound to reverse over time, there's no use building career plans around the flavor of the day. You'd rather go with your gut than listen to a bunch of pundits claiming that they know what they're talking about. Sooner or later, what we thought to be the truth will turn out to be a myth.

# Solutions to Overcoming the Biggest Obstacles

Okay everyone, take a deep breath. We've said our fears out loud. We've listed all the reasons we're afraid to go after a recession-proof career. Let's congratulate ourselves on the honesty. Some folks, nobody reading this book of course, never even admit what's scaring them about change. You're already ahead of the game because you've faced your fears. I'm not one to leave you hanging, so let's conquer our fears together. It's time to revisit the nine fears from the last section but turn those obstacles into stepping-stones. So here's our new list of nine, but this time we're talking solutions instead of obstacles. Now that's a turn toward positive thinking.

## Solution #1: Change on Your Own

Not liking change does not mean you can live without it. You can ignore the need for change for months or even years, but sooner or later circumstances will require it. So if you shy away from changing your career now, a future reorganization or layoff may necessitate change anyway.

I've come to realize it's better to initiate your small change on your own terms than to deal with major change on someone else's terms. Even if career change scares you, imagine how much scarier it will be when it happens against your will. I'd rather know the change is coming than have it sprung on me at an inopportune time.

## Solution #2: Decide to Take Action

You may think that as long as you don't decide something, the world will just wait for you. That's not how it works. Not making a decision actually counts as a decision. In other words, you're deciding not to take action.

The result is that circumstances take place around you. These circumstances have an impact on you and act as a decision. Once I realized that not deciding counts as a decision, I vowed never to let circumstances decide for me. I recommend the same course of action for you. Take your time to make a sound decision, but never fool yourself into thinking you have an eternity to formulate your plan.

## Solution #3: Position Yourself Well

A recession *can* be so deep-rooted that everyone seems to suffer. But keep in mind that the *national* unemployment rate rarely climbs above 10 percent. So, despite all the bad news, more than 90 percent of workers in America are still gainfully employed.

As you can see, the odds are still heavily in your favor to keep a job. But why not double or triple your odds by migrating toward an industry that seems above the fray? Getting yourself in an industry poised for growth will almost certainly help your chances of holding down a steady paycheck.

## Solution #4: Value Your Skills

Just because you enter customer information into a computer at a car dealership doesn't mean you can work only for car companies. Stop thinking of yourself as a car industry employee and start thinking of yourself as a data entry specialist.

It's amazing how career opportunities can open for you when you think beyond your current industry. Make a list of your transferable skills. Then see which ones best match the recession-proof industries covered in this book. You'll soon find you're more qualified than you first believed.

> **Career Caveat**
>
> Your perception can influence your reality. So if you see yourself as a technical specialist in only one area, that's how you'll come across in interviews. The more you think about transferable skills and how you can succeed in multiple settings, the more confidence you'll display and the better your odds of making a positive change.

# Solution #5: Listen to Those Bosses

If one boss gives you a bad performance review, it may just be a mismatch of leader and employee. If every boss has the same feedback, it's time to look in the mirror. As much as you want to believe you're misunderstood, all these bosses can't be entirely wrong.

Look for the common themes in your performance reviews. If you've heard the same things over and over, there's probably some validity to the feedback. Either figure out a development plan or get yourself in a career where your weaknesses won't be a factor. Just don't go on blaming your bosses for pointing out what could well be the truth.

# Solution #6: Control What You Can

You never really know exactly what a hiring leader is looking for. The job ad or description may not tell the whole picture. Invariably, there are intangibles that simply can't be listed. It's easy to self-sabotage before the interview even begins. But maybe, just maybe, what you perceive as your interview deal breakers aren't all that relevant to the interviewer.

I'm a big believer in strong interview preparation. Play to your strengths and then let the interview chips fall where they may. We all have one or two areas that we know hurt our chances, including the other people interviewing for the same job. So put your weaknesses *and* your strengths nose to nose with the competition and you may be pleasantly surprised.

# Solution #7: Up-Skill Yourself

If your skills are overly technical, particularly in a fading field, it's time to search for the next big thing. There must be something on the rise that's replacing your aging skills. Do your homework to see what's on the horizon.

Then don't be afraid to take a class, go for extra training, or earn a degree at night. By the time your technical skills are completely out of demand, you'll be ready to transfer into the up-and-coming field. Because you've found such a new technical skill, the competition will likely be light; other folks won't yet have the necessary training. This is your chance to capitalize and make a smooth transition to a new, recession-proof career.

> **In Their Own Words** _____
>
> Company compliance is going global, and that means English is not the only language of choice required to do business around the globe. When I saw my company actively moving into the Latin American market, I began taking Spanish lessons. My rapidly improving language skills have opened career doors for me as I've taken a larger role in our South American compliance operations.
>
> —Jeff, compliance lawyer for Fortune 500 company

## Solution #8: Play Up Your Resumé Gap

The days of the steady corporate climb are long gone. From raising a family to taking a sabbatical, more people than you think have resumé gaps. It's time to embrace, rather than fear, your time away from the grind.

Learn how to turn this gap into a captivating human interest story. For example, time away from work to care for a sick relative is clearly relevant to a future career in health care. What better backstory for an aspiring registered nurse than to bring personal bedside skills to the table? This positive spin on your time away from traditional work can actually make you stand out from a plain vanilla interviewee.

## Solution #9: Believe in Something

You may believe that not every trend pans out, but there are certain truths that seem to stand the test of time. There's no getting around the aging population and their need for increased medical care. There's no denying the supply and demand gap in the education department.

So while fads may come and go, long-term trends are not likely to reverse anytime soon. So listen for the longevity of predictions and latch on to those expected to stay steady for years to come. This will get you off the flavor of the day and on to a reliable trend you can believe in.

# Drowning Out the Negativity

Believe it or not, not everyone is going to support your recession-proof journey. The very people you call family, friends, and colleagues may not be in your corner. I know what you're thinking. The people who love and care about you want only the best for you. So why would they ever stand in the way of you making positive changes to improve your career prospects? In a perfect world, they wouldn't. But life doesn't work that way, so let's discuss the negativity that may come your way as you journey toward a recession-proof career.

For starters, let's look at the top five reasons your supporters may not support your recession-proof metamorphosis:

1. **Jealousy**

   If you've ever had co-workers, you know all about negativity. There is something about chitchatting among the cubicles that brings out the gossip and negative thinking in all of us. People love to dish on what ails them.

   If you're taking positive steps to improve your career prospects, beware of sharing them at work. You'll find a handful of negative thinkers telling you that you're making the biggest mistake of your life. This outlook is most likely based in jealousy. So if you must talk about your plans, be ready for a negative response and be ready to drown it out.

2. **Old patterns**

   Old patterns and habits can be hard to change. If you've been going through the motions in a dead-end career, don't underestimate how hard it may be to break out of your routine. Unfortunately, it's not just you that needs to break the old patterns. Friends and family are used to this version of you, too. They've come to know and love a version of you floating through your career without much direction.

   When you take charge of your career, those old patterns will pull you back to your old ways. It's not that loved ones don't want you to succeed. It's just that they're so used to the current version of you that this new and improved model seems strange. People prefer familiar to strange, even if familiar is actually worse than strange.

3. **Fear of change**

   We're not talking about *your* fear of change here. We're talking about *other* people's fears. Questions such as "What if you're making a big mistake?" and "Maybe the grass won't be greener" are likely to hit you in the face.

Anytime you make a decision, someone is going to think you're making a mistake. Sometimes this fear-based thinking turns out to be right. But in most cases, your worst fears, and those of your friends and family, never materialize. So it's okay to listen to the fears of your loved ones, but don't let them stop you in your tracks. Remember, this is your life and your career at stake.

4. **Misguided expertise**

   You're bound to know a colleague, boss, or mentor who knows more about your career, industry, and job than you. These so-called experts have a wealth of knowledge about trends and forecasts. You may have relied on these folks in the past as you contemplated prior career moves. So this support team has been a good thing.

   Keep in mind that sometimes the expertise is more of a guess. Sometimes the people who know more than you don't actually know more about *what's right for you*. So take the expert advice, give it a fair shake, but don't let it be the final say in your career plan.

> **Career Caveat**
>
> Just because some expert advice is misguided, don't underestimate the power of the person sharing the advice. You may disagree wholeheartedly, but don't forget to show respect to someone who can easily influence your career. There are ways to disagree without damaging an important relationship. This is critical if you don't want to turn an ally into an enemy.

5. **Misguided power**

   This issue most commonly rears its ugly head from current and former bosses. You work or have worked for these folks; this gives them a certain power over you. They give you daily direction and tell you what to do. This is okay in a day-to-day work setting, but the power shouldn't cross over into controlling your career moves.

   Unfortunately, too many bosses believe they have the right to order you around daily as well as over the long haul of your career. If you work under a controlling boss, chances are he or she won't support your journey toward bettering yourself. If you're in this situation, either keep your career plans to yourself or talk to your boss without allowing him or her to influence you too much. Remember, the controlling boss wants to keep you around because you do valuable work. Your recession-proof outlook is not necessarily in his or her best interest.

Now, what do we do about all of this negativity? I'm not one to leave you hanging. So without further ado, here's my plan for drowning out negativity so you can move forward with your recession-proof career game plan. Arm yourself with these five strategies and you'll be well on your way to brushing negativity aside and landing in the recession-proof promised land.

## Do Your Homework

Flying by the seat of your pants is not exactly a career strategy. If you're going to make changes, and if you're sharing those changes with other people, arm yourself with the data, logic, and rationale for change. People love to poke holes in ill-conceived plans. It's harder to do so when you have statistics and data to bolster your decision.

So use this book and others, relevant websites, and industry organizations to build your case for change. When it comes time to go public with your plans, you'll be confident you're on the right track. This homework can make all the difference in overcoming the challenges sure to come your way.

## Embrace the Negativity

Sometimes we all wish we could make a decision without telling our family, friends, and colleagues. We know the negativity is coming our way, so why not save everyone the pain and just keep our plans secret? Sounds promising—but the truth will come out eventually.

So I say embrace the negativity. You've already done your homework (see previous section), so why not just come clean, face the music, and tell the world? You can systematically tell your friends, family, and colleagues you'll be making some changes and just get it over with. Some folks will surprise you and support you immediately. For those who don't jump on your bandwagon of change, keep reading!

## Be Clear and Consistent

The last thing you want to do is waver. Negative people look for chinks in your armor. They see you lacking confidence and assume it means that you doubt your own plan. You appear only partially on board with your idea, so why should they fully support you?

If you've done your homework and know where your career is headed, you must plow ahead. Save the unsettling thoughts for the positive people who can help you through it. When you are around the negative thinkers, stay the course and come across as steady in your recession-proof pursuit. Otherwise, those chinks will turn into wide openings and the negativity will engulf you.

### Another Path _____

Even if you don't have the confidence from the outset, follow the old axiom to fake it until you make it. Be clear and consistent in your beliefs, even if you don't completely believe in yourself from the start. Sooner or later, your confidence will catch up to the positive results coming your way.

## Anticipate the Pullback

We all know about taking two steps forward and one back. Most careers encompass a series of positive and negative moves. Often we don't even know if we've made a good decision until years later.

As you build momentum toward a recession-proof career, it's entirely possible that some of the jobs you take will actually take you a step backward. That's okay and should be expected. You can always course correct and learn from your mistakes. But don't ever let these small missteps ruin an otherwise upward trajectory to recession-proof bliss. Also, don't let the negative thinkers say "I told you so" when a bad move materializes. These naysayers may be right at the moment, but you'll be back on track with your next career move.

Be generous and spread the wealth. As you learn more about how to recession proof your career, take others on your journey. Not only will you feel good about helping others, but you just may find motivation in working as part of a bigger team. You won't be alone in your quest for the right career. You'll have some like-minded folks enjoying the ride by your side.

There's comfort in numbers. Don't be afraid to find those positive folks, share your knowledge, and better yourselves as a team. You will soon find all of your careers flourishing as you push yourselves to new levels.

There you have it, a foolproof, five-part plan to drown out the negativity and move forward with your recession-proof plans. Now that negativity is no longer pulling you down, let's get to work on finding and keeping the right recession-proof career for you.

## The Least You Need to Know

◆ There are some legitimate fears and concerns associated with finding and keeping a recession-proof career.

◆ Acknowledge obstacles before they prevent you from making necessary changes.

◆ Once your fears are on the table, you can design strategies to turn the obstacles into recession-proof stepping-stones.

◆ Expect and accept negativity from friends, family, and colleagues as you make changes.

◆ You can keep key relationships intact without letting negativity stop you from landing a recession-proof career.

# Part 2

## Here's to Your Health

We all know health-care costs are rising. We also know people continue to see more doctors, try new medical drugs, and strive for better overall health. It's no wonder the medical industry continues to be on the rise while other industries falter. If you've ever thought about seeing patients, assisting medical professionals, dispensing medications, or researching new treatments, then this is the part for you.

We'll begin with a look at the recession-proof folks who lend a helping hand to medical professionals. We're talking about the people who help doctors, dentists, and veterinarians get the job done. From there, you learn about the people and drugs that keep us healthy. Professions such as registered nurses, paramedics, and pharmacists are all covered. Finally, we cover the people who work on our minds, bodies, and souls, including physical therapists, counselors, and personal appearance workers.

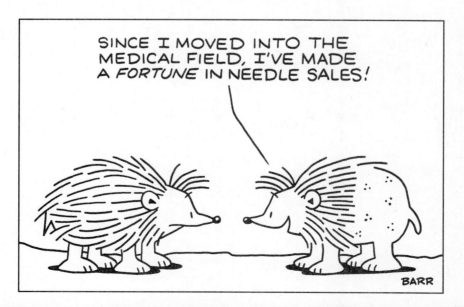

# Chapter 5

# Medical Professionals Need a Hand

## In This Chapter

- Why assisting medical professionals is a great way to improve your own career prospects

- What it takes to land and keep a job as a physician assistant or dental hygienist

- Where to find health-care jobs if you're interested in the business or technology side of the industry

- How you can build a healthy career track record by entering and maintaining patient records

- How to recession proof your career by helping veterinarians care for family pets

We all need a little help every now and then. Who among us can make it in this topsy-turvy world all alone? The medical profession is no different. Physicians, dentists, and veterinarians could never get their jobs done without assistants and hygienists. Somebody has to make preliminary diagnoses, administer basic medical procedures, and be that second pair of hands in the operating room.

Assisting medical professionals is not just about standing next to a trained professional in a white coat. The business side of medicine is equally vital to delivering outstanding patient care. After all, someone has to manage doctor's office operations to keep things running smoothly. Let's not forget the importance of recordkeeping, too. The last thing you want is for the doctor to make an errant diagnosis after reviewing the wrong file.

This chapter covers recession-proof careers built around lending a helping hand. You learn about physician assistants and surgical technologists who practice medicine under the watchful eye of physicians and surgeons. You read about dental hygienists who make your teeth shine and your gums plump and pink. From there, we go to the business and technology side of health care, learning about medical and health services managers and the information technology (IT) professionals who help plan and coordinate the delivery of health care. Finally, you discover that veterinary technologists and technicians do for veterinarians what nurses do for doctors. By the end of this chapter, you'll wish you had *two* right hands to capitalize on all the recession-proof medical opportunities around.

# Physician Assistants

Have you ever been treated in a doctor's office by someone other than the doctor? If so, chances are you've met a physician assistant. Working under the watchful eye of physicians and surgeons, physician assistants are trained to examine and diagnose patients.

## Outlook for Physician Assistants

| | |
|---|---|
| Current Number of Employees | 66,000 |
| New Jobs Created by 2016 | 18,000 |
| Expected Job Growth by 2016 | 27% |
| Geographical Hotspots | Nevada, Oregon |
| Average Annual Earnings | $62,000–$89,000 |

*Sources: U.S. Bureau of Labor Statistics National Employment Matrix, State Occupational Projections*

The most common duties performed by physician assistants include:

◆ Order an x-ray and help interpret the results

◆ Treat scrapes, sprains, and strains

- Ask patient questions to record medical histories

- Make house calls or hospital visits and report back to a supervising physician

The nature of your day will vary greatly depending on the kind of physician assistant you choose to be. Work in a doctor's office and you'll spend your day going in and out of patient rooms. Assist a surgeon, and you may be spending hours on your feet in the operating room. Score a job in a hospital and you're in for irregular night and weekend hours. Be sure to think about which scenario best suits your preferred working environment.

**Another Path**

How would you like to work in a career poised for 35 percent growth with only half of the educational requirements of a physician assistant? Consider a career as a medical assistant. The two professions are often confused. Medical assistants focus on administrative work; physician assistants diagnose and treat. The work may be different, but as a medical assistant you're still helping a doctor's office run smoothly.

## You Must Be Certifiable

Your passion to help requires both a formal education and state licensing. In a nutshell, you're looking at five steps to become a physician assistant:

1. You'll need to complete at least two years of college. Courses in biology, chemistry, and social sciences will help show your interest in the field.

2. During or after those two years of schooling, be sure to gain some real-world health-care experience.

3. Two years of college, plus the work experience, will open doors for you into a two-year, full-time physician assistant program.

4. After graduating from an accredited physician assistant program, you'll need to pass the Physician Assistant National Certifying Examination.

5. To keep your certification, you'll need to complete 100 hours of medical education every two years. You'll also need to retake the certification exam every six years to keep your credentials.

## How About Some Special Assistance?

Physician assistants are not bound to careers in physician offices and operating rooms alone. The need for physician assistants is growing rapidly at teaching hospitals. You might even consider this a double recession-proof strategy. After all, education and health care are both recession-proof industries.

You can increase your earnings by pursuing further education in a physician assistant specialty area. While you'll still be under the supervision of a physician, you can delve into such specialties as internal medicine, pediatrics, or even emergency medical care. The more specialized you become, the more indispensable you'll be!

When considering a specialty, don't lose sight of anticipated trends in the health-care industry. Two of the biggest trends are the shift from inpatient to outpatient care and the move from acute care to prevention and wellness.

Imagine a job working in a medical trailer that pulls up alongside a company to administer preventive screenings on site. Or picture working at a miniclinic right inside your local drugstore to help provide outpatient medical services. The more you understand where health care is headed, the better your odds of keeping a job over the long haul.

# Surgical Technologists

When I was six, I underwent hernia surgery. I remember vividly that the surgeon was not the only one in the operating room. This really nice guy, a surgical technologist, got me ready for my operational debut. Surgical technologists, also called operating room technicians, assist in surgical operations under the supervision of surgeons and other medical staff.

## Outlook for Surgical Technologists

| | |
|---|---|
| Current Number of Employees | 86,000 |
| New Jobs Created by 2016 | 21,000 |
| Expected Job Growth by 2016 | 24% |
| Geographical Hotspots | Maryland, Utah |
| Average Annual Earnings | $30,000–$44,000 |

*Sources: U.S. Bureau of Labor Statistics National Employment Matrix, State Occupational Projections*

Common responsibilities include the following:

◆ Prepare the operating room by setting up surgical equipment and instruments

◆ Get patients ready for surgery by washing, shaving, and disinfecting the site of the operation

◆ Transfer patients to the operating room and help them get comfortable on the operating table

◆ Keep an eye on patient vital signs and charts to make sure everything is on track during a procedure

◆ Pass instruments to surgeons and care for specimens removed from patients

Most surgical technologists work in hospitals—about 70 percent of them, actually. But physicians who perform outpatient surgery also hire surgical technologists. You can even go for an ambulatory surgical center and live a life and career on the move. In fact, the 30 percent of surgical technologists who work *outside* hospitals are expected to see the greatest increase in employment opportunities in coming years.

The Commission on Accreditation of Allied Health Education Programs (CAAHEP) recognizes more than 400 surgical technologist programs around the country. That's an average of eight per state, so there's no excuse for not finding a suitable school reasonably nearby. You'll earn a certificate, diploma, or Associate's degree after completing a 9- to 24-month program offered by one of the 400 junior colleges, community colleges, vocational schools, or hospitals accredited by the CAAHEP.

Because most employers prefer to hire certified surgical technologists, it's worth getting your license. The National Center for Competency Testing (NCCT) can help you earn the Tech in Surgery Certified (TS-C) designation. The other route is through the Liaison Council on Certification for the Surgical Technologist. Here you'll walk away with a Certified Surgical Technologist (CST) designation after passing a national certification exam. Either way, continuing education and/or future exams are required to keep your certification current.

**Another Path**

Surgical technologists can advance to certified surgical technologists with specialized education. You'll earn a cool new title: surgical first assistant. Now your job is to help the main surgeon carry out a safe operation by controlling blood flow and preventing hemorrhaging during the operation. Not a bad title to strive for if you're a surgical technologist looking to expand your skill set.

The best way to get ahead is to specialize and become the go-to surgical technologist for a particular type of surgery. Imagine a world-renowned cardiologist refusing to perform open-heart surgery without you in the room. Now that's a recession-proof strategy that will pay serious dividends.

# Dental Hygienists

The last time I went to the dentist, my hygienist told me I need to do a better job flossing and to make sure to brush the teeth in the upper left corner of my mouth. Turns out you can make a recession-proof living helping people plaque-proof their teeth. Dental hygienists clean teeth, teach patients about oral care, and look for problem areas to report to the dentist.

## Outlook for Dental Hygienists

| | |
|---|---|
| Current Number of Employees | 167,000 |
| New Jobs Created by 2016 | 50,000 |
| Expected Job Growth by 2016 | 30% |
| Geographical Hotspots | Idaho, Utah |
| Average Hourly Earnings | $25–$36 per hour |

*Sources: U.S. Bureau of Labor Statistics National Employment Matrix, State Occupational Projections*

More specifically, dental hygienists are responsible for the following:

◆ Remove plaque and tartar buildup during a cleaning

◆ Educate patients on good oral hygiene practices

◆ Take dental pictures with an x-ray machine

◆ Record teeth or gum abnormalities for the dentist

As you can imagine, dental hygienists work in dentist offices. Safety protocol is part of the job. The last thing you want is inadvertent exposure to x-rays, dental compounds, or anesthetic gases. So you have to be comfortable with a daily wardrobe that includes rubber gloves, a safety mask, and scrubs.

Many hygienists work for multiple dentists part-time. That's because some dentists may only need a hygienist a few days per week. So it's common to work for one dentist on Monday, Tuesday, and Wednesday, and another dentist who offers late Thursday appointments or weekend hours.

## In Their Own Words

Americans cut back on virtually everything during recessions. However, 173 million people are lucky enough to have dental insurance. They can see their dental hygienist for a cleaning, check-up, and x-rays twice per year with little or no out-of-pocket expense. Low patient costs, coupled with a desire by Americans to feel better, healthier, and younger, explain why the dental hygiene field remains a recession-proof career choice.

—Dr. David Eidman (www.gratefuldentistry.com); from personal e-mail with the author

Before you can clean your first tooth, you'll need three things:

1. A high school diploma

2. A degree from an accredited dental hygiene school

3. A state license granted after passing an examination

Nearly 300 dental hygiene programs are offered throughout the United States. In some cases, programs are looking for relevant high school coursework, including biology and chemistry. So don't goof off when it's time to dissect a frog or turn on that Bunsen burner. Other schools require at least one year of college before applying to the program. While in school, you'll undergo a mix of both clinical and classroom training. You can expect to dive into such varied subjects as pharmacology, anatomy, and physiology. After completing the required coursework, you'll walk away with either an Associate's degree or certificate. Either one opens the door to a dental hygienist job at a private dental practice. Of course, that door remains open only if you can pass the licensure examination. You'll need to pass both a written and clinical examination to get licensed in the state in which you plan to practice.

Though working for a dentist is a great place to start, your career does not have to plateau there. If you're willing to continue your dental education, you can earn a Bachelor's or Master's degree. Now the career door will swing open even wider and you can score jobs in research, teaching, or clinical practice.

If the schooling and licensing sounds like a bit much to you, then consider the dental assistant route instead. You'll still work closely with dentists, but can land a job without the extra schooling. Many dental assistants learn on the job and spend their days sterilizing equipment, laying out instruments, and making patients comfortable in the dental chair. You can always work up to dental hygienist as your career progresses.

# Medical and Health Services Managers

Though health care is all about helping people, it's still a business. That means the industry needs people to make it run smoothly. That's where medical and health services managers come in. Their job is to coordinate, direct, and manage the delivery of health care in hospitals, doctor's offices, nursing homes, and other health-care facilities.

## Outlook for Medical and Health Services Managers

| | |
|---|---|
| Current Number of Employees | 262,000 |
| New Jobs Created by 2016 | 43,000 |
| Expected Job Growth by 2016 | 16% |
| Geographical Hotspots | Nevada, Texas |
| Average Annual Earnings | $57,000–$95,000 |

*Sources: U.S. Bureau of Labor Statistics National Employment Matrix, State Occupational Projections*

More specifically, medical and health services managers …

◆ Seek efficiencies and implement improvements in the delivery of health care.

◆ Formulate strategies to attract patients, improve revenue, and grow the business.

◆ Ensure all federal, state, and local government regulations are adhered to in the delivery of health care.

◆ Analyze the quality of care, feedback from patients, and other factors to improve service.

◆ Manage facility personnel, finances, and payroll to keep the operation running smoothly.

More than one in three medical and health services managers work in hospitals. About one in five work at a doctor's office or nursing care facility. The balance earns their money working for the government, home-care services, and community care facilities.

As health care grows more complex, medical and health services managers are increasingly required to be jacks-of-all-trades. One minute your job is all about controlling costs to meet hospital budgets. The next minute you're rolling out a brand-new technology system to store patient records. Two minutes later you're in an interview to recruit new talent. Recession-proof medical and health services managers combine solid experience in the health-care field with strong business acumen.

So how far do you want to take your medical and health services management career? Requirements range all the way from a high school degree and on-the-job training to Master's and doctoral degrees. For example, you can likely break into the business with nothing more than a high school degree if you want to work in a physician's office or nursing facility. You'll be starting at the bottom of the food chain, but you'll learn invaluable health-care skills to build your resumé.

If you want more of a standard entry-level position at a hospital or health-care facility, you'll need a Bachelor's degree. Coursework in health-related topics will help demonstrate your interest in the field and improve your odds of scoring your first big career break. If you dream of being the head honcho, or at least moving up the ladder, then a Master's degree in health administration will be in your future. Nearly 75 programs around the country offer accredited programs.

> **Career Caveat**
>
> Medical and health services managers do work in the business world, but the job is hardly a 9-to-5 deal. When was the last time you went to a hospital and the door was locked? Most health-care facilities operate around the clock, which means business emergencies can occur mid-afternoon or in the middle of the night. You'll have to be prepared for that call at 3 A.M. to deal with an unexpected administrative development.

Do you want to make your medical and health services management career truly recession proof? Many medical professionals are specialists. Make your specialty a well-rounded business background—from finances to human resources to technology. Your repertoire of business skills will be highly transferable. So if your hospital cuts staff, you can always reinvent yourself at a corporation or small business.

# Medical Records and Health Information Technicians

Doctors seem to have memories of steel. They come in to see you and they know your entire medical history. This encyclopedia-style memory would not be possible without a medical record. That's where medical records and health information technicians come in. Their job is to enter patient health information, ensure its accuracy, and provide doctors with all the patient information needed to make effective diagnoses and treatment plans.

## Outlook for Medical Records and Health Information Technicians

| | |
|---|---|
| Current Number of Employees | 170,000 |
| New Jobs Created by 2016 | 30,000 |
| Expected Job Growth by 2016 | 18% |
| Geographical Hotspots | Nevada, Utah |
| Average Annual Earnings | $22,000–$36,000 |

*Sources: U.S. Bureau of Labor Statistics National Employment Matrix, State Occupational Projections*

Basically, medical records and health information technicians carry out the following tasks:

◆ Enter all initial patient information to capture everything there is to know about a new patient

◆ Load results of any CAT scans, lab tests, or other diagnostics to round out patient information

◆ Fill out medical information needed to file health-care claims with insurance carriers

◆ Document medical procedures and decisions in the event any legal action ensues

Medical records and health information technicians need strong organization skills and attention to detail. If organizing stuff floats your boat, then this career may be right up your alley. Unlike most medical professions where bedside manner and patient interaction are critical, medical records and health information technicians have little daily patient contact. In most cases you're looking at a standard 35- to 40-hour work week. However, some hospitals, open 24/7, will be looking for workers to take night and weekend shifts. That's your ticket to overtime pay if you want a few extra dollars in your pocket.

Breaking into the field requires an Associate's degree from a community college or junior college. You can earn your degree full-time, at night, or even through accredited online programs. You'll definitely want to take courses in relevant topics such as coding; statistics; database management; and even medical topics such as anatomy and physiology.

If you really want to be marketable, strive to become a Registered Health Information Technician (RHIT). You can earn the certification by graduating from a two-year Associate's program accredited by the Commission on Accreditation for Health Informatics and Information Management Education (CAHIIM). Your ticket to certification comes through CAHIIM. Nearly 250 CAHIIM-accredited schools exist in the United States. Each one opens the door to the American Health Information Management Association (AHIMA) written examination. So just to summarize, if you want to be an RHIT, you'll need CAHIIM to open the door to AHIMA. Now that's a mouthful!

**Another Path**

Hospitals and physician offices are not the only places that maintain records. Credit card companies keep consumer records, retail stores have customer records, and hotels retain guest records. So don't feel locked down to the medical field if you master data entry and maintenance. Your skills will be in high demand in more industries than you ever imagined.

## Go the Specialty or Management Route

Your ticket to more money and more responsibility is to either specialize or move up the ladder. For example, coding and cancer are two of the most popular specialties for medical records and health information technicians. Coders are responsible for assigning proper medical codes for insurance purposes. These codes determine the reimbursement a hospital or physician's office will get from the insurance company. With hundreds of codes out there, it's not an easy specialty to master. Or you can also specialize in cancer registry. Here your job is to review patient records and reports to assign codes for the diagnosis and treatment of cancer.

Instead of specializing, the other way to go is moving up the ladder into management and supervisory roles. So you can go from coder to overseer of a team of coders. Now you're calling the shots, and that's a great way to recession proof your career.

## Expand Your Information Technology Skills

Have you been watching the news? The government has slated more than $19 billion for health IT investments. Because medical records and health information technicians will benefit from this cash outlay, you'll want to make sure you stay on the cutting edge of IT skill development. This will minimize the risk of your job getting outsourced or automated.

### In Their Own Words

Most medical industries are at least a decade behind in IT, so there are big growth opportunities for people who understand both health care and information technology. Keep in mind there is intense pressure for companies to control costs and improve efficiencies. You need to up-skill constantly so a lower skilled person or robot doesn't replace you.

—Dr. Harry Greenspun, Executive Vice President and Chief Medical Officer, Perot Systems Healthcare Group

How can this $19 billion health IT investment help you recession proof your career? Much of the money is slated to help create an electronic health information network. The move from a paper-based to fully integrated, automated health information network will require workers both to implement and to manage the software and programs created. Learn these new technologies and you'll be on the cutting edge of health care IT, and therefore in high demand for years to come.

# Veterinary Technologists and Technicians

You love your cat Fluffy, or your dog Teddy, or your goldfish Seymour, or even your boa constrictor Athena. That love means you want state-of-the-art veterinary care should a pet health problem arise. You depend on a well-trained veterinarian to do his or her job. But did you know that veterinarians depend on quality veterinary technologists and technicians? These professionals do for veterinarians what nurses do for physicians. The job of a veterinary technologist or technician is to perform the routine laboratory and clinical procedures so that veterinarians can do the more complex work.

## Outlook for Veterinary Technologists and Technicians

| | |
|---|---|
| Current Number of Employees | 71,000 |
| New Jobs Created by 2016 | 29,000 |
| Expected Job Growth by 2016 | 41% |
| Geographical Hotspots | Arizona, Florida |
| Average Hourly Earnings | $10–$16 per hour |

*Sources: U.S. Bureau of Labor Statistics National Employment Matrix, State Occupational Projections*

More specifically, veterinary technologists and technicians have these responsibilities:

- Perform medical tests to aid in diagnosing medical conditions and diseases in pets

- Carry out lab tests such as blood work and urine samples to uncover medical problems

- Take and develop x-rays

- Record a pet's medical history by asking the owner questions

- Assist a veterinarian in carrying out a medical procedure on a pet

Your love for animals may be the driving force behind jumping into this career. It can be tremendously rewarding to see the smile on a pet owner's face when you help restore little Nicky to health. However, you'll also have to bear up under sad stories. Euthanasia, or putting a pet to sleep, is common for unwanted, older, or diseased pets.

Nine out of ten veterinary technologists and technicians work for a veterinarian. The rest of the jobs can be found at animal shelters, zoos, pet grooming stores, and government agencies.

The expected 41 percent growth in the field puts this profession at the top of the charts for recession-proof careers. So why the dramatic growth? It comes down to three factors. First, people get attached to their pets. Dougie the dog becomes part of the family and pet owners are increasingly willing to do anything to prolong a pet's life. Second, technology is advancing the preventive and curative procedures available to veterinarians. Affluent pet owners are taking more and more advantage of these new services available. Finally, shelters, clinics, and hospitals are increasingly searching for skilled technicians rather than veterinary assistants.

**Career Caveat**

Do you know that sign that says "Beware of Dog"? We all know dogs can bite from time to time. Even the friendliest dogs can lose their cool and take a chomp from an unsuspecting leg. Abandoned dogs in shelters and clinics may have been abused, posing a greater risk for biting behaviors. If you choose this path, you'll have to watch your fingers, arms, and legs to keep a tooth from autographing your skin.

While technicians and technologists perform essentially the same duties for veterinarians, the educational paths are different. Entry-level technician positions require a two-year Associate's degree from an American Veterinary Medical Association (AVMA) accredited community college. Here you'll work with live animals in laboratory and clinical settings to gain the experience necessary for the profession. Technology programs take four years instead of two and culminate in a four-year Bachelor's degree in veterinary technology.

Whether you go the technician or technology route, you'll need official certification to score a job. Governed by the Board of Veterinary Examiners or state agencies, you'll earn credentials after passing a written, oral, and practical test. Many states use the National Veterinary Technician (NVT) exam. For these states, you can have your passing scores transferred if you choose to change your state of employment.

So how do you advance your career? You can't exactly count on Puffy the poodle to fill out a positive customer feedback card. Over time, you can undertake private clinical work at an animal hospital. Now you'll be involved in testing cutting-edge medical pet treatments and maybe even finding a cure for a deadly disease. You may be working with pets, but it's possible to uncover a treatment that actually crosses over to human health. Imagine helping Micky the monkey get better and stumbling on a cure for a human ailment. That ought to recession proof your career for years to come!

## The Least You Need to Know

♦ Staff members who surround doctors and dentists are as recession proof as the medical professionals themselves.

♦ You can successfully work in the medical field without ever interacting with patients.

♦ If you love the business side of health care, then consider working as a medical and health services manager.

♦ Strong computer skills can be translated into a recession-proof career as a medical records technician or other health IT professional.

♦ Helping veterinarians care for family pets can keep you in a job for years to come.

# Chapter 6

# The People and Medications That Keep Us Healthy

## In This Chapter

- The connection between the rising demand for medical attention and recession-proof careers in the medical field

- How to figure out which medical career best suits your personality, education, and passion

- What it takes to take care of people as a registered nurse, licensed practical nurse, or home-care aide

- Vital statistics on working as an emergency medical technician or paramedic

- How to build a career developing or dispensing medications and health-related products

Health-care premiums may be on the rise, but so is the demand for medical services in the United States. It's not just the 80 million baby boomers who need extra medical care. Elderly patients and kids alike are using new drugs, trying cutting-edge treatments, and going for more surgery than ever before. The sky-high demand for medical attention equals a recession-proof medical goldmine for you.

What's that you say? The sight of blood makes you queasy? The good news is that an aversion to blood and needles does not rule out all of the careers covered in this chapter.

This chapter covers a variety of recession-proof careers sure to grow as the demand for medical services increases. You'll learn the educational and training requirements, salary trends, job outlook, and geographical hotspots for such careers as registered nurses (RNs), home-care aides, emergency medical technicians (EMTs), pharmacists, and medical scientists. But before we dive into the career details, let's help you narrow in on the medical career that best fits your personality, education, and interests. After all, an EMT and an RN don't share many commonalities on the job.

# What Do You Care For?

So many caretaking choices, so little time. How do you decide among options that range from registered nurse to pharmacist? These careers may share a common industry, but the daily routines couldn't be more different. To focus your thoughts, here's a quick three-question quiz to uncover your passions and qualifications.

1. Which work environment sounds most appealing?

   (A) Working in a home taking care of one patient

   (B) Working in a hospital caring for multiple patients

   (C) Working in an ambulance and handling emergencies

   (D) Working in an office or drug store to produce/dispense drugs

2. What level of education do you possess or would you be willing to obtain?

   (A) No high school degree

   (B) High school or vocational degree

   (C) College degree

   (D) Advanced or specialized degree

3.  Which set of tasks sounds most interesting to you?

    (A) Cooking for an elderly person and changing bed linens

    (B) Checking patient vital signs and administering medications

    (C) Rushing to a car accident scene and attending to victims

    (D) Interacting with drug store clientele and dispensing drugs

Here's a breakdown of what your answers likely mean:

*   *A* answers indicate a preference and skill set match as a personal and home-care aide.

*   *B* answers match careers as an RN or licensed practical nurse.

*   *C* answers indicate you might enjoy a career as an EMT or paramedic.

*   *D* answers point toward careers as a pharmacist or medical scientist.

If your answer choices were *B*, for example, don't feel locked into an RN career. I just wanted to guide your thinking as you learn more about the careers discussed in this chapter.

# Registered Nurses

Have you ever been laid up in a hospital and pushed that little button by the side of your bed for assistance? Chances are, an RN came rushing in to adjust your bed, provide some comfort and nourishment, or administer a basic medical procedure. RNs are responsible for treating and educating patients while also providing guidance and support to patients' family members.

## Outlook for Registered Nurses

| | |
|---|---|
| Current Number of Employees | 2,500,000 |
| New Jobs Created by 2016 | 587,000 |
| Expected Job Growth by 2016 | 23% |
| Geographical Hotspots | Texas, Utah |
| Average Annual Earnings | $48,000–$70,000 |

*Sources: U.S. Bureau of Labor Statistics National Employment Matrix, State Occupational Projections*

More specifically, here are some of the most common tasks performed by RNs:

- Monitor a plan of care and administer medications

- Teach a post-discharge care plan to patients and family members

- Enter vital signs and medical history into a computer

- Perform tests, evaluate results, and offer preliminary diagnoses to a doctor

Nearly 60 percent of RNs work in hospitals where the nurses follow strict protocol to prevent potentially dangerous interactions with patients. One minute you're serving harmless watermelon Jell-O to a patient, and the next you're in contact with hazardous medications, infectious diseases, and syringes. You'll want to take sanitation and sterilization seriously to minimize inadvertent contact with harmful materials.

Of course, you don't have to limit your job search to hospitals. As an RN, you'll be in high demand in physician offices, outpatient care centers, and home health services. Temporary employment agencies are even seeking RNs who can fill short-term staffing needs at health-care establishments.

## License to Care

Your passion for caring will require some education and licensing. First you'll need to commit to one of three educational paths:

1. Over 700 nursing programs offer four-year programs to earn a Bachelor of Science degree in nursing (BSN).

2. More than 850 RN programs offer two- and three-year Associate's degrees in nursing (ADN) through community and junior colleges.

3. Various hospitals offer three-year diploma programs to become an RN.

Regardless of the nursing program you choose, you'll need to pass a national licensing examination after you graduate. Known as the NCLEX-RN, this exam is required by all 50 states and the District of Columbia to obtain a nursing license. Don't worry, if you move, you probably won't have to retake the test. Many states honor licensing exam scores from other states.

**Another Path**

How would you like to recession proof your health-care career without committing two, three, or four years to education? Consider becoming a licensed practical nurse (LPN). With just one year of training, you'll be qualified to care for patients under the supervision of a physician or RN. It's not a bad shortcut if your dream is to care for the sick, disabled, or injured without hitting the books for seemingly endless semesters.

## What's the Special of the Day?

Specializing is common for RNs, and the advanced certifications vary depending on the area of specialty. For example, a nephrology nurse specializes in kidney treatment; a geriatric nurse works with the elderly. You can even specialize by treatment type, such as a long-term care nurse who provides health services to a patient with a chronic condition.

Have you ever wanted to be the chief? Well, by taking on additional management responsibilities you can advance from assistant to director and even to chief nurse. To get to the top, you'll likely need a graduate nursing or health services administration degree.

You can even make a jump to the business side of the RN profession. Insurance companies, pharmaceutical manufacturers, and managed care companies are always looking for RNs to fill marketing, consulting, and quality assurance roles.

RN skills also translate outside the medical community. Forensics nurses are called upon to investigate crime and accident scenes. Do you prefer courtroom dramas? Legal nurse consultants partner with lawyers in preparing for medical-based cases. Can you speak in front of 500 folks without shaking in your boots? Then you'll thrive as a prominent RN speaker by leading public seminars on various diseases, conditions, and treatment plans. The bottom line is that your RN skills can translate into investigative, legal, and even public-speaking fields. Talk about recession proofing your career!

# Personal and Home-Care Aides

Let's say your mom, now 82 years old, is showing signs of physical impairment. You weigh the options. Mom could move to an expensive nursing home, she could share a common roof with you for the first time in 40 years, or you could hire a home-care aid. The rising popularity of seeking in-home care for those you love helps explain why the personal and home-care aide industry is expected to double in size by 2016.

Home-care aides typically work with elderly, disabled, or ill people to help them stay in their homes rather than having to move to a health facility.

## Outlook for Personal and Home-Care Aides

| | |
|---|---|
| Current Number of Employees | 767,000 |
| New Jobs Created by 2016 | 389,000 |
| Expected Job Growth by 2016 | 51% |
| Geographical Hotspots | Minnesota, North Carolina |
| Average Hourly Earnings | $7–$10 per hour |

*Sources: U.S. Bureau of Labor Statistics National Employment Matrix, State Occupational Projections*

Here are some of the most common responsibilities for personal and home-care aides:

◆ Provide housekeeping services including laundry, bed linen changes, mopping, and vacuuming

◆ Plan meals for special diets (i.e., diabetic), shop for ingredients, and cook the food

◆ Accompany clients to doctor appointments or on errands

◆ Help groom clients including bathing, shaving, and dressing for the day

◆ Offer daily companionship, friendship, and psychological support

The explosive growth for personal and home-care aides can be attributed to the fact that many elderly patients prefer to receive care in the familiar confines of their own homes. Additionally, hospital and nursing home care can be cost prohibitive, making home care a favored option. Home care is also an excellent option for patients who need everyday assistance of the nonmedical variety.

The National Association for Home Care and Hospice (NAHC) offers national certification for personal and home-care aides. This is a voluntary certification and many workers choose on-the-job training instead. In many cases, home-care aides work under the supervision of social workers or RNs who monitor the overall care plan. Don't worry, they won't be breathing down your neck like a micromanaging boss. Instead, their job is to provide the medical expertise to complement your home-care skills. It can actually be comforting as a home aide to know someone is there to help you manage medications, oversee nutritional plans, and coordinate physician visits.

## In Their Own Words

I've been Miriam's caretaker for over five years. After a lifetime as a social butterfly, she's now confined to a wheelchair and battles Alzheimer's disease. My job includes housekeeping, cooking, grocery shopping, grooming, and helping dispense medication. I even accompany Miriam to museums, cafes, and shops to get her out of the house. After all these years together, I care for Miriam as if she were my own mother.

—Rosana, home-care aide for Miriam

Being a home-care aide is a bit like dating. You can choose to be monogamous or to see other people. Some aides develop long-standing relationships with one client. Others prefer to visit multiple clients in the same day or week. Still others partner with a second aide to provide round-the-clock client support in shifts. The beauty of the occupation is you can translate your skills to working with newborns and disabled children; many of the responsibilities overlap.

# Emergency Medical Technicians and Paramedics

You're cruising through town in your car butchering the lyrics to your favorite song when a siren starts blaring. You pull over to the side of the road, curious about the emergency racing by. What you probably didn't realize is that the employees in the ambulance work in a recession-proof career. Emergency medical technicians (EMTs) and paramedics are typically the first ones on the scene after a 911 call is placed.

## Outlook for EMTs and Paramedics

| | |
|---|---|
| Current Number of Employees | 201,000 |
| New Jobs Created by 2016 | 39,000 |
| Expected Job Growth by 2016 | 19% |
| Geographical Hotspots | Nevada, South Carolina |
| Average Annual Earnings | $21,000–$35,000 |

*Sources: U.S. Bureau of Labor Statistics National Employment Matrix, State Occupational Projections*

Responsibilities include the following:

◆ Provide immediate medical attention in varied emergency situations, such as car accidents, strokes, and childbirth

◆ Coordinate with police and physicians to determine the best course of treatment on the scene

◆ Immobilize a patient on a stretcher to prevent further injuries or complications

◆ Care for sick or injured patients while transporting them to the nearest hospital or medical facility

**Career Caveat**

Being an EMT or paramedic is nothing like a routine desk job. Be prepared to work irregular hours and night shifts; emergencies are not limited to 9 to 5. Also, you have to be comfortable handling the full gamut of emergencies, from simple bruises to horrible traffic accidents. Make sure you can employ lightning-quick thinking skills because your decisions can mean the difference between life and death.

As an EMT or paramedic, you'll typically work in teams of two or three. Patient care involves checking vital signs, administering care, and driving the ambulance. Once at the hospital, your job is to transport the patient to the emergency department while conveying your observations from the emergency to the attending physician.

Breaking into the field requires a high school diploma to enter a formal EMT training program. Basic certification requires a mix of coursework and on-the-job emergency room or ambulance training. At the more advanced levels, you'll need an Associate's degree, as well as extensive clinical and field experience. Regardless of your level, all 50 states have some type of certification requirement. More specifically, you can advance to one of three levels as an EMT or paramedic:

1. **EMT—Basic:** You provide straightforward on-the-scene care and handle ambulance transport.

2. **EMT—Intermediate:** You can offer more advanced patient care on the scene, although this varies by state.

3. **EMT—Paramedic:** You are qualified to dispense medications on the scene and even administer complex diagnostic medical tests.

As an EMT or paramedic, you can work for a private ambulance service, your local government, the fire department, or an area hospital. If airborne care is your cup of tea, consider trading in the ambulance for a helicopter. Imagine the rush of flying into a remote mountainside to save the day for a stranded hiker—that's the stuff of Hollywood movies!

# Pharmacists

There's just something about a street corner in the center of town that screams, "Put a drug store here!" Every time a new drug store springs up, so does a sign saying "Pharmacist Wanted." From dispensing drugs to advising patients and warning about side effects, pharmacists offer full-service drugs and medication consulting.

## Outlook for Pharmacists

| | |
|---|---|
| Current Number of Employees | 243,000 |
| New Jobs Created by 2016 | 53,000 |
| Expected Job Growth by 2016 | 22% |
| Geographical Hotspots | Arizona, Nevada |
| Average Annual Earnings | $83,000–$108,000 |

*Sources: U.S. Bureau of Labor Statistics National Employment Matrix, State Occupational Projections*

More specifically, pharmacists carry out these tasks:

- Dispense prescription medications to customers

- Advise patients on the side effects and interactions of drugs

- Mix ingredients to form medications and compounds

- Counsel customers on general health-related topics including diet and nutrition

- Oversee and lead a pharmacy staff of technicians, cashiers, and other positions

Breaking into a pharmacy career requires a Doctor of Pharmacy degree from a college of pharmacy. You'll learn the ins and outs of every drug under the sun, as well as how to communicate effectively with physicians and store patrons. Most pharmacy programs integrate real-life training, with approximately 25 percent of your time spent working directly in drug stores under experienced pharmacist supervision.

### Another Path

Perhaps you love the idea of working in a drug store but don't have the stomach for a Doctor of Pharmacy degree. Consider a career as a pharmacy technician. You'll be the pharmacist's right hand, helping to count pills, label bottles, work the cash register, and answer incoming calls. Pharmacy technician opportunities are expected to grow 32 percent by 2016, so jobs *will* be available.

While 62 percent of pharmacists work in drug stores, this is not the only employment option. Nearly 25 percent of pharmacists choose to work in hospitals. Beyond drug stores and hospitals, nontraditional pharmacy careers are growing in popularity. If you're willing to go for a Master of Science degree or Ph.D., you might land a job as a university professor or as a researcher for a drug company. That's when even bigger bucks start rolling in!

Specializing is another way to go if you want to get ahead and establish your pharmacy niche. For example, you can choose to focus on home health care drug monitoring and be responsible for preparing medications administered in the home. You can also specialize in a specific drug therapy. Got a soft spot for caring for patients suffering from mental illness? Consider specializing as a psychiatric pharmacist. Want to help those battling cancer? Maybe oncology pharmacy is the way to go. Whatever specialty you choose, you'll sleep well knowing your career is expected to grow 22 percent by 2016.

# Medical Scientists

If you dream of gracing the cover of a national magazine in appreciation of your breakthrough medical discovery, then medical scientist could be the right career path for you. Medical scientists research diseases, viruses, and bacteria to uncover new medical treatments and drugs.

## Outlook for Medical Scientists

| | |
|---|---|
| Current Number of Employees | 92,000 |
| New Jobs Created by 2016 | 18,000 |
| Expected Job Growth by 2016 | 20% |
| Geographical Hotspots | Nevada, South Carolina |
| Average Annual Earnings | $45,000–$88,000 |

*Sources: U.S. Bureau of Labor Statistics National Employment Matrix, State Occupational Projections*

Medical scientists are likely to be involved in the following:

- Carry out research in an effort to control or even eliminate a deadly, infectious disease

- Formulate new vaccines to prevent the onset of a particular disease or condition

- Conduct clinical trials on new drug therapies to test effectiveness and unwanted side effects

- Pen a technical piece for a medical journal on the pros, cons, and outlook for a new treatment

Where do medical scientists work their magic to cure diseases, invent new drugs, and vaccinate us against harmful viruses? More than one third choose to work in colleges and universities where research is the name of the game. More than 25 percent of medical scientists work for scientific research and development service firms. Another 10 percent work for pharmaceutical and medicine manufacturing companies. The balance work for hospitals and other health facilities.

A Ph.D. is the minimum educational requirement if you want to be a medical scientist. The one exception is if you work as an epidemiologist. An epidemiologist is a medical scientist who researches the spread of dangerous diseases and investigates prevention strategies. Epidemiologists can get by with a Master's degree in public health, although *some* employers require a Ph.D. or medical degree.

If you want to be a medical scientist, choose a science major. You'll want to complete courses in chemistry, biology, physics, and mathematics. Then the big question is whether to go the Ph.D. or medical degree route. The Ph.D. route will suffice if you want to focus on researching basic life processes and medical problems. The medical degree option will be required if you want to test drug therapies on human patients or perform invasive procedures of any kind.

**Another Path**

If you want to be on the cutting edge of medical science, give some thought to biotechnology. It's a rapidly growing field if you're interested in DNA and genes. Scientists are increasingly involved in sequencing human genes to understand their function. Solving this DNA mystery may lead to cures for some of the most challenging diseases, including Parkinson's disease, Alzheimer's disease, and maybe even cancer and AIDS.

Some medical scientists choose to earn both a Ph.D. and a medical degree. That is a serious educational commitment, but it's a strong recession-proof strategy if you have the time.

What signs indicate that your medical science career is on the rise? Well, greater independence in your research and a larger research budget are sure signs your superiors believe in your talents. If you work in a university setting, earning tenure is about as recession proof as it gets. In a business setting, you can always strive to advance from medical scientist to the leader of a team of medical scientists. It's more responsibility, but the more valuable you become, the less likely your name will be called at the next round of layoffs.

## The Least You Need to Know

- The rising demand for medical services represents a recession-proof goldmine for medical-based careers.

- A fear of blood and needles does not necessarily rule out a career in health care.

- If you enjoy taking care of others, consider a career as a registered nurse, personal and home-care aide, or licensed practical nurse.

- You can recession proof your career by learning how to dispense medications and counsel drug store customers.

- Researching and developing the next generation of drug therapies can keep you employed for years to come.

# Therapy for the Mind, Body, and Soul

## In This Chapter

◆ How to get work as a counselor to help people overcome emotional, family, and career-related challenges

◆ What it takes to work as a physical therapist for injured people or those suffering chronic pain

◆ How to put yourself to work as an occupational therapist—and help other people regain or learn work and life skills

◆ Why working as a barber, manicurist, skin-care specialist, or other personal appearance worker is a recession-proof choice

We all know our minds, bodies, and souls have a way of making their own agenda. You may feel great physically, but an emotional problem keeps you up at night. Or you have your head on just right, but that car accident has left your back out of whack. It's these daily—and lifelong—struggles that keep therapists and counselors off the unemployment line.

In this chapter, we start with all kinds of counselors, including those who keep marriages together, help addicts overcome drugs and alcohol, and even guide students in choosing a college. From there, we delve into both occupational and physical therapists. In their own ways, each helps patients resume "normal" daily life. Finally, we talk about personal appearance workers who make everyone from movie stars to average citizens look their best. By the end of this chapter, you'll know which recession-proof careers best keep the mind, body, and soul in sync.

# Counselors

When I was 19 years old, I scored a camp counselor job at a local day camp. I spent my days throwing footballs to adolescents, teaching the fine art of belly flops, and breaking up arguments over who gets the last ice cream bar. This is not the kind of counselor we're talking about in this section. Instead, we're referring to counselors who help people with family, mental, and career-related problems.

## Outlook for Counselors

| | |
|---|---|
| Current Number of Employees | 635,000 |
| New Jobs Created by 2016 | 136,000 |
| Expected Job Growth by 2016 | 21% |
| Geographical Hotspots | South Carolina, Tennessee |
| Average Annual Earnings | $29,000–$55,000 |

*Sources: U.S. Bureau of Labor Statistics National Employment Matrix, State Occupational Projections*

Specifically, we're covering the following types of counselors:

- Marriage and family therapists who help couples and their children overcome emotional conflicts, communication breakdowns, and interpersonal struggles

- Substance abuse counselors who counsel individuals battling alcohol and drug addictions, gambling problems, and eating disorders

- School counselors who evaluate special needs in younger children and advise older students on college and career choices

- Career counselors who offer job assistance outside the school setting for people who are unemployed or looking to make a career change

- Mental health counselors who help people cope with challenges such as depression, obsessive-compulsive behavior, or bipolar disorder

The counseling field as a whole is recession proof and deserves its place in this book. Regardless of whether you're helping people overcome addictions, emotional problems, or family struggles, it's all about helping people put their lives in order.

The variety of counselors means the work environment varies greatly. Devote your time to kids and you'll likely work out of a school. Set up a private practice, either in your home or in an office, and your time is spent seeing clients throughout the day. Go the mental health or substance abuse route, and your nameplate just may hang outside a hospital office door.

Chances are you'll need a Master's degree to get your career off the ground. Supervised clinical experience will also be required to obtain your degree. Some states accept a Bachelor's degree alone, provided you take the required counseling courses in college. Where you live and work will dictate what kind of degree you need.

Earning a license to practice requires different steps, depending on your area of specialty. For example, if you want to be a school counselor, you'll likely need a state school counseling certification. Go the nonschool route and a Master's degree, plus at least two years or 3,000 hours of supervised clinical experience, will earn you that coveted license.

**Another Path**

People with birth defects or those suffering serious injuries from car crashes and accidents often need counseling. If helping this group cope sounds rewarding to you, consider becoming a rehabilitation counselor. You'll help people make peace with a physical deformity while giving the emotional tools to increase a client's capacity to function on a daily basis.

You can grow your career and your bank account in two ways. First, gain a following. If you become known as the couples' counselor who can save a marriage, you'll have clients banging down your door to ward off divorce. Or if you can show a gambling addict how to spend Friday night at the dinner table instead of at the blackjack table, word will spread of your counseling abilities. Second, you can advance to supervisory, research, or teaching roles. Groups of counselors need a leader, the field always needs breakthrough therapy techniques, and new counselors want to learn from the best. You can keep your practice and delve into leading others, researching methods, or teaching. Now that's quite a recession-proof one-two punch!

# Physical Therapists

I'm embarrassed to admit it, but I once pulled my back bending over to pick up a tissue. I'd like to say I had manhandled a shark the day before, but it's not true. After eight sessions with a physical therapist, my tissue-induced back problem was solved. Physical therapists help improve mobility, decrease pain, and restore functionality to patients suffering from injuries or diseases.

## Outlook for Physical Therapists

| | |
|---|---|
| Current Number of Employees | 173,000 |
| New Jobs Created by 2016 | 47,000 |
| Expected Job Growth by 2016 | 27% |
| Geographical Hotspots | Arizona, Florida |
| Average Annual Earnings | $55,000–$78,000 |

*Sources: U.S. Bureau of Labor Statistics National Employment Matrix, State Occupational Projections*

More specifically, physical therapists do the following:

◆ Test a patient's strength and range of motion to create a treatment strategy

◆ Help patients rebuild muscle and improve flexibility through targeted exercises

◆ Reduce swelling and relieve pain through electrical stimulation, heat, or cold

◆ Teach patients how to use assistance devices such as crutches or walkers

◆ Conduct examinations, document patient progress, and adjust treatment plans accordingly

As a physical therapist, there's a 60 percent chance you'll be working in a hospital or a fellow physical therapist office. But you can also score a job working in a nursing facility, physician office, or even see patients in their homes.

The aging population is the biggest factor driving the positive career outlook for physical therapists. Chronic and debilitating diseases drive the increased need for therapeutic services. It's no wonder Arizona and Florida, two favored retirement destinations, are the geographic hotspots of the future for physical therapists.

> **In Their Own Words**
>
> While a doctor may save your life, a physical therapist can make it more livable by reducing pain and improving quality of function. Further, a physical therapist will likely spend more time with a patient in one visit than their physician will spend in an entire month. This creates an interdependency that keeps physical therapists in high demand.
>
> —Marc Madison, owner, Ridgewood Physical Therapy

Let's say you're in college and see physical therapy as the recession-proof career for you. Here's a quick snapshot of the steps that can make it happen:

1. As an undergraduate, you'll want to take relevant courses, including anatomy, chemistry, and physics.

2. While in school, volunteer or get paid to work in the physical therapy department at a hospital or therapist's office.

3. As graduation approaches, apply to one of over 200 accredited physical therapy education programs.

4. In two years you can earn a Master's degree or in three years go for a Ph.D.

5. Pass both national and state exams and you'll be licensed to launch your physical therapy career.

So you've followed the steps and your career is underway. How exactly do you advance your career? First, attend continuing education classes to expand your knowledge. Depending on the state in which you practice, this may be more of a mandate than a good idea. Some states require continuing education to maintain your physical therapy license.

The best bet to recession proof your career is to continue to learn new therapy techniques and technologies. The broader the scope of services you provide, the less likely you are to lose business to the therapist down the block. You can also choose to specialize in a particular area of physical therapy. It's always good for a business to be known as the therapist of choice for a certain condition. Of course, affiliating with local hospitals and clinics can also keep a steady flow of new patients banging on your door.

# Occupational Therapists

My uncle Sol read *The New York Times* cover to cover every single day of his life. I begged him to be a contestant on *Jeopardy*. His encyclopedic knowledge would have put him in the Tournament of Champions. Age and medical complications threatened to put his paper-reading streak in jeopardy. It was an occupational therapist who helped him regain the ability to enjoy his favorite pastime. Occupational therapists work with patients suffering from mental, physical, or developmental challenges to help them recover their daily life or work routines.

## Outlook for Occupational Therapists

| | |
|---|---|
| Current Number of Employees | 99,000 |
| New Jobs Created by 2016 | 23,000 |
| Expected Job Growth by 2016 | 23% |
| Geographical Hotspots | California, Massachusetts |
| Average Annual Earnings | $50,000–$74,000 |

*Sources: U.S. Bureau of Labor Statistics National Employment Matrix, State Occupational Projections*

The most common roles performed by occupational therapists include these:

◆ Help patients perform daily routine tasks such as cooking, showering, and grooming

◆ Teach physical exercises to help a patient regain manual dexterity lost in an accident or through disability

◆ Collaborate with an employer to modify a work environment so it's suitable for an employee with a disability

◆ Improve decision-making, problem-solving, or other life skills with the help of a computer program

◆ Demonstrate the use of wheelchairs and other aids for patients suffering from permanent disabilities

Job opportunities abound in hospitals. It's common for recovering patients to be sent to rehab wings or facilities to regain physical and mental acuity. Therapist offices and nursing care facilities also offer ample career opportunities.

If answering to a boss is not your thing, you can also go it alone. Many occupational therapists run their own practice, making their money driving from home to home to see patients. I recommend loading your iPod and plugging it into the car adaptor or finding a favorite radio station for all the driving in your future.

### Another Path

Do you like the idea of helping to eliminate pain from people's lives? Occupational therapy is not the only answer. Consider some spine-tingling career stability as a chiropractor. Chiropractic care is covered by more insurance companies than in the past, so people with back pain are increasingly turning to chiropractors for spine adjustments. You can work with a hospital or physician office or even go it alone, which is what more than 50 percent of chiropractors choose to do.

## How to Master the Skills

To make occupational therapy your occupation, you'll need a Master's degree, half a year of supervised field work, passing grades on both national and state exams, and a license. I know it seems like a lot; let's break it down so it seems less daunting. More than 100 schools around the country offer Master's degree programs in occupational therapy. You can also go the combined undergraduate/Master's route if you know early on this is the career for you. Around 65 programs offer the combo platter. You'll want to take high school courses in chemistry, health, and physics to improve your odds of acceptance into a combo program.

With your Master's degree in hand, six months of field work should be next on your list. View this as an apprenticeship—a chance to work under the watchful eye of an experienced professional. After 180 days, you'll build the confidence to be on your own and put your talent to the test. That's when it's time for one final test, the national certification exam. Passing scores earn you the title of Occupational Therapist Registered (OTR). Now you can really hit the ground running, although in some states you'll need some additional certifications and education to treat patients.

## Find Your Niche

Becoming the occupational therapist of choice for the human race is a noble aspiration, but may not be realistic. Specializing is more likely to net you a group of recession-proof clients. For example, you can work with the littlest of little ones, infants and toddlers. As soon as parents notice developmental delays, a call to the occupational therapist is high on the list. Sticking with a love for kids, you can also target school-age children who need therapeutic help.

On the opposite end of the spectrum, elderly patients are a great way to go, too. The aging baby boomer population will surely increase demand for therapeutic services. Helping elderly patients lead productive, active lifestyles can be rewarding.

Specializing by age is not your only option. If mental health is more up your alley, consider working with patients who are mentally ill or emotionally unstable. Teaching daily coping skills can be rewarding to help these patients go about their daily routines.

# Personal Appearance Workers

They say death and taxes are two sure things in life. If you think about it, haircuts should be on the list, too. Last time I checked, hair has a preference for continuous growth. But this section is about more than barbers and hair stylists. Careers focused on personal appearance are in growth mode. That includes manicurists, pedicurists, makeup artists, and even skin-care specialists.

## Outlook for Personal Appearance Workers

| | |
|---|---|
| Current Number of Employees | 825,000 |
| New Jobs Created by 2016 | 117,000 |
| Expected Job Growth by 2016 | 14% |
| Geographical Hotspots | Varies by specialty |
| Average Hourly Earnings | $8–$14 per hour |

*Sources: U.S. Bureau of Labor Statistics National Employment Matrix, State Occupational Projections*

Typical roles for professionals focused on appearance enhancement include the following:

◆ Barbers who cut, trim, and style hair for mostly male clientele

◆ Hair dressers and stylists who perform more intricate hair-care procedures such as perms, coloring, and styling

◆ Manicurists and pedicurists who keep nails clean, healthy, and polished

◆ Makeup artists who help news people, actors, and other performers look their best for TV, movies, and the stage

◆ Skin-care specialists who offer a range of services, from facials to massages and full body treatments

Nearly half of all personal appearance workers are self-employed. This may mean owning your own barbershop or salon and controlling your destiny. Or an increasingly popular option for personal appearance workers is to lease space from a salon owner. This way, you still feel like you own your business but without the overhead and ownership risk.

When it comes to makeup artists, the most likely employment option is a movie or television studio, or even theater company. Of course, you can also walk through your local department store and find makeup artists eager to paint your face with the newest "it" color.

Depending on your personal appearance career of choice, the training and licensing required varies. Barbers and cosmetologists first must complete a state-licensed program in barber or cosmetology school. You're looking at nine months of full-time school (or more months of part-time school) to earn your Associate's degree. All in all, there are four basic steps to get your career in gear.

> **Career Caveat**
>
> Personal appearance jobs are not for folks who like to sit at a desk from 9 to 5. You'll likely be on your feet most of the day. Come to think of it, you'll be on your feet nights and weekends, too. After all, these are the most convenient times for many people to schedule haircut, manicure, and skin-care appointments.

1. You must be at least 16 years old.

2. You must have a high school diploma or earn your GED.

3. You need to graduate from a state-licensed program.

4. You need to pass a state licensing test consisting of a written exam plus a demonstration of cutting and styling skills.

If you don't have nine months to birth your barber or cosmetology career, consider hairstyling, makeup, manicures, and pedicures. Generally, minimal vocational or even on-the-job training is all you'll need to get started. Sure you'll start with the most basic of responsibilities, say washing hair or cleaning manicure tables. Soon enough you'll advance to more challenging tasks working directly with customers.

So how do you go from washing hair, sweeping the floor, or cleaning out pedicure tubs to a personal appearance empire? There are three basic ways to advance your career. First and foremost, build a following. Have you ever noticed how one barber can have an empty chair while the next has a waiting list five people deep? People care about their looks and they're willing to wait for superior service. Word of mouth is also huge in building a clientele. Do your job, do it well, learn the latest tricks of the trade, and watch word spread of your personal appearance prowess.

The next route to success is teaching newbies what you know. Barber and cosmetology schools, as well as vocational programs, are always looking for teachers. So master your skills, build that following, and then supplement your income giving back to others who are just starting out. You can also cross over into personal appearance marketing. The companies that produce new shampoos, fresh-scented gels, and the hottest nail polish colors need people to stir up interest at local hair and nail salons. This could be a perfect fit if spending all day in one salon is not for you. You'll spend your working hours popping in and out of salons, earning hefty commissions every time you make a sale.

## The Least You Need to Know

- Becoming a counselor, regardless of specialty, is a good recession-proof choice.

- Physical therapy is the way to go if removing pain, improving flexibility, and strengthening muscles sounds rewarding.

- Consider working as an occupational therapist if you enjoy helping people regain daily work and life skills.

- If helping people look and feel their best puts a smile on your face, then working in the personal appearance field is right for you.

# Part 3

## Learn to Teach

The gap is growing between those who need to learn and those who are trained to teach. Our country badly needs more teachers to educate our youth. The federal government is pouring billions of dollars into education, hoping to lure more and more talented people into the profession. Our country's leaders have made it clear they do not want to fall farther behind the rest of the world in giving our youngsters the educational tools they need to succeed.

All of these trends add up to the simple fact that teaching is recession proof. You can specialize by age group, or you can specialize by subject. In this part, we even talk about special education teachers and substance abuse counselors. Basically, if you want to help students learn or overcome life's mental and emotional challenges, then this is the recession-proof part for you.

# Chapter 8

# The People Who Shape Our Children

## In This Chapter

- ◆ How child-care workers can thrive in good times and bad
- ◆ Why preschool teachers are working in the fastest-growing educational age group of all teachers
- ◆ What it takes to build a stable career teaching kindergarten, elementary, and middle school children
- ◆ Why the people who assist teachers are just as recession proof as the teachers themselves

Much of your own career success can likely be traced to the positive influence of your teachers. From the toddler years through middle school you learned how to play well with others, multiply and divide, and even memorize the periodic table. You probably didn't realize that the people teaching you were in recession-proof careers.

That's right—child-care workers; as well as preschool, kindergarten, elementary, and middle school teachers; and teacher assistants are working on solid ground. This chapter is all about the training, education, and advancement opportunities for the folks who shape our youth. If you're interested in working with toddlers, teenagers, or in between, then this is the chapter for you.

You'll notice we don't touch on secondary school teachers in this chapter. That's because, with the exception of math and science teachers (covered in Chapter 10), high school teacher openings are expected to grow at a much slower rate than teaching positions at other grades. In fact, according to the U.S. Department of Labor, high school teaching positions will grow at only a 5 percent rate through 2016. The teaching levels covered in this chapter are poised for 13 percent growth and more. So let's get started on reviewing the teaching opportunities poised for double-digit growth.

# Child-Care Workers

Let's get one thing straight about child-care workers and recessions. You're probably thinking that when the economy sours, families view the nanny as an expendable luxury. That's probably true for stay-at-home parents who use child-care workers for a parenting break or to get stuff done around the house. However, there is an opposing recession trend regarding child-care workers that keeps them in business. Many parents fear losing their jobs during a recession. This leads to extra hours in the cubicle to make a good impression. It also leads to single-income families choosing to become dual-income families to diversify and expand their earning potential. The bottom line is that hiring someone to watch the kids is critical to free up parents to earn the money to put food on the table.

Now that we understand the potential for child-care workers, let's dive into the nature of the work, training requirements, and advancement opportunities. Child-care workers nurture children who are not yet ready for formal schooling. So, we're generally talking about infants through roughly age three. The actual age when parents enroll kids in formal schooling varies by location and by parental preference.

## Outlook for Child-Care Workers

| | |
|---|---|
| Current Number of Employees | 1,388,000 |
| New Jobs Created by 2016 | 248,000 |
| Expected Job Growth by 2016 | 18% |
| Geographical Hotspots | Louisiana, Utah |
| Average Annual Earnings | $15,000–$22,000 |

*Sources: U.S. Bureau of Labor Statistics National Employment Matrix, State Occupational Projections*

Basic responsibilities of child-care workers include all of the following:

◆ Care for children when parents are away or at work

◆ Attend to basic children's needs, including preparing and serving meals, dressing the children, and changing diapers

◆ Plan activities to stimulate and entertain kids

◆ Teach children to be social and to play well with others

◆ Help kids explore personal interests, develop early talents, and learn new life skills

There are basically three kinds of child-care workers. The breakdown comes from where you work. The first type of child-care worker spends the day in the child's home. Home-based child-care workers attend to the child's needs throughout the day. Some child-care workers set up shop in their own home. In this situation, one or more kids are dropped off at your home. The third possibility is working at a child-care center. In this scenario, parents deliver children to the center on the way to work.

**Another Path**

The majority of child-care workers focus on the littlest of little ones. However, there is also a market for supervising older children before and after school. This means you can break into the child-care field even if diaper changing isn't your thing. Remember, most schools end by 3 P.M. Very few parents can leave work that early to care for their kids.

## A Child-Care Worker's Day

Working in a family home is a very different day compared with running a child-care center from your home or working at an actual child-care center. Let's talk about the pros and cons of each career choice. Working for one family is great for child-care workers who want to devote time to shaping one child or a group of siblings. You can really dedicate yourself to caring for and influencing the early years of the child or children you work with every day. Additionally, you'll likely build a relationship with the family and may even feel like a member after some time on the job. The downside is the social aspects of the job and the child-care resources available. Spending your day with little ones who can't exactly communicate may make you feel isolated. Additionally, you're at the mercy of whatever books, toys, and games the parents choose to purchase for the home. This may or may not be sufficient to do the job to the best of your ability. Still, with the right personality, energy, and creativity, a great nanny can make a big impact.

On the flip side, you can choose to run a child-care center from your home or work at an established center. Now you'll go from caring for one baby or a few siblings to an entire center full of little ones. You'll also likely partner with at least one other child-care worker to keep an eye on all of the kids under your watch. As you can imagine, the stimulation from all these kids can be exciting and rewarding, but also extremely challenging and frustrating. Picture 10 kids running around with at least one child crying at any one time. However, the right organization skills, patience, and a loving disposition make this an ideal role.

Wherever you choose to work, let's make an important distinction between child-care workers and preschool teachers, which are discussed in the next chapter. The job of a child-care worker is mostly focused on attending to basic needs; preschool teachers focus more on teaching as opposed to attending. Your preference should help dictate whether you pursue a child-care worker or preschool teacher position. In some cases, the job responsibilities overlap. For example, helping a toddler grasp and hold objects could be considered attending to basic needs. However, you're also teaching a life skill as a preschool teacher might do.

## Training and Advancement

Unlike kindergarten, elementary, and middle school teachers—about whom you'll read later in this chapter—many child-care worker jobs require little more than a high school degree. Requirements do vary by state, so you'll want to inform yourself about your state guidelines before pursuing a child-care worker job.

In general, requirements for child-care workers in private homes are less than those for child-care workers in centers. When parents hire a child-care worker for their home, the most important factor is parent comfort. Parents want to build trust with you, see you in action with their young ones, and feel comfortable leaving you alone with their pride and joy. This comfort level is usually much more important than formal child-care training. Few states even regulate child-care workers in the home, so this is another reason formal training is less common among these workers.

If you choose to work in a child-care center, you're more likely to be regulated by the state. Requirements can vary from a high school degree to a national Child Development Associate (CDA) credential to college courses or a degree in early childhood education. Many child-care centers form their own training requirements. This can include prior child-care work experience, specialized on-the-job training, or even an Associate's degree in early childhood education.

Licensing is important for child-care centers to stay in good graces with the state. These licensing requirements hold for formal child-care centers and those run out of your home. Background checks for all employees, immunizations against infectious diseases, and CPR training are the most common requirements for child-care centers to maintain a license.

If your goal is moving up the child-care employment chain, there are a few ways to accomplish the mission. First, doing a great job for a family often leads to more hours and higher pay. The birth of another child can also raise your income. If you work in a child-care center, you can move up to supervise other teachers or even get involved in administrative duties. You can also package up your child-care experience to go work for a nanny agency or other child-care referral service. Helping parents find the right care options for their beloved kids is a great way to transfer your child-care skills to a new job.

# Preschool Teachers

If only other years of school were like preschool. When learning occurs primarily through playing, you're bound to have a great day at school. If only we could all be paid to play when we enter our working years. Preschool teachers work with students generally under the age of five.

## Outlook for Preschool Teachers

| | |
|---|---|
| Current Number of Employees | 437,000 |
| New Jobs Created by 2016 | 115,000 |
| Expected Job Growth by 2016 | 26% |
| Geographical Hotspots | Louisiana, Utah |
| Average Annual Earnings | $23,000 |

*Sources: U.S. Bureau of Labor Statistics National Employment Matrix, State Occupational Projections*

Primary responsibilities include the following:

◆ Guide early language and vocabulary development through interactive exercises

◆ Improve social skills by teaching children how to play effectively with each other and to work as teams

◆ Introduce cause-and-effect concepts by showing students the results and consequences of actions they take

◆ Begin basic math concepts such as counting rocks, blocks, or balls

Unlike kindergarten, elementary, and middle school teachers, preschool teachers follow a less structured approach. You can't exactly expect a group of three-year-olds to stare at the blackboard all morning. Instead, preschool teachers focus on small-group learning, one-on-one instruction, and even creative approaches to introduce a new concept. For example, students might learn the alphabet by singing a song instead of by rote memorization.

**Career Caveat** _____

As a preschool teacher, you just might be the very first teacher experience for a toddler. Don't underestimate the profound impact you can have on kids at this young, impressionable age. You're responsible for shaping their early learning style, social skills, and initial view of education. Take this role seriously because your influence will start either positive or negative momentum for each student you teach.

What makes preschool education so different from kindergarten and beyond? The biggest variable is the students' capacity to learn from traditional methods. As a preschool teacher, you have to be comfortable teaching through song, games, rhyming, and other creative outlets. So much of your success hinges on entertaining and captivating the students. What traits can help you succeed as a preschool teacher? Five basic characteristics will give you the best odds of success.

1. **Kid-based communication**
   You can't just rely on logic when dealing with little kids. You need to speak, listen, and act in a way the little ones can relate to and appreciate.

2. **Patience**
   Parents know even one kid can drive you bonkers on a given day. If you have from 5 to 20 little ones around you, the need to hold it together is critical.

3. **Creativity**
   Attention spans of children under five years old are limited. You must continuously find new and inventive ways to explain concepts.

4. **Parent relationship skills**
   This will be the first time many parents leave their kids in an environment other than the home. It's your job to recap the day and make parents feel a part of the educational experience.

5. **Fairness**
   You're going to work with the most outgoing kid, the shy kid, and everything in between. An even-handed approach is key, so little ones don't feel you're playing favorites.

As you might imagine, requirements for preschool teachers vary by state. In general, you'll find the requirements more stringent for public preschool teachers than for private preschool teaching positions. Some states require a Bachelor's degree in early childhood education. Other states seek an Associate's degree for official certification. In some states, you'll actually need certification by a nationally recognized organization. The most common type of national certification is the Child Development Associate (CDA) credential. Earning your credential takes three steps. The first step is completion of required classroom training. Next, you'll need demonstrated experience working with children. Finally, to earn your credential, you'll need to pass an independent competence assessment.

If you're debating which age group you want to teach, take a closer look at preschool education. Of all the teaching levels, preschool education has the highest predicted growth rate (26 percent) through 2016. Why the superior growth projections? For starters, many states are implementing programs to improve early childhood education. Second, the demand from parents to instruct their kids from the earliest of ages continues to increase.

Finally, religious organizations and community centers continue to add preschool programs to expand their services and to meet increased demand for early education. So if working with the littlest of the little sounds like fun to you, now's the time to consider a recession-proof career as a preschool teacher.

# Kindergarten, Elementary, and Middle School Teachers

Let's talk about children who are anywhere from 5 to 14 years old. These are some seriously important educational years. Everything from spelling and reading through geography and science enters a child's brain during these years. It's no wonder kindergarten, elementary, and middle school teachers are so critical. It's also not surprising to find out it's a recession-proof career choice.

## Outlook for Kindergarten, Elementary, and Middle School Teachers

| | |
|---|---|
| Current Number of Employees | 2,384,000 |
| New Jobs Created by 2016 | 310,000 |
| Expected Job Growth by 2016 | 13% |
| Geographical Hotspots | Varies by grade level |
| Average Annual Earnings | $44,000–$49,000 |

*Sources: U.S. Bureau of Labor Statistics National Employment Matrix, State Occupational Projections*

In general, kindergarten, elementary, and middle school teachers are responsible for these duties:

◆ Conduct classroom activities, including presenting lesson plans and administering exams

◆ Meet with parents to discuss student progress, strengths, and educational development areas

◆ Supervise extracurricular student activities after regular school hours

◆ Accompany students on field trips to local museums, zoos, and other places of interest

◆ Help identify students with learning disabilities or physical challenges who may need specialized classes

The specific roles of kindergarten, elementary, and middle school teachers differ, mainly because of student age. For example, kindergarten teachers focus more on structured play than formal lesson plans. Meanwhile, the majority of elementary school teachers instruct one group of children in multiple subjects—math, science, history, reading, and language arts. At the elementary level, there may be specialists, but typically only for music, art, and physical education. So a music teacher, for example, is likely to interact with children in several grades throughout the day.

At the middle school level, specialization is common. Here your job is to help students delve deeper into the subjects learned in elementary school. If you're a history teacher, for example, you'll teach the same lesson to four or five groups of students each day. While you won't get to build deeper relationships with just one class of 25 kids, you will get the chance to touch the lives of more total students compared to an elementary teacher.

> ) **In Their Own Words**
>
> The range and intensity of cognitive, physical, hormonal, and social/emotional changes that adolescents experience in the middle school years require educators who are fundamentally creative, caring, enjoy multi-tasking, can be gentle but firm, and have a great sense of humor. In my experience, I find that many middle school teachers are actually looking to redeem their own adolescence gone wrong!
>
> —Kevin Jacobson, Middle School Division Head, Windrush School

## Having What It Takes

Let's talk about the qualities that make a great kindergarten, elementary, or middle school teacher. For starters, you have to have a keen interest in shaping, influencing, and guiding children in their most formative years. Second, the United States is increasingly multicultural. An ability to relate effectively to people from various racial, ethnic, and religious backgrounds is important. In fact, many schools now require cultural training to help teachers effectively teach and work with the variety of students' and parents' backgrounds. Third, patience is key, especially when dealing with misbehaving or unruly kids. You have to be comfortable maintaining control and disciplining, as necessary.

One decision you want to make is whether to work in a public or private school. The biggest advantage of private schools is the chance to teach smaller classes. A disadvantage in public school is that teachers sometimes feel intense pressure to prepare students to achieve mandated standardized test scores, especially in the later elementary years and in middle school.

## Learning to Teach

What does it take to break into a kindergarten, elementary, or middle school teaching career? If you choose public school, you'll need a Bachelor's degree from a teacher education program. In such a program, you'll take basic courses including math, science, art, and so on. You'll also take more philosophical courses such as teaching methods, the psychology of learning, and philosophy of education. Proficiency with computers is critical and is part of most teacher education programs. So much of learning today is through computer programs and the Internet. You'll have to be up to speed on the latest educational tools to guide your students in class.

With degree in hand, a one-year internship is common. Here you'll get firsthand experience in the classroom under the supervision of an experienced teacher. Putting theory from your college courses to practice in the classroom prepares you for official certification. The state Board of Education where you want to work typically offers the necessary certification. You can get licensed to teach early childhood ages, elementary grades, or middle school grades. So what does it take to earn your certification? Generally, landing and maintaining a teaching career has these four requirements:

1. **Bachelor's degree**
   You need a Bachelor's degree from an accredited teacher education program.

2. **Internship**
   One year of supervised teaching under an experienced educator fulfills this requirement. This step may not be required at the kindergarten level.

3. **Subject proficiency**
   Study your subject areas of expertise carefully because you need to be able to demonstrate proficiency before earning the right to teach others. The older the age group you want to teach, the more important this step is.

4. **Master's degree**
   Depending on where you teach, you may need to work toward a Master's degree to maintain your license after landing your first job.

### Another Path

Many states now offer alternative licensure programs to ease the shortage of teachers for specific subjects. You can become a history teacher, for example, if you have a Bachelor's degree in history, even if you never completed the education courses required for a traditional teaching license. Alternative licenses open the door for you if you want to change careers by applying a long-lost college degree to a classroom setting.

So let's say you have your license and you have your teaching job. How might you move up the ladder to earn more responsibility or greater pay? For starters, you can work toward more administrative responsibility. This may entail getting involved in school budgets, overseeing parent conferences, or even tracking enrollment figures. You can also go the supervisory route. This could include overseeing a group of teachers or mentoring new, inexperienced teachers. After all, someone's got to teach newbies the ropes. Whether you choose to move up or simply become an outstanding teacher, working toward tenure is a great recession-proof strategy. While it won't guarantee job security, it certainly eliminates the possibility of losing your job without just cause or due process.

One final consideration is whether you want to work full-time or part-time. At the elementary and middle school levels, you will likely work the 9- or 10-month school year with summers off. You can use this time to rest and recharge or land a summer job as a camp counselor. At the kindergarten level, jobs are more likely to be part-time because in most states, students don't attend school all day. You can work up to full-time if you teach one class in the morning and another class in the afternoon. If you work part-time or have summers off, consider using your free time for continuing education classes. The more you learn, the more you can teach. Now that's a great way to build some serious job security.

# Teacher Assistants

Think back to your own school days. Do you remember that second person in the room helping your teacher get the job done? The helper in the room was likely a teacher assistant. Teacher assistants provide the educational and clerical support necessary to free up a teacher's time for lesson planning and teaching.

## Outlook for Teacher Assistants

| | |
|---|---|
| Current Number of Employees | 1,312,000 |
| New Jobs Created by 2016 | 137,000 |
| Expected Job Growth by 2016 | 10% |
| Geographical Hotspots | Nevada, Texas |
| Average Annual Earnings | $16,000–$26,000 |

*Sources: U.S. Bureau of Labor Statistics National Employment Matrix, State Occupational Projections*

The primary responsibilities of a teacher assistant include the following:

- Support children who need extra help to learn lesson plans created by teachers

- Watch over students during free time, recess, and at lunch in the cafeteria

- Chaperone on field trips

- Record grades and student progress in databases and computer systems

- Help teachers grade test papers, check homework, and maintain student attendance records

- Stock classroom supplies and organize teaching materials to keep instructional sessions running smoothly

Keep in mind that around 40 percent of teacher assistants work part-time. The job is still recession proof, but may be better suited for you if full-time work is not your goal. The other 60 percent of teacher assistants do work full-time during the school year. So you can expect summers off for either an extended break or the chance to earn extra dollars from June through August.

## Another Path

The educational requirements for teacher assistants are somewhat similar to those of both child-care workers and even library assistants. So if your particular school cuts back on teaching assistant jobs, or you want to supplement part-time teaching assistant work, check out your local child-care facility or public library. You just may find an easy transition from one career to the other.

The variety of employment options for teacher assistants is greater than you might think. You can, of course, be conventional and work in an elementary or middle school setting. You'll balance both instructional and clerical duties. If you choose to work with older kids in middle school, specializing in a subject is quite common. You'll also perform more elaborate tasks, including computer lab work, special projects, and preparing student exhibits.

The traditional school setting is not your only option. You can also choose to work with special education students. You'll still attend to students' educational needs. However, you'll also get involved in physical help including feeding, grooming, and other life skills. This is a great option if working with children suffering from emotional or developmental disabilities sounds rewarding to you.

## Learning to Help the Teacher

What it takes to break into a teaching assistant role varies by state and by school district. You'll want to review the specific requirements where you plan to teach, but in general, one of these three paths will be your ticket into the profession:

1. **High school diploma and on-the-job training**
   Education beyond twelfth grade may not be necessary as long as you've completed some high school coursework in child development.

2. **Minimum of a two-year college degree**
   Several colleges around the country offer Associate's degrees and certificate programs to prepare graduates for teacher assistant jobs.

3. **Passing grades on state or local assessments**
   Many states and local school districts have developed teacher assistant exams to qualify for the profession.

Educational and training requirements are not all it takes to be an effective teacher assistant. Certain personality traits are particularly helpful, too. First and foremost, you have to be willing to follow the direction of the teacher. To the students, you and the teacher have to present a unified front to keep control of the classroom. Communication skills are also a must. You have to relate effectively both to adults and students. Finally, attention to detail is critical. The teacher you support is depending on you to keep student records, classroom supplies, and lesson plans organized.

There are two primary ways to advance your career as a teacher assistant. The first is through experience. The more helpful you become and the more tasks you can take over for the teacher, the more valuable you become. The second advancement strategy is to work your way up to teacher. If you work part-time or have summers off, the free time is there if you want to pursue the required teacher training. In fact, some schools will even offer tuition reimbursement or extra time off to pursue a teaching degree.

One more educational trend is paving the way for increased demand for teacher assistants. Schools are increasingly held accountable for the quality of education provided. This is most often measured through standardized testing because it's considered a fair and uniform national educational assessment vehicle. Teacher assistants play a vital role in helping students prepare for these tests, and thereby improve a school's quality performance rating. Helping students so that a school's ranking improves is a great way to recession proof your career.

## The Least You Need to Know

- Child-care providers have a variety of opportunities as more households become dual income. They have the flexibility to choose between working with one family in the child's home, running their own program at home, or working at a child-care center.

- Preschool teachers are expected to be the fastest-growing teaching segment over the next several years.

- Like preschool teachers, kindergarten teachers depend on structured play and activities to teach children the skills they need to be good learners.

- Elementary and middle school teachers shape students in the formative years—from ages 5 through 14.

- Working as a teacher assistant is a rewarding, child-oriented career that requires less education and training than a teaching career.

# Chapter 9

# Specialty Teachers and Counselors

## In This Chapter

- How to make a living as a university professor or technical education instructor

- Why it pays to enrich the lives of others by teaching life skills and hobbies people want to develop

- What it takes to educate youths who suffer from developmental impairments, learning disabilities, and emotional problems

- How to help people suffering from addictions and behavioral disorders get back on their feet

Pre-K through high school teachers are critical to educating our country's youth. However, there is a world of education required beyond the standard school curriculum. This chapter is about all the other kinds of education that help well-adjusted, socially stable adults.

We start with university teachers and vocational instructors. These are the folks responsible for continuing your education beyond the high school years. From there, we review self-enrichment instructors who teach both important life skills and self-development competencies. Next, we talk about special education teachers who work with disabled and emotionally disturbed children. Finally, we cover substance abuse and behavioral disorder counselors who help our youth overcome addictions and behavioral problems to get their lives back on track.

The beauty of the careers discussed in this chapter is that they're both recession proof and highly rewarding. These careers can be trying, but they bring satisfaction in the knowledge that you are positively influencing someone's life.

# Postsecondary and Vocational Teachers

Postsecondary and vocational teachers are college, junior college, and technical school teachers. Postsecondary educators teach students who are working toward a degree, certificate, or certification to improve their career skills.

## Outlook for Postsecondary and Vocational Teachers

| | |
|---|---|
| Current Number of Employees | 1,672,000 |
| New Jobs Created by 2016 | 382,000 |
| Expected Job Growth by 2016 | 23% |
| Geographical Hotspots | Arizona, Utah |
| Average Annual Earnings | $40,000–$80,000 |

*Sources: U.S. Bureau of Labor Statistics National Employment Matrix, State Occupational Projections*

Postsecondary teachers are responsible for the following:

◆ Write formal lesson plans to instruct students

◆ Present material in front of the class, in a lecture format or informal setting

◆ Evaluate student progress through exams, research papers, and in-class participation

◆ Work with individual students to address unique needs, provide extra help, and answer questions

◆ Perform research in an area of expertise and stay current on the latest trends and developments

By 2016, more than 2 million postsecondary teachers are expected to be employed in the United States. This 23 percent anticipated job growth stems from two main factors. First, student enrollments continue to rise, particularly with the U.S. government's commitment to furthering educational programs. Second, many current postsecondary teachers will soon reach retirement age.

These 2 million postsecondary teaching opportunities are segmented into many specialties at both the university and vocational level. Here's a list of the top 10 specialties, starting with the area that is projected to have the most jobs by 2016:

1. Health specialties teachers

2. Graduate teaching assistants

3. Vocational education teachers

4. Art, drama, and music teachers

5. Business teachers

6. English language and literature teachers

7. Education teachers

8. Biological science teachers

9. Math teachers

10. Nursing instructors and teachers

The training, advancement opportunities, and earnings differ for university faculty versus vocational teachers. So let's take these one at a time to understand what it takes to build a recession-proof career in each endeavor.

## College and University Faculty

The majority of postsecondary teachers work as college and university faculty. Organized into departments based on academic subjects, college and university faculty typically teach multiple classes built around an area of expertise. Class sizes can range from formal lectures in front of hundreds of students to small-group seminars or even one-on-one supervised laboratory work. Face-to-face interaction is no longer the only way to deliver content; distance learning programs are growing in popularity. Faculty can teach courses over the Internet as students watch and participate virtually around the globe.

Teaching at a university is not solely about educating students. Typical responsibilities also include both administrative and research requirements. For example, most university faculty members serve on administrative committees that oversee university policies, budgets, and academic issues. Further, teachers are often required to perform independent or joint research both to further their understanding of their field and to get published in relevant academic journals and websites. The institution you work for designates the percentage of your time spent on teaching, administration, and research.

### Career Caveat

Going for tenure at a university used to represent the ultimate in career stability. However, the number of tenure-track positions is declining as universities seek greater flexibility in dealing with changing economic circumstances. Though tenure is still a great goal, continual high performance is your best bet for achieving long-term job security as a university-level teacher.

If your goal is to become a full-fledged, tenure-track university professor, you'll need a doctoral degree. In addition to the years of formal schooling, you're also looking at a dissertation requirement. This is a written report based on extensive research in your field of interest. But don't worry, a doctoral degree is not the only way to break into university education employment. Many two-year colleges and certain disciplines at four-year universities accept candidates with Master's degrees. Of course, if you have the Master's degree, you'll want to couple it with some live teaching experience to land a great job.

Salaries for full-fledged university faculty will be on the high end of the average income for all postsecondary teachers. In fact, the average salary hovers just over $72,000 per year. The good news for university teachers is that your teaching salary is typically only one form of income. Many professors parlay their subject matter expertise into multiple streams of income, including book royalties, corporate consulting fees, and paid writing or research for publications. Additionally, there are some nice benefits to working on campus, including free access to university facilities, reduced tuition requirements for your kids, and even paid sabbaticals.

## Career and Technical Education Teachers

If you want to teach high school graduates, but the university academic requirements seem steep, consider becoming a career or technical education teacher. You'll still be helping shape the minds and skills of students, just in a different setting. Instead of teaching folks working toward four-year degrees, you'll focus on students looking for specialized training in a particular field. Examples include dental hygienists, mechanics, and cosmetologists.

Unlike the formal university setting, these classes are taught in a hands-on, less formal way. For example, if you're teaching students to become x-ray technicians, you'll be focused less on theory, more on actual hands-on demonstrations and practice using the required equipment.

The educational requirements for a career or technical education teacher are much less than those needed for a university faculty candidate. Typically you're looking at a Bachelor's degree plus at least three years of experience working in the field you want to teach. Some technical specialties will require a graduate degree as well. On the flip side, there are fields where a license or certificate is the only requirement to demonstrate your qualifications and land a job.

With so many fields, it can be hard to decide what you want to teach. One great strategy is to home in on a recession-proof industry. In your hands you hold a book outlining several of them. Working as a recession-proof technical education teacher educating students in a recession-proof industry (such as nursing, for example) is what I call a double recession-proof strategy!

# Self-Enrichment Teachers

I've heard it said before that self-enrichment classes are the first to go in a down economy. After all, who has money to take self-improvement classes when times are tough? It turns out the opposite is true. When the going gets tough, the tough get educated. Laid-off workers with severance packages and even nervous employed workers feel the need to learn additional skills. That's why self-enrichment teachers always find work, even in a recession.

## Outlook for Self-Enrichment Teachers

| | |
|---|---|
| Current Number of Employees | 261,000 |
| New Jobs Created by 2016 | 60,000 |
| Expected Job Growth by 2016 | 23% |
| Geographical Hotspots | Arizona, South Carolina |
| Average Hourly Earnings | $11–$23 per hour |

*Sources: U.S. Bureau of Labor Statistics National Employment Matrix, State Occupational Projections*

Typical job responsibilities include the following:

- Teaching a series of classes on an academic subject of interest such as literature

- Providing one-on-one instruction for a particular skill such as time management

- Offering group instruction for a recreational subject such as pottery

Self-enrichment teaching is more about learning than obtaining a degree or certificate. Students have the desire to learn a specific skill and are seeking an expert who can share what he or she knows. In some cases, the skill can be learned in one session. For example, a cooking class focused on the newest barbeque techniques might require only a single two-hour class. Other, more technical skills require longer teaching periods. Students may sign up for multiple, weekly one-hour lessons with homework assignments in between.

**Another Path** _____

Instead of viewing self-enrichment teaching as a primary career, you can also view it as a source of supplemental income. Think of it like a safety net if your primary job falls through or you don't get an anticipated raise. All you have to do is figure out how to repackage your expertise into a class for which people would be willing to pay.

Because self-enrichment education often occurs during nonworking hours, you'll likely be teaching your classes on nights and weekends. But in-class training is only one way you can deliver your expertise to eager students. Thanks to the Internet, multiple teaching avenues can build your income. Following are the top five ways you can use the Internet to teach self-enrichment subjects:

1. **eBooks**
   Take your expertise and package it in a 25- to 50-page eBook in a portable document format (PDF), which readers then open using the freely available Adobe Reader or various other programs. There's no cost to produce the eBook because it's delivered electronically to buyers.

2. **Audio CDs**
   Audio CDs are similar to eBooks except that instead of writing your expertise, you speak about it. You can record a 30- to 60-minute seminar and deliver it either electronically as an audio file or through the mail as a traditional CD.

3. **Teleseminars**

   Get a group of eager students to dial into a conference call number and listen to your expertise over the phone. Typically you'll record the teleseminar so folks who miss the call can listen to the recording at their leisure.

4. **Small-group mentoring**

   Typically more expensive than teleseminars, small-group coaching involves a small group of students who get hands-on training directly from you. The hand-holding learning approach is attractive for students who want extra access to you.

5. **One-on-one coaching**

   The ultimate high-end approach to sharing your expertise is to offer personalized one-on-one coaching. Students pay you for a session or string of sessions to master a skill or technique.

The beauty of self-enrichment education is that your expertise is your ticket to teaching. In most cases, academic and training requirements are unnecessary if students believe in your abilities to teach. Years of piano practice as a child can easily translate into an adult piano-teaching career. You can also specialize through a train-the-trainer approach. Here you teach aspiring experts how to train others. It's basically like having an army of experts out and about who have learned from you. Not a bad way to pass along your personal talents to a world of eager experts in training.

# Special Education Teachers

Special education teachers are critical for the education and development of children with mild or severe mental disabilities. These teachers work with disabled children and youths both to educate them and to teach basic life skills.

## Outlook for Special Education Teachers

| | |
|---|---|
| Current Number of Employees | 459,000 |
| New Jobs Created by 2016 | 71,000 |
| Expected Job Growth by 2016 | 15% |
| Geographical Hotspots | Kansas, Maryland |
| Average Annual Earnings | $38,000–$61,000 |

*Sources: U.S. Bureau of Labor Statistics National Employment Matrix, State Occupational Projections*

In general, the basic responsibilities of a special education teacher include the following:

◆ Modify the standard educational curriculum to meet the unique needs of the student

◆ Arrange special accommodations for students who might need oral or audio assistance to take exams

◆ Guide the development of a student suffering from emotional disturbances or mental disabilities

◆ Help a disabled student adjust to and thrive in social settings

Special education teachers are considered recession proof for several reasons. First, developmental and emotional or behavioral disabilities are now diagnosed at an earlier age, so special education teachers are needed sooner rather than later. Second, medical advances have enabled more children to survive major illnesses and accidents even though they might still need special attention. Finally, many school districts report difficulty in finding qualified special education teachers, so the career is always in demand.

**Career Caveat**

Special education is not the field for folks lacking patience. Students with disabilities and emotional problems require extra attention, a caring hand, and repetition of even basic concepts. It can, of course, be extremely rewarding to shape the life of such a student. Just make sure you have the fortitude and endurance to handle the job.

So what does it take to score a job as a special education teacher? All states require a combination of both academic training and official certification. Let's start with the academic requirements. Colleges across the country offer undergraduate and graduate programs in special education, culminating in a Bachelor's degree, a Master's degree, or even a doctoral degree. You're typically looking at a minimum of five years of education, including your undergraduate years. During those four years of undergraduate work, you'll take relevant courses in educational psychology, child development, and disability education. The fifth year of the program involves teaching special education in a classroom supervised by a certified teacher.

Before you can officially become a special education teacher, you need to earn your license. Requirements vary by state, but typically fall into one of three categories:

1. **General education credential**
   Many states require special education teachers first to earn a general education credential. From there, you'll train toward a specialty such as behavioral disorders.

2. **Teacher preparation program**

   Some states look for a combination of education and on-the-job training to earn your license. You'll need to accumulate a specified amount of educational credits plus a minimum number of supervised working hours.

3. **Alternative licensing routes**

   Some states offer alternative licensing programs to attract people who may not fulfill traditional licensing standards. You'll earn a provisional license that enables you to get to work right away while working toward your traditional license.

Special education teachers can advance their careers in one of two ways. First, you can advance to the supervisory or administration level. Second, you can continue your education and qualify as an instructor to teach other aspiring special education teachers.

In addition to seeking advancement opportunities, you can also choose to specialize. For example, you can choose to work with a specific age group, anywhere from toddler through high school students. You can also specialize by where you work—in a school, at a social assistance agency, or in a hospital. Finally, specialization can come in the form of choosing a specific ailment. Some of the most common specialties include working with physically disabled students, with the hearing impaired, or with children who are mentally disabled. However you choose to advance or specialize, you'll sleep well knowing you're in a recession-proof industry and helping teach those less fortunate than yourself.

# Substance Abuse and Behavioral Disorder Counselors

There are very few things tougher to watch than a young person struggling with addiction. Anything from drugs to alcohol to eating disorders can quickly derail an otherwise promising young life. Substance abuse and behavioral disorder counselors work with people struggling to overcome addictions and disorders.

## Outlook for Substance Abuse and Behavioral Disorder Counselors

| | |
|---|---|
| Current Number of Employees | 83,000 |
| New Jobs Created by 2016 | 29,000 |
| Expected Job Growth by 2016 | 34% |
| Geographical Hotspots | Illinois, Utah |
| Average Annual Earnings | $27,000–$43,000 |

*Sources: U.S. Bureau of Labor Statistics National Employment Matrix, State Occupational Projections*

Basic responsibilities of these counselors include the following:

♦ Counsel individuals battling addictions and disorders to help identify the associated behavioral problems

♦ Work in one-on-one or group settings to help people talk through their problems and figure out a game plan to solve those problems

♦ Offer coping strategies to friends and family affected by the addictions and disorders of their loved ones

♦ Teach classes or seminars on addiction and disorder prevention strategies and ideas

While substance abuse and behavioral disorder counselors may work with many age groups, for the purpose of this chapter we're talking about those who work with young people. Counselors at a more general level were already covered in Chapter 7.

If this kind of work interests you, where can you score a job as a substance abuse and behavioral disorder counselor? The school counselor route is a great way to go. You'll have an office at the local school. You'd work the traditional 9- or 10-month school year with summers off. Or you might work all year round because addictions and disorders don't stop in the summer. Rather than work in schools, you can also go the private practice route. You'll meet one-on-one with clients throughout the day to offer personalized assistance. Finally, you can score a job at a community health organization or hospital. In this case, counseling in both solo and group settings is common.

### Another Path

If substance abuse and behavioral disorders are not your cup of tea, but you still want to counsel others, consider becoming a mental health counselor. The education and training are similar, but you'll be working with individuals and families to treat mental and emotional disorders. You'll help people cope with maladies such as depression, stress, and low self-esteem.

The education and training you'll need depends on where you want to work. Requirements differ for counselors who want to work in school versus private practice settings. If you want to work in a school setting, you'll need to start with a college degree from a university's department of education or psychology. If you know you want to work as a substance abuse and behavioral disorder counselor, you can even specialize in this area as you earn your degree. With undergraduate degree in hand, you'll need to enter a Master's degree program, which will take one or two years. You'll probably get on-the-job training during your graduate work. Then you're ready to be a school counselor.

If you want instead to go the private practice route or to work in a group practice, the requirements are different. Almost every state has a licensing requirement that governs counselors. You'll typically need a Master's degree in counseling followed by either two years or 3,000 hours of supervised clinical experience. With degree in hand and supervised experience complete, you'll qualify to take a state exam to earn your license. Once you open your practice or join an existing one, you'll need to take continuing education classes to maintain your license. Keep in mind that requirements do vary by state. In fact, some states actually will license a substance abuse and behavioral disorder counselor with only a high school diploma and certification. You'll want to review the educational, training, and certification requirements for your state before you commit your time to earning a license.

You've got that degree in hand, you've earned your license, and your recession-proof career is underway. So how do you keep moving up the ladder, taking on more responsibility, and raising your income? There are three basic ways you can advance your career as a substance abuse and behavioral disorder counselor:

1. **Become a supervisor**
   Oversee a team of substance abuse and behavioral disorder counselors. You'll need to develop your leadership skills, of course, but you'll also be shaping the development of less-experienced counselors.

2. **Become a teacher**
   With additional training, you can help aspiring counselors earn their own credentials. In fact, you can go the hybrid route, continuing to counsel troubled youth while also training other counselors. Now you've got the best of both worlds. You get to influence young lives while also helping future counselors eventually to do the same.

3. **Become a researcher**
   Like any field, the arena of substance abuse and behavioral disorders benefits from new research findings. If you want to be on the cutting edge of the latest counseling techniques, strategies, and diagnoses, then become a researcher. Depending on how scientific you want to get with it, you may or may not need additional training to enter the research field.

The beauty of landing a job as a substance abuse and behavioral disorder counselor is that your skills are highly transferrable to other forms of counseling. While this field is expected to be recession proof, you can always transfer to another counseling specialty if the clients dry up. With a little extra training, you can transfer your skills to work as an educational school counselor, family therapist, or mental health counselor.

Of course, before you make the change you'll want to investigate the specific educational and licensing requirements for your state. The good news is that substance abuse and behavioral disorder counselor opportunities are expected to grow 34 percent by 2016. That's the highest predicted growth rate for any of the counseling specialties. Based on that projection, you're unlikely to run out of work!

## The Least You Need to Know

◆ The nation's emphasis on educating future generations makes university professors and technical educators recession proof.

◆ In downturns, people often look to advance their life and business skills, making it a good time to be a self-enrichment teacher.

◆ Working as a special education teacher can be physically and emotionally draining, but also extremely rewarding.

◆ Helping our youth overcome addictions and behavioral disorders is a great way to give back to the community and earn a stable income.

# Chapter 10

# Math, Science, Adult Literacy, and Online Teachers

## In This Chapter

- Why math and science teachers are the fastest-growing group of teachers around

- How teaching English as a second language and other adult literacy concepts is a stable career choice

- How you can make a living as a teacher without leaving your home

- Where you can find alternative tracks to becoming a teacher

In the last two chapters, we covered everything from preschool to post-secondary teachers. We even discussed recession-proof specialty teaching careers such as behavioral counselors and self-enrichment teachers. Now it's time to delve into some specialty subjects and teaching techniques that are in growth mode.

We'll start with a look at math and science teachers. Of all the subjects in school, our government is pouring the most funding into improving student performance in math and science. We cover the teachers who help adults and out-of-school youths read, write, and speak English. From there, we review online and distance learning teachers who can instruct a student body from the comfort of a home office. Finally, we close with some alternative tracks to entering the teaching profession, such as Teach for America.

The goal of this chapter is to show you some specialty subjects and teaching methods that can help recession proof your career. This way, you'll know it's not just about choosing which age group to teach, but also what and how you teach them. By the end of this chapter, perhaps you will have discovered some new and different recession-proof paths to becoming a teacher.

# Math and Science Teachers

Have you heard anything about the United States' $5 billion "Race to the Top" initiative? Basically, it's our country's attempt to encourage each state to improve the quality and number of its math and science teachers. Embedded in this $5 billion initiative are some important factors that make math and science teachers recession proof for years to come:

♦ States are encouraged to implement alternative routes into math and science teaching professions.

♦ States are expected to upgrade math and science teacher training programs and then reward and promote the most effective teachers.

♦ New science labs will be constructed and old ones will be renovated to create state-of-the-art research facilities.

♦ More scholarships will be awarded to promising math and science teachers to lower financial training burdens.

♦ Internationally benchmarked standards will be created to measure U.S. math and science education progress against that of other countries.

Talk about a serious investment in building math and science teachers for the future. The U.S. government is basically asking everyone from politicians to philanthropists to scientists to get involved in building a future generation of top-notch science and math teachers. This clear government investment and focus is why math and science teachers are the most recession proof of all the recession-proof teaching careers discussed in this book.

| | |
|---|---|
| Average annual earnings for math and science teachers, grades K–12 | $44,000–$49,000 |
| Average annual earnings for postsecondary math and science teachers | $40,000–$80,000 |
| Shortage in math and science teachers expected by 2015 | 280,000 |

*Sources: Business Higher Education Forum, U.S. Bureau of Labor Statistics National Employment Matrix*

Do you still need further proof that our country is focused on improving math and science student performance? Under Secretary of Education Margaret Spellings' leadership, the United States Congress enacted the American Competitiveness Initiative. The goal is to strengthen math and science education and encourage high schools to offer more challenging and advanced math and science curricula. Clearly, with billions in funding and national initiatives underway, math and science teachers are needed now more than ever before.

Clearly, there is a major demand for math and science teachers to meet not only the anticipated teacher shortfall but the ambitious goals of our government. With that in mind, let's review what it takes to break into and succeed in the fields of math and science.

> **In Their Own Words**
>
> Our country is beginning to understand that there is a greater demand for higher competency levels in math and science to compete globally and, therefore, a greater need for math- and science-related teachers.
>
> —Margaret Spellings, former U.S. Secretary of Education and President of Margaret Spellings and Company; from an interview with the author

## Math Teachers

According to the book *Great Jobs for Math Majors* by Stephen E. Lambert and Ruth J. DeCotis (McGraw-Hill, 2005), "Teaching mathematics requires much more than just knowing mathematics. Even though the subject is mathematics, the most important concern in teaching it is not just having the skills and information but being able to instill appreciation and enjoyment of math in all its myriad forms." In other words, success as a math teacher is not just about mastering the skills you need to teach math. You also need to think from the student's perspective and understand how to build an appreciation for math skills into the mind of everyone you teach. Math pervades our daily lives. Important life skills—from balancing a checkbook to figuring out the tip in a restaurant—require an understanding of basic math concepts.

In previous chapters, we covered how to break into teaching careers in general. Now let's talk about math teaching professions specifically. If you want to teach at the elementary through secondary school level, you'll need a Bachelor's degree, most likely in education. The higher the age group you want to teach, the more likely it is that your college concentration or even major should be in a math-related field. In fact, according to Margaret Spellings, former Secretary of Education, "early and middle school teachers increasingly need to have much better math, science, and specialty areas; it's no longer just about a focus on reading." For you, this means that even for teachers of younger students, many states are increasingly looking for specialized teachers, not just generalists. If you want to go the math route, then the more math-specific credentials you have, the better your shot of landing a job at any grade level. This is most true at the postsecondary level, where a Ph.D. may be your only ticket in the door at most universities.

Of course, you may be wondering how it's possible to break into a math teaching career when you went to college years ago and majored in philosophy. The good news is that many states are opening alternative doors to math teaching professions in response to the nationwide shortage of teachers. New Jersey is one such state offering a program to facilitate career change into the math field. Known as Traders to Teachers, the program is designed to turn unemployed finance professionals into math teachers within three months. The program is sponsored by Montclair State University in New Jersey and results in a public school certification to teach math upon program completion.

## Science Teachers

Science differs from math in that much of the learning is hands-on, especially at middle school levels and beyond. You remember the Bunsen burner, don't you? For that reason, teaching science is about both theoretical and practical lessons. You have to explain the concepts and then help students bring those ideas to life with lab experiments.

To teach science at the elementary level, a Bachelor's degree and teaching certification suffice. At the middle or high school level, you're more likely to need a Bachelor's degree in your specific field of science. In fact, according to the National Science Teacher's Association (NSTA), more than half of science teachers have a Master's degree. Many states even require you to work toward your Master's degree within a certain time frame after entering the profession.

Beyond the Bachelor's or Master's degree, you'll also need your official certification. We covered the certification requirements in Chapters 8 and 9, so I won't repeat them here. Needless to say, state requirements may vary, so you'll want to check with your state's Department of Education to ensure that you fully understand the steps necessary to earn and keep your teaching certification.

# Adult Literacy and Remedial Education Teachers

Adult literacy and remedial education used to be a field geared toward Americans who did not graduate high school or those who passed through the school system without acquiring the fundamental skills needed to find meaningful work. In recent years, there's been a shift as non-English speakers and immigrants have filled up these classes. The job of adult literacy and remedial education teachers is to instruct adults and youths to read, write, speak English, and master basic math skills.

## Outlook for Adult Literacy and Remedial Education Teachers

| | |
|---|---|
| Current Number of Employees | 76,000 |
| New Jobs Created by 2016 | 11,000 |
| Expected Job Growth by 2016 | 14% |
| Geographical Hotspots | Arizona, Nevada |
| Average Annual Earnings | $33,000–$57,000 |

*Sources: U.S. Bureau of Labor Statistics National Employment Matrix, State Occupational Projections*

The career category consists of three main teaching professions:

1. **Adult basic education (ABE) teachers**
   For adults and youths whose educational skills are at or below an eighth-grade level, adult basic education teachers help raise student skills to middle school ranks.

2. **Adult secondary education (ASE) teachers**
   For students who wish to obtain a General Educational Development (GED) certificate or high school equivalency credential, adult secondary education teachers provide the learning tools necessary to succeed.

3. **English literacy teachers**
   For adults and youths with limited English language skills, English literacy teachers help students learn to read and write English. Many of these instructors are referred to as English as a second language (ESL) teachers.

Regardless of the subcategory, adult literacy and remedial education teachers encounter a variety of students. Some simply need to learn effective study habits to build the confidence to catch up to their peers academically. Other students have learning or physical disabilities that have slowed their academic progress. Still other students are held back simply by not understanding how to read or write English. Because students in the same class have different proficiency levels, it's important for you—as the teacher—to assess each student individually. Then you can customize a learning plan based on the student's starting point and academic goals.

Many of the students you'll teach will be adults. This means the typical adolescent discipline issues are absent. Detention, speaking to kids after class, and trips to the principal's office will likely not be part of your job description. However, your working hours will probably differ from the typical teaching gigs in public schools. Many adult students want to learn after work and on weekends. Both evening and weekend classes will be part of your life. In fact, many adult literacy and remedial education teachers work part-time. You can actually hold a full-time job in a related career and still find the time to teach on nights and weekends.

### Another Path

The skills required to excel as an adult literacy and remedial education teacher are similar to those of a special education teacher (covered in Chapter 9). In fact, students with physical and learning disabilities can end up with either teacher. It's nice to know you can always transfer your skills between these two recession-proof careers.

Breaking into the field will require a Bachelor's degree at a minimum. Many employers prefer or even require a Master's degree, too. The kinds of classes you'll want to take to prepare for your career include courses on teaching adults, teaching different cultures, and teaching disabled students. If you want to focus on ESL teaching, you should also consider courses in language acquisition theory and linguistics. It wouldn't hurt to know one or two languages besides English. Knowing the native language of your students facilitates early communication, before their English skills improve under your tutelage.

Most states require professional continuing education classes. Depending on the state in which you teach, these classes may be classroom courses or online. You'll also be required to obtain and maintain a license to teach in this field, particularly if you work for a state- or government-sponsored program. Depending on where you work, earning a license may require attaining a public school teaching license, completing a teacher training program, acquiring a Bachelor's degree, and/or working toward a specific license for adult education teachers.

After you break into the field, how do you advance your career? If you're working part-time, you can always seek full-time opportunities. You can also look for multiple part-time roles that would add up to a full-time income. You can also advance to an administrator or coordinator role, helping set up programs and oversee teachers.

ESL teachers account for the biggest growth opportunity for this career category. The immigrant population continues to increase, and more of these residents need English skills to land jobs. States with large populations of English learners offer the most career opportunities for ESL teachers. California, Florida, Texas, and New York are the states with the highest percentages of immigrant populations.

Adult literacy and remedial education teachers tend to do well in recessions. Why is that? Employers in general are more selective when hiring employees. In a down economy, with increased competition for fewer jobs, companies expect higher qualifications. So job-seekers who want to rise to the top of the hiring pool will be inclined to further their education.

If adult literacy and remedial education sounds like the right career choice for you, there are a few skills you'll need to succeed. First, much of the teaching, particularly in ESL, is done via computer. So you'll need to be familiar with the latest computer teaching technologies. Second, many of your students will not speak English. In fact, it's quite possible your class will be filled with students speaking many different languages. You'll need to be creative in finding nonverbal and other ways to communicate effectively with the class. Finally, many of these classes are voluntary, with coursework rarely graded. You'll need to motivate the class in nontraditional ways. Threatening the class with a pop quiz probably won't work with this type of student.

# Online and Distance Learning

According to the U.S. Distance Learning Association (USDLA), distance learning is defined as "the acquisition of knowledge and skills through mediated information and instruction. Distance learning encompasses all technologies and supports the pursuit of lifelong learning for all. Distance learning is used in all areas of education including Pre-K through grade 12, higher education, home school education, continuing education, corporate training, military and government training, and telemedicine."

## Fast Facts About Online and Distance Learning

| | |
|---|---|
| Total enrollment in college-level distance education courses | More than 12 million |
| Annual growth in students enrolling in online classes | 400,000 students |
| Percentage of postsecondary institutions offering online classes | 66% |
| Total number of college-level programs designed to be completed solely through online and distance education | More than 11,000 |
| Number of states offering state-sponsored online learning programs | 38 |

*Sources: The U.S. Distance Learning Association (USDLA), North American Council of Online Learning*

Online and distance learning merges advances in technology with the need to meet growing twenty-first-century educational needs. Schools conducted virtually enable a collaborative forum-type environment with the ability to learn at a student's own pace. With younger generations relying so heavily on technology, it's no wonder distance learning programs are growing at record paces. After all, if our youth are going to communicate all day via computer technology, why not promote education through this popular channel, too?

### Career Caveat

Many online and distance learning teachers are part-time instructors. So this is not necessarily the career for you if working at one institution, with fixed hours, is your desired teaching setup. However, if you like the variety and the chance to work with many age groups through many schools, then consider the field.

The explosive growth in online and distance learning signifies a recession-proof teaching opportunity for you. No longer will the formal classroom be your only venue for teaching students and adults. All you need is a computer and a camera to reach millions of students. Okay, so it's a bit more complicated than that—but let's take a closer look at online and distance learning opportunities.

According to the U.S. Department of Education's Institute of Education Sciences, online and distance learning is a "formal education process in which the students and instructor are not in the same place." Think about that for a moment. You're a teacher, reaching hundreds or even thousands of students, and you may never have a single face-to-face meeting. That is a true testament to the power of the Internet. However, it also presents a few logistical challenges:

◆ You miss the camaraderie of having a group of students together experiencing a lesson.

◆ You lose the instant feedback from students because you can't "read" the faces and reactions of folks following your lesson online.

◆ You must effectively combine audio, visual, and interactive components in an online environment.

The good news is that online learning software is becoming more sophisticated. This means many programs now enable students to follow a PowerPoint presentation while hearing audio. Students can even get in virtual queues to ask questions of the instructor. In other words, the online experience is getting closer to recreating what students could once experience only in a classroom.

One thing that is the same in online and traditional classroom teaching is the requirements to break into the field. If you want to teach university classes online for course credit, you need the same qualifications as a traditional university professor. If you want to teach vocational classes, you need the same credentials as a classroom-based vocational instructor. Whichever direction you want to go, simply flip back to Chapters 8 and 9 to read the specific educational and training requirements.

Beyond the educational requirements, let's also cover the skill sets that make an online or distance learning teacher effective. We know from previous chapters what it takes to succeed as a teacher in general, but let's look at online and distance learning skills specifically. Three main qualities are likely to lead to success:

1. **Ability to connect with a disparate audience**
   Holding the attention of students can be difficult when they're together. Now you're talking to a class spread around the country or globe. You'll need to be able to hold student attention without making eye contact.

2. **Willingness to communicate via e-mail**
   All of the questions students ask will be e-mailed. It's not as if students can raise their hand in a classroom. So you need to be comfortable handling issues and responding to student questions via e-mail and message boards.

3. **Personal satisfaction without immediate gratification**
   Many teachers particularly enjoy the instant gratification of student laughs and knowing looks. From this perspective, teaching online can make a teacher feel a bit isolated. In the absence of visual evidence, you have to know in your heart that you're having an impact on students.

It's also worth mentioning that the Southern Regional Education Board (SREB) has done an outstanding job outlining the skills and competencies needed to teach online. According to SREB, an online teacher should meet five specific criteria. Briefly put, you should have the proper credentials, make your credentials or qualifications known and easily accessible, understand your subject matter, know how to teach it so students will grasp the information, and commit to lifelong learning to keep your skills current. Now that's a nice, succinct way to describe what it takes to succeed in the world of online and distance education.

Ultimately, if you have the skills described and enjoy teaching through online media, then distance learning just may be the perfect recession-proof career choice for you.

# Additional Paths to Teaching

In this and the previous two chapters, we've covered all kinds of teaching careers. You've learned about everything from preschool teaching to postsecondary, and even online distance learning. I'll close this chapter with a look at some alternative ways to break into the teaching profession. The more avenues to making your teaching career a reality, the better your odds of landing a recession-proof educational role.

## Teach for America

You probably know that educational opportunities are often limited for students who live in low-income, typically urban, areas. Teach for America is an organization striving to reverse this educational inequity. The organization looks for promising leaders willing to commit to two years of teaching in disadvantaged locations throughout the United States. According to the Teach for America website, here are the criteria by which candidates are judged:

- Demonstrated past leadership and achievement—achieving ambitious, measurable results in academic, professional, extracurricular, or volunteer settings

- Showed perseverance in the face of challenges

- Possess strong critical thinking skills—making accurate links between cause and effect and generating relevant solutions to problems

- Skilled at influencing and motivating others

- Proven organizational ability—planning well, meeting deadlines, and working efficiently

◆ Possess understanding of and desire to work relentlessly in pursuit of our vision

◆ Have respect for students and families in low-income communities

This is a program particularly enticing if you're a soon-to-be or recent college graduate. That's because you can get placed in a teaching position immediately after completing a summer training program with Teach for America. Then, during your two-year commitment, you can work toward a full, state-recognized teacher certification.

Teach for America also works with both graduate programs and employer sponsors. This means you can bridge your Teach for America experience into a relevant graduate program or a future job with one of the sponsoring organizations. Check out www.teachforamerica.org for more details.

## Troops to Teachers

Sponsored by the U.S. Department of Education and the U.S. Department of Defense, Troops to Teachers helps military personnel make the transition to teaching in public schools. It's a fantastic program if you're in the military and wondering what you'll do when your service period ends. This program is a bridge into a recession-proof teaching career. Working with Troops to Teachers requires three steps:

1. **Troops to Teachers registration**
   By linking with Troops to Teachers, you're eligible for financial assistance in your pursuit of a teaching certificate. To earn the assistance, you have to commit to teaching for a minimum of three years in a high-needs school district.

2. **Teacher certification requirements**
   Every state has its own certification process. Decide on the state where you want to work and Troops to Teachers helps you identify the certification steps necessary to earn your teaching credentials.

3. **The job search**
   Troops to Teachers has a wealth of job searching resources to assist your transition from military service to teacher. While you ultimately need to perform well in an interview to land a position, Troops to Teachers puts you in the best possible position to get the gig.

Visit www.proudtoserveagain.com for more information on Troops to Teachers and how to get started. You'll find you can pursue all three steps simultaneously to speed up your transition from the military to a teaching profession.

# Charter Schools

Nearly 3,000 schools have opened since the early 1990s that operate with freedom from many of the typical public school regulations. These schools establish a "charter," which lays out the school's mission, goals, and success measures. In exchange for this freedom, charter schools are held accountable for meeting the success measures outlined in the charter. Ultimately, charter schools are accountable to the sponsor that grants funds, to parents who send their kids to the school, and to the local citizens who are funding the program with tax dollars.

As an aspiring teacher, which scenario sounds more appealing?

♦ **Scenario #1:** You have some autonomy over the curriculum you teach and are judged based on student success measures established by teachers and school administrators.

♦ **Scenario #2:** You have minimal autonomy over the curriculum, and you are judged based on numerical testing benchmarks of student performance established by the state and federal government.

If scenario #1 sounds more appealing, then you just might prefer working in a charter school over a traditional public school. You'll need generally the same schooling and certification as a public school teacher. But you may find the increased control over what and how you teach a rewarding aspect of the profession.

# The Least You Need to Know

♦ There's extra job security for those who specialize in teaching math and science to students in grades K through 12.

♦ You can build a recession-proof career helping adults learn to read, write, and speak English.

♦ Online and distance learning programs are opening up avenues for teachers who don't want to pursue traditional 9-to-3 classroom teaching roles.

♦ Programs such as Teach for America help open alternative doors to becoming a teacher.

# Part 4

# Climate Control

We've talked, in previous parts of this book, about health-care professions and numerous teaching professions. Now it's time to talk about environmental professions. You're probably familiar with white-collar and blue-collar jobs. Did you know green is the new "it" color? That's right, you can earn a recession-proof living wearing a green collar to work and helping the environment.

If you have an interest in wind, solar, nuclear, and other forms of energy, then this is the part for you. You also learn about utilities careers poised for significant growth in the years to come. This part even introduces you to some cutting-edge professions, such as nanotechnology. Get ready to go green, help the environment, and find a stable career.

# Chapter 11

# The Science of Going Green

## In This Chapter

◆ How studying the formation and structure of Earth can lead to recession-proof employment

◆ Why your desire to improve the environment by reducing air pollution or contaminated drinking water can be a stable career choice

◆ How to weather economic recessions by reporting on the weather as an atmospheric scientist or meteorologist

◆ Why working with the newest technologies such as biofuel, biotechnology, and nanotechnology can be a great way to work on the front lines of scientific research

If you looked forward to science class in high school, then this is the chapter for you. The only difference is we're going to talk recession-proof science. After all, if I'm going to help you break into the science field, the least I can do is guide you to a stable one. So this chapter is all about the research and applied science fields that are sure to grow over the next several years.

We begin with geoscientists who study Earth, look for geological trends, and help secure a healthy planet for future generations. Next, we cover environmental scientists and hydrologists. From reducing air pollution to ensuring sources of clean water, these two professions have us covered. From there, we talk about atmospheric scientists. While you see these folks on the evening news, many work for the federal government and in private-sector jobs analyzing climate and weather trends. Finally, we close with some of the hottest, cutting-edge science around, including biofuel, biotechnology, and nanotechnology. Talk about working on the front lines of scientific research.

By the end of this chapter, you'll understand the nature of the work, educational requirements, salary ranges, and advancement opportunities for the most promising science careers around. So let's flash back to those fun days in earth science and geology, and then flash ahead to the best recession-proof careers around.

# Geoscientists

Between Earth's rocks, volcanoes, oceans, and streams, there is so much to study and research. In fact, Earth is so massive, an entire recession-proof career is devoted to studying the different aspects of our planet. Geoscientists are scientists who devote themselves to studying the composition and structure of Earth. Many geoscientists search for natural resources and work closely with environmentalists to preserve the environment. That's where the connection between geoscientists and going green comes in.

Geoscientists are commonly categorized into two broad categories. Geologists study the earth's physical structure, its substance (that's where the rocks come in), its history, and the forces that act on it. Meanwhile, geophysicists study Earth's surface, oceans, atmosphere, and gravitational forces. These two subspecialties are even further divided into career specialties.

## Outlook for Geoscientists

| | |
|---|---|
| Current Number of Employees | 31,000 |
| New Jobs Created by 2016 | 6,800 |
| Expected Job Growth by 2016 | 22% |
| Geographical Hotspots | Colorado, Montana |
| Average Annual Earnings | $52,000–$101,000 |

*Sources: U.S. Bureau of Labor Statistics National Employment Matrix, State Occupational Projections*

The most common include the following:

- **Mineralogists:** Classify precious stones and minerals based on their composition and structure

- **Sedimentologists:** Research sand, mud (silt), and clay to understand their nature and origin

- **Glacial geologists:** Study movement of ice sheets and glaciers in cold climates

- **Paleomagnetists:** Interpret continent sediments and fossil mangnetization in rocks to explain continent and sea floor movement

- **Geomagnetists:** Devise models to explain Earth's origin by measuring magnetic fields

- **Seismologists:** Detect earthquakes and find fault lines using seismographs and other instruments

As you can see, if you have a love for continents, the sea floor, glaciers, fossils, or any other wonders of our planet, there's a recession-proof career for you. Where might you land work as a geoscientist? Almost one quarter of all geoscientists work for architectural and engineering firms. About 20 percent work for oil and gas extraction companies. Many of the rest are employed by state agencies and the federal government. A few geoscientists go it alone as self-employed consultants to industry or government.

Geoscientists spend their days in offices, laboratories, and in the field. This mix can keep the job interesting and varied. For example, for part of the day you're behind a computer putting together a research proposal. Then it's out into the field to conduct experiments. By day's end you may be back in the lab studying the materials you scooped up in the field. Of course, travel can be a big part of the job. After all, the earth is a big place. Depending on what you choose to study, you may spend considerable hours on ships, climbing in the mountains, or hiking across remote field sites.

Breaking into the geoscience field is likely going to require a Master's degree. If you really want to achieve a high-level research position or university professor job, you'll need a Ph.D. to open the door. You can set yourself up for the career by majoring in

**Another Path**

While many geoscientists are on the cutting edge of the green movement, a large percentage works in the petroleum and natural gas industry. If you're interested in the extraction of petroleum and natural gas, geoscience isn't the only way to go. You can also consider a career as a surveying technician or petroleum engineer.

geoscience in college. Many universities offer both Bachelor's and Master's degrees in the field. You'll study such varied topics as mineralogy, paleontology, and structural geology. You can still break into the field if you major in a related, relevant field. Good choices include physics, engineering, and computer science. Just be sure you've taken some geoscience courses to demonstrate your interest in the subject.

Beyond the educational requirements, you'll likely need a license from your state's licensing board. Requirements vary by state, but you'll need a combination of the right education, work experience, and passing scores on a state-sponsored exam.

With degree and license in hand, how do you move up the ranks among geoscientists? Traditionally, your first positions will be as a research assistant or laboratory technician. However, as you prove yourself, you may assist on more difficult assignments or even lead your own projects. After that, the most senior positions will oversee a team of researchers while reporting to top executives or clients.

Doing great work to advance your career sounds good, but what skills does it take to make it happen? The most successful geoscientists possess the following five skills:

1. **Logical thinking**
   Much of your job is about examining evidence and searching for logical explanations. You have to be good at compiling research and logically thinking through the implications of your findings.

2. **Spatial skills**
   The earth is three-dimensional, so thinking spatially and understanding relationships among Earth's components is critical to analyzing water and continents.

3. **Oral and written communication skills**
   Doing the research is one thing; explaining your findings is something else. You'll need to write up and present research findings either to satisfy clients or to meet research grant requirements.

4. **Interpersonal skills**
   Most geoscientists work on teams that include engineers, technicians, and other scientists. Relating to and working effectively within your broader team is critical.

5. **Computer skills**
   We're not talking about typing in a word-processing program in this profession. Geoscientists use complex data analysis, modeling, and geographic information systems to do their jobs.

With the education, licensing, and skills needed, you're on your way to success as a geoscientist. There are also some macro-factors in your career favor. As the honorable Dr. Stephen L. Johnson, former administrator of the U.S. Environmental Protection Agency, puts it, "The nation and world [are] at a significant point in time when environmental concerns, energy needs, and economic hardships are all coming together." This focus on energy conservation, environmental protection, and responsible use of our planet's finite resources opens the door to a multitude of recession-proof geoscience positions.

# Environmental Scientists and Hydrologists

How would you like a job in which you protect the environment, find water and energy sources, help avoid planetary hazards, and improve indoor air quality? All of these noble causes fall under the career fields of environmental scientist and hydrologist.

## Outlook for Environmental Scientists and Hydrologists

| | |
|---|---|
| Current Number of Employees | 92,000 |
| New Jobs Created by 2016 | 23,000 |
| Expected Job Growth by 2016 | 25% |
| Geographical Hotspots for Environmental Scientists | Montana, Utah |
| Average Annual Earnings for Environmental Scientists | $43,000–$74,000 |
| Geographical Hotspots for Hydrologists | Florida, Nevada |
| Average Annual Earnings for Hydrologists | $51,000–$82,000 |

*Sources: U.S. Bureau of Labor Statistics National Employment Matrix, State Occupational Projections*

The careers are often grouped together, but the roles are somewhat different:

◆ **Environmental scientists:** Conduct research to find and eliminate hazards that could have a negative impact on people, animals, and the environment

◆ **Hydrologists:** Study the nature, properties, and distribution of both surface and underground water

That covers the two jobs in a nutshell, but let's delve a little deeper to understand these two career choices more fully. As an environmental scientist, you'll observe air, water, and food sources looking for ways to preserve the environment. You'll be on the front lines of efforts to conserve, recycle, and replenish our environment's resources. You'll find ways to clean contaminated land, to limit negative impacts of construction on the environment, and to design environmentally friendly waste disposal sites.

If you go the hydrologist route, then your career is all about water. You'll study precipitation levels, water movement throughout the planet, and how water goes from oceans to the atmosphere and back again. You'll also be on the front lines of researching and identifying changes in water cycles, flow rates, and overall water quality.

### Career Caveat

As an environmental scientist or hydrologist, you may be working in extreme conditions. Travel to some of the hottest and coldest spots around the world is common. So if you really want to be on the front lines of research and scientific investigation, you have to be comfortable traveling to remote spots and enduring trying climate conditions.

You can sometimes break into the environmental scientist or hydrologist field with a Bachelor's degree in earth science. Increasingly, entry-level and mid-level positions require a Master's degree in a relevant field such as hydrology or environmental science. This is especially true if you want to work for private companies and federal agencies. If you choose to go the teaching route at a university, then you'll ultimately need a Ph.D.

There are also specific courses you'll want to take if you're looking to become an environmental scientist or hydrologist. For environmental scientists, class work in environmental legislation, chemistry, geologic data, and inorganic compounds will all be useful for your future career. For hydrologists, classes in chemistry, mathematics, water conservation, and geophysics all pave the way for entry into the field.

After you clear the education hurdle, where are the best places to find work? According to the U.S. Department of Labor, career opportunities for environmental scientists and hydrologists are somewhat similar, but the percentages in each employment venue differ. For environmental scientists, local and state governments employ 35 percent of workers, 21 percent work in consulting services, 15 percent work for architectural and engineering firms, 8 percent work for the federal government, 2 percent are self-employed, and 19 percent work for other, miscellaneous entities. For hydrologists, the federal government employs 28 percent of workers, 26 percent work for architectural and engineering firms, 21 percent for state agencies, 18 percent work in consulting services, 2 percent are self-employed, and 5 percent work for other, miscellaneous employers.

The most important point regarding environmental scientists and hydrologists is the anticipated 25 percent growth by 2016. This tremendous growth stems from the following factors:

◆ Continued population growth is placing increased demands on both the environment and on water resources.

◆ New laws continue to increase regulations on keeping our water and air clean.

◆ Newer construction builders are increasingly relying on environmental professionals to help plan and construct energy-efficient structures.

◆ The continued migration toward coastal living means hydrologists are increasingly needed to monitor and help prevent floods and landslides.

◆ Waste minimization and recycling initiatives require environmental consultants who can help companies dispose of or re-use waste responsibly.

Put these five factors together and it's easy to see why environmental scientists and hydrologists are working in a recession-proof career. Still, there is a path to advancement worth noting to fully understand what it takes to build your career. Many entry-level positions will be in field exploration or research assistance. Here you're helping a lead scientist get the job done. This is a great time to build a mentoring relationship. After all, your boss likely held your job at an earlier point in his or her career.

As you gain experience, you can move up to more complex assignments. You can even enter leadership positions in which you run your own projects and manage a team of scientists. From there, you can advance to the most senior positions in which you seek project funding, "sell" new projects, and get more involved in the business end of the profession.

# Atmospheric Scientists

You wake up on a brisk Friday morning with thoughts of the weekend. You have a fun barbeque planned with about 50 friends and family swinging by your house. You've ordered the food, you've cleaned the patio furniture, and the extra napkins are on hand. Your one lingering concern is the weather. This is the very point where your life intersects with a recession-proof career—atmospheric scientist. Commonly referred to as meteorologists, atmospheric scientists study the atmosphere's motions and characteristics and how these factors impact our environment.

## Outlook for Atmospheric Scientists

| | |
|---|---|
| Current Number of Employees | 8,800 |
| New Jobs Created by 2016 | 900 |
| Expected Job Growth by 2016 | 11% |
| Geographical Hotspots | Georgia, Texas |
| Average Annual Earnings | $56,000–$94,000 |

*Sources: U.S. Bureau of Labor Statistics National Employment Matrix, State Occupational Projections*

The most common responsibilities for atmospheric scientists include the following:

◆ Predict the weather and share weather forecasts on television and through the Internet

◆ Investigate and interpret past climate trends to anticipate future weather patterns

◆ Participate in studies to tackle such challenges as global warming, ozone depletion, and droughts

◆ Study the impact of air pollution to find ways to reduce pollutants and improve air quality

Atmospheric science is also further broken down into distinct career specialties. You are probably most familiar with operational meteorologists. These are the folks you see on television sharing the weather forecast for the upcoming week. Most atmospheric scientists work in this specialty area. Many other atmospheric scientists focus on the research end of the field. For example, physical meteorologists study the transfer of energy, light, and sound in the atmosphere, as well as the formation of clouds, rain, and snow. Synoptic meteorologists use computers and math models to create new weather forecasting tools. Climatologists analyze climate variations from hundreds and thousands of years ago to identify weather patterns. Finally, environmental meteorologists study air pollution and water shortages to find solutions to those problems.

As you can imagine, weather is a 24/7 business. That means many professionals in this career work long hours, nights, and weekends. You never know when a big storm is going to hit. You have to be ready to report the latest news as it happens. More regular hours are possible if you work in research-based as opposed to reporting-based weather professions. After all, studying storms from hundreds of years ago doesn't quite have the same sense of urgency as reporting an impending snowstorm.

Whether you want to be on the front lines of weather reporting or in the backroom research lab, you'll need to meet some academic requirements to get your career in gear. Most entry-level positions, particularly for the U.S. government, require a Bachelor's degree. You don't have to major in meteorology, but you do need to complete at least 24 semester hours of atmospheric science courses. You can major in meteorology if you find one of the hundred programs accredited by the American Meteorological Society. There are some atmospheric classes required by the National Weather Service if your goal is to gain employment with that organization.

**Another Path**

The beauty of this career choice is that much of the early training is similar to two other careers covered in this chapter—geoscientists and environmental scientists. So with a little extra training, you can jump from one recession-proof career to another.

If your goal is to work in operational meteorology, then a Master's degree will open up more employment opportunities and higher pay. The Master's degree is also necessary if you want to focus on applied research and development. If you want to go for a major research position or teach at the university level, then a Ph.D. is your ticket to these job opportunities.

Another factor in your education is how you want to specialize over time. Many meteorological disciplines actually combine two skills. For example:

◆ If you want to be a broadcast meteorologist on television or the radio, you should take speech and communication classes in addition to the standard atmospheric courses.

◆ If you want to work for a weather-consulting firm, then supplement your atmospheric classes with business courses.

◆ If your goal is to work in a weather-related career for the U.S. government, be sure to take policy and government affairs classes.

Choosing your weather-related specialty should incorporate an understanding of where the jobs lie. The federal government is the single biggest employer of meteorologists, employing 37 percent of those in the field. Many of these employees work specifically in National Weather Service stations around the country or in research and management positions. The U.S. Department of Defense and Armed Forces also employ hundreds of atmospheric scientists. The balance of meteorologists are spread across consulting firms, broadcast positions, and scientific research organizations.

Beyond where the jobs lie, you also want to know which categories are in growth mode. While the federal government is the largest employer of meteorologists, employment opportunities are expected to remain flat over the next several years. Private sector opportunities, however, are very favorable. New and advanced research is improving weather forecasting capabilities. Climate-sensitive industries, such as farming, construction, and transportation, will be clamoring for this information to gain a competitive edge and plot their work.

# Cutting-Edge Scientists

If you have a desire to work in science and want to be on the cutting edge of research and development, then this section is for you. Three of the newest technologies are biofuel, biotechnology, and nanotechnology. While each could be its own chapter—or even a book—I want to give you a taste of these emerging technologies. Let's take them one at a time to understand why each is in growth mode.

## Biofuel

Biofuels are fuels manufactured from agricultural derivatives. Imagine the possibility of turning crops into an energy source. That's precisely what happens when ethanol is produced from corn. While the true costs and environmental concerns associated with biofuel can be debated, it does represent a clear alternative to our country's heavy dependence on oil.

If biofuel sounds promising to you, then working as an agricultural scientist is the career for you. But this is not the only way to get in on this growing field. Because much of the biofuel is produced on farms, there's a hands-on way to get involved, too. In fact, if you have extensive experience in traditional farming, you can transfer these skills to this growing industry.

## Biotechnology

Many new drugs and vaccines, as well as disease-resistant crops, exist because of biotechnology. Similar to biofuel, agricultural scientists are on the cutting edge of working with biotechnology. These scientists have actually found ways to alter the genetic makeup of plants and crops, making them resistant to commonly detrimental diseases.

The field extends beyond crops into the medical community. There's a branch of bio-technology that works with DNA and genetics to find new medical applications that may lead to vaccines, cures, and ways to fight diseases. As the population continues to age, you'll see even more dollars funneled into research in this exciting area.

## Nanotechnology

Nanotechnology is the study of new structures that are no bigger than the size of an individual atom. At this tiny level, materials can be manipulated to produce amazing new feats. The National Nanotechnology Initiative (NNI) oversees the collective efforts to find breakthroughs through nanotechnology. According to their website, www.nano.gov, "the power of nanotechnology is rooted in its potential to transform and revolutionize multiple technology and industry sectors, including aerospace, agriculture, biotechnology, homeland security and national defense, energy, environmental improvement, information technology, medicine, and transportation. Discovery in some of these areas has advanced to the point where it is now possible to identify applications that will impact the world we live in." Now that's an amazing promise of what's to come in the next several years. When you've got a technology that can influence so many important areas in our country's future, you're clearly working in a recession-proof field. All of the research funding pouring in will continue to generate the need for more workers in the field.

## The Least You Need to Know

- Geoscientists know everything about the properties of our planet and make a recession-proof living in the process.

- Environmental scientists and hydrologists are on the front lines, keeping air pollution down and drinking water safe.

- Meteorologists, particularly the ones who work in private industry, are in growth mode.

- It's never a bad idea to learn about and work with some of the newest technologies, including biofuel, biotechnology, and nanotechnology.

# Engineering a Green Future

## In This Chapter

- ◆ How to tackle air pollution, waste management, and other health hazards as an environmental engineer

- ◆ Why civil engineers are on the cutting edge of constructing environmentally friendly buildings

- ◆ How agricultural engineers discover the most efficient uses of biological resources

- ◆ Why nuclear engineers—and, more specifically, nuclear power reactor operators—may be working on one of the fastest-growing alternative energy sources

Engineering is a large and varied profession. In fact, there are more than 1.5 million engineers in the United States. These professionals include a variety of specialties such as chemical engineers, electrical engineers, petroleum engineers, and mechanical engineers. While there are more than 15 directions you can take your engineering career, not all of them are recession proof.

This chapter is all about those engineering specialties that are both resistant to economic downturns and most connected to building a green future for our country. We start with environmental engineers who tackle the most daunting environmental challenges, including global warming and ozone depletion. From there, we cover civil engineers who work to make sure buildings are environmentally friendly. Next we cover agricultural engineers who work with crops to find the most biologically efficient ways to produce and store food. Finally, we cover nuclear engineers—specifically, nuclear power reactor operators—who carefully follow safety procedures and maintain equipment.

So if your goal is to engineer a bright future for generations to come, then you want to read the following sections on recession-proof engineering careers. It's nice to know you can protect both your job and the environment at the same time.

# Environmental Engineers

You probably do your part to help the environment. Maybe you recycle soda cans, pick up stray garbage in the park, or turn off lights to save electricity. Did you know you could make a living developing solutions to environmental problems? That's right, environmental engineers create solutions regarding waste disposal, air pollution, water contamination, and many other public health issues.

## Outlook for Environmental Engineers

| | |
|---|---|
| Current Number of Employees | 54,000 |
| New Jobs Created by 2016 | 14,000 |
| Expected Job Growth by 2016 | 25% |
| Geographical Hotspots | Nevada, Tennessee |
| Median Annual Earnings | $70,000 |

*Sources: U.S. Bureau of Labor Statistics National Employment Matrix, State Occupational Projections*

The main responsibilities of an environmental engineer include the following:

◆ Analyze hazardous waste materials to understand the true danger of the contaminants

◆ Develop policies and regulations to reduce pollution and environmental hazards

◆ Study the potential environmental impacts of proposed construction projects

- ◆ Test air and water samples to determine the level of toxicity

- ◆ Tackle some of the biggest environmental challenges, including global warming, ozone depletion, and acid rain

- ◆ Help clients comply with local, state, and federal environmental guidelines for their business ventures

Of all the engineering specialties, environmental engineers are expected to have one of the highest employment growth rates in the coming years. The expected 25 percent growth stems from three primary factors. First, environmental regulations continue to evolve, and more engineers will be needed to manage the growing list of policies. Second, Americans are paying more attention than ever before to controlling and preventing environmental hazards. This spotlight on the environment is driving an increased need for talented folks in related professions. Finally, the desire to prevent future environmental problems is resulting in a greater need for engineers to devise proactive approaches to potential hazards.

Let's take a look at a day in the life of an environmental engineer. It's important to get a sense of daily working conditions before committing to a career choice. So here's a hypothetical look at a random Tuesday for an environmental engineer. You arrive at your desk to scan environmental newsbreaks and chug a morning cup of decaf. Right away, two stories catch your attention. First, the Environmental Protection Agency has issued new air pollution guidelines for U.S. factories. Anyone opening a factory in the next few years will face tighter restrictions on smokestack emissions. Second, a research scientist in Belgium has made startling progress on new ways to slow down ozone layer depletion.

The breaking news is fascinating, but you have work to do, starting with a 9 A.M. client call. A new health-care facility wants to open near a government-protected bird sanctuary. You've been asked to determine whether construction of the new facility will have a negative impact on the bird population. On the call are representatives from the health-care facility and local government regulators who are eager to protect the town's natural beauty. You offer to head over to the sanctuary to collect air samples later this morning. You'll analyze the air

**Another Path**

How would you like to work in the environmental engineering field without the educational requirements of an environmental engineer? Consider working as an environmental engineering technician. You'll help control environmental hazards, reduce air pollution, and increase recycling efforts by working closely with environmental engineers to get the job done.

now and then again by mixing in the proposed construction materials for the health-care facility.

By lunchtime you're grabbing a bite on the way to the airport. You're on the way to Washington, D.C. You've been invited to sit on the board of a new government-sponsored global warming task force. You'll meet with top scientists, activists, and engineers, and then participate in a panel discussion in front of a live audience. On the flight, you review a client proposal for your boss. Apparently, one of the local restaurants has been issued a citation for improper waste dumping. The restaurant wants your firm to help get them back in compliance. Quite a busy day. You'll get to bed by 10:30 P.M. with a smile on your face knowing you've done your part to improve the environment.

If this sounds like the right career path for you, then you'll need to know what education is required to break into the field. It comes down to three basic requirements:

1. **Bachelor's degree in engineering**
   Collegiate engineering programs are overseen by the Accreditation Board for Engineering Technology (ABET). You'll want to be sure to apply to a program accredited by ABET. Undergraduate programs look for strong skills in math, science, and the humanities as a prerequisite for acceptance. In the average four-year program, the first two years will be general studies, including basic science and engineering courses. In the last two years you'll want to specialize in environmental engineering courses to demonstrate your passion for the subject.

2. **Professional engineer licensing**
   All 50 states require licensing for engineers who want to perform service for the public. The professional engineer (PE) license requires a Bachelor's degree from an ABET accredited school, at least four years of relevant work experience, and passing grades on a state examination. The exam is broken into two parts. The first covers engineering fundamentals while the second test covers principles and practices of engineering. Many states also require continuing education classes to maintain your license.

3. **Graduate training for education and research positions**
   If you want to enter a teaching or research-based position, then you need to continue your education beyond the undergraduate level. Most research positions will seek Master's level graduates at a minimum. College professor opportunities in engineering are reserved primarily for Ph.D. holders. If you want to go the Master's route, some ABET-accredited schools offer five-year programs in which you earn both your undergraduate and Master's degrees.

According to the American Academy of Environmental Engineers (AAEE), you can earn a specialty certification if you can demonstrate proven expertise in any of these environmental engineering subjects:

- ◆ Air pollution control
- ◆ Hazardous waste management
- ◆ Industrial hygiene
- ◆ General environmental engineering
- ◆ Radiation protection
- ◆ Solid waste management
- ◆ Water supply and wastewater engineering

With proven expertise in one of these specialties, you'll be awarded the title of Board Certified Environmental Engineer (BCEE) or Board Certified Environmental Engineering Member (BCEEM). The AAEE oversees annual recertification programs for these two certifications through mandatory continuing professional development. You'll even get listed in the annual edition of *Who's Who in Environmental Engineering* (published annually by AAEE). Now that's a great way to keep your name out there and your expertise in high demand.

# Civil Engineers

Have you ever driven across a well-designed bridge, travelled through a tunnel carved through a mountain, or marveled at the layout of your city's airport? Chances are you were admiring the work of a civil engineer. The job of a civil engineer is to design and oversee construction of roads, tunnels, bridges, buildings, airports, and even sewage systems. In many cases, a primary focus for civil engineers is to ensure that construction projects meet local, state, and federal environmental regulations.

## Outlook for Civil Engineers

| | |
|---|---|
| Current Number of Employees | 256,000 |
| New Jobs Created by 2016 | 46,000 |
| Expected Job Growth by 2016 | 18% |
| Geographical Hotspots | Nevada, Utah |
| Median Annual Earnings | $69,000 |

*Sources: U.S. Bureau of Labor Statistics National Employment Matrix, State Occupational Projections*

According to the American Society of Civil Engineers (ASCE), there are 12 civil engineering specialties or communities of practice. These include the following:

1. Air and space

2. Architectural engineering

3. Construction and materials

4. Disaster reduction

5. Environmental

6. Geo-technology

7. Maritime technology

8. Power generation

9. Structural

10. Transportation

11. Urban planning

12. Water resources

It's clear from this list that there's a wealth of specialty areas for civil engineers. In fact, the profession is so big it accounts for approximately one in six of all practicing engineers. The good news is that the civil engineering profession is expected to grow another 18 percent by 2016. The biggest factor driving this growth is the desire by the U.S. government and private industry to overhaul the nation's infrastructure. From repairing roads to replacing bridges and other public structures, employment opportunities abound for civil engineers.

### In Their Own Words

While climate change is certainly the greatest challenge any of us will face in our lifetimes, it also opens up infinite possibilities for individuals who are creative, ambitious, and forward thinking. While we represent less than 5 percent of the world's population, we account for 25 percent of greenhouse gas emissions. We as Americans need to lead the way on climate change solutions, and as such open up a wide range of career paths.

—Harriet Shugarman, Executive Director and Founder, Climate Mama, and certified trainer on Al Gore's Climate Project; from personal e-mail with the author

We could devote an entire chapter to breaking down civil engineering specialty areas. Instead, I've chosen a few in particular to help you understand the types of jobs available. A scan of online job listings shows the following openings as examples:

- **Geotechnical civil engineer:** Help clients understand and mitigate underground conditions and other below-the-surface hazards on construction projects to reduce worker safety risks, public safety issues, and construction delays

- **Maritime engineering assistant:** Work aboard a ship in the engine room to assist the lead engineer in keeping the ship's engine controls and functions running smoothly

- **Regional logistics program manager:** Work on project funded by the Department of Homeland Security to improve regional resilience to future natural disasters

- **Senior water resources engineer:** Complete complex technical assignments involving surface water hydrology, groundwater testing, surface water planning, and flood minimization projects

- **Bridge inspection engineer:** Conduct safety inspections to ensure that bridge construction projects meet local, state, and federal guidelines

Clearly the opportunities in civil engineering are varied and diverse. From working with water to bridges to disaster relief, you can find your specialty and build a promising, recession-proof career. Let's talk about breaking into the field and continuing education opportunities to specialize and advance.

Similar to environmental engineers, you'll need a Bachelor's degree in engineering from a program accredited by the ABET for entry-level positions. Your first two years of a four-year program will involve general engineering courses. In the final two years, you can specialize in courses related to civil engineering. With more than 1,800 university programs in the United States offering engineering degrees, you'll want to investigate which programs focus on industrial versus theoretical aspects of civil engineering. If you want to get to work right after school, then consider industrial-based programs. If your goal is to go on to graduate work in civil engineering, then a more theoretical-based program is right for you.

The same licensing requirements as described in the environmental engineering section also apply to the civil engineering career track. You'll need a Bachelor's degree, relevant work experience, and passing grades on the state exam to earn your civil engineering license. Once your career is off the ground, staying in touch with ASCE is important for your continuing education. According to their website, www.asce. org, the society "holds more than 300 seminars and computer workshops each year on a wide variety of technical, management, and regulatory topics. These seminars are held in more than 45 cities across the United States. In addition, ASCE offers customized on-site training, live interactive web/teleconference seminars, and many distance learning programs, including online courses, and courses on CD, videotape, and audiotape." In other words, there are multiple and diverse opportunities to keep your skills current to further recession proof your civil engineering career.

# Agricultural Engineers

Would you believe that in the early 1900s more than half of the world's population was involved in production of our food supply? According to the American Society of Agricultural and Biological Engineers (ASABE), developed countries can now produce enough food with the labor of only 2 percent of the population. Much of that advancement is thanks in part to the work of agricultural engineers. Often called agricultural and biological engineers, these professionals are all about helping to produce more food, energy, and goods as resources become more scarce.

In fact, the ASABE website (www.asabe.org) does an outstanding job explaining the challenge that lies ahead for agricultural and biological engineers as well as the continued high demand for the profession. According to the website, "As world population swells, more food, energy, and goods are required. But our limited natural resources demand that we produce more with less, that higher productivity does not degrade our environment, and that we search for new ways to use agricultural products, by-products, and wastes. Biological and agricultural engineers are responding with viable, environmentally sustainable solutions, the success of which is expanding career opportunities in renewable energy, food safety, bioprocesses, and more."

## Outlook for Agricultural Engineers

| | |
|---|---|
| Current Number of Employees | 3,100 |
| New Jobs Created by 2016 | 300 |
| Expected Job Growth by 2016 | 10% |
| Geographical Hotspots | Nebraska, North Dakota |
| Median Annual Earnings | $66,000 |

*Sources: U.S. Bureau of Labor Statistics National Employment Matrix, State Occupational Projections*

Agricultural and biological engineers meet these challenges through all of the following job responsibilities:

- ◆ Design crop storage equipment, structures, and agricultural machinery

- ◆ Develop techniques to conserve soil and water in the production of agricultural products

- ◆ Discover and test renewable energy sources for producing food more efficiently

- ◆ Reduce or manage waste materials and toxic hazards, which can be byproducts of food production

- ◆ Research safe food-production techniques to reduce occurrences of contaminated food

We know about the challenges facing agricultural and biological engineers. What exactly makes the profession recession proof? Three main factors drive the continued demand for this specific engineering specialty. First, the expanding population continues to fuel the need for increased crop yields. Second, the desire to expand renewable energy usage means crops such as corn will continue to be produced at record rates. Finally, cost-conscious crop producers are always looking for new and less expensive ways to produce crops and generate more revenue. Considering these three major factors, it's clear agricultural and biological engineers will be needed for years to come.

If you want to break into the agricultural and biological engineering field, you're going to need those same educational requirements previously covered for environmental and civil engineers. Just in case you jumped right to this section, let's quickly cover the three requirements to score a job:

**Another Path**

Crossing over from the engineering to science field is quite possible in the agricultural arena. This is especially true if you've aimed your undergraduate studies to the more theoretical aspects of agricultural and biological engineering. You can then consider repackaging your skills to become an agricultural or food scientist.

1. **Undergraduate engineering degree**
   You'll need a Bachelor's degree in engineering from an accredited school. You'll take two years of basic engineering courses and then it would be wise to specialize in some agricultural and biological classes to make your case for specializing in this field.

2. **Professional licensing**

   ABET is your ticket to earning the professional engineer license and having an important credential for job interviews. You'll need the Bachelor's degree, four years of work experience, and passing grades on the state exam. Many entry-level engineering positions give you basic engineering experiences while you work up to the four-year working requirement for a license.

3. **Graduate degree**

   The big question for you is whether you want to go down the research or industrial engineering path. Four years of working in the field may help you decide whether you prefer to work in the field or teach. If you want to stay on the industrial path, then you may not need further education, although some jobs will seek candidates with Master's degrees. If you want to teach, however, you'll likely need a Ph.D. for most positions at universities.

If you're just beginning to explore agricultural and biological engineering, attending the annual ASABE conference is a great way to dive into the field before committing. Check out www.asabemeetings.org to learn about the annual conference. In this three-day conference, you'll hear lectures from renowned engineers in the field, attend breakout sessions on current industry issues, and network with people already in the industry.

You may also be wondering who exactly needs agricultural and biological engineers on staff. This is not a job where you're destined to be working in the crop field every day. As the ASABE website points out, agricultural and biological engineers are needed in a multitude of industries including consumer products, aerospace, food and beverage, and government agencies. Here's a recent list from the ASABE website of various companies employing agricultural and biological engineers:

| | |
|---|---|
| 3M | Grinnell Mutual Reinsurance |
| Abbott Labs | John Deere |
| AGCO | Kellogg's |
| Anheuser Busch | Lockheed Martin |
| Archer Daniels Midland | M & M Mars |
| BASF | Morton Buildings |
| Briggs & Stratton | NASA |

| | |
|---|---|
| Campbell's Soup | New Holland |
| Caterpillar | Ralston Purina |
| Case Corp. | Sunkist |
| Exxon Mobil | U.S. Department of Energy |
| Florida Light & Power | U.S. Environmental Protection Agency |
| Ford Motor Co. | |

When you can make a living with such varied organizations as Campbell's Soup and the Environmental Protection Agency, you know you're onto a career with many options. That's a great way to build a recession-proof career.

# Nuclear Engineers

Though nuclear engineering is recession proof, like the other industries discussed in this book, the growth projections for the field by 2016 are only 7 percent. So the industry is stable, but the job growth isn't as promising as in other career choices. For that reason, I want to share some brief information on nuclear engineering, but then I'll focus on a specific subcareer choice within nuclear engineering. Nuclear power reactor operators are poised for 11 percent growth in the coming years. I'll cover this career choice within nuclear energy so you know the specific job choice with the most promising future.

First, though, let's talk about nuclear engineering in general. Engineers in this career are responsible for researching and developing systems and processes related to nuclear energy and radiation.

## Outlook for Nuclear Engineers

| | |
|---|---|
| Current Number of Employees | 15,000 |
| New Jobs Created by 2016 | 1,100 |
| Expected Job Growth by 2016 | 7%–11% |
| Geographical Hotspots | Maryland, South Carolina |
| Median Annual Earnings | $90,000 |

*Sources: U.S. Bureau of Labor Statistics National Employment Matrix, State Occupational Projections*

Common roles include the following:

♦ Design and operate nuclear power plants

♦ Produce nuclear fuel and manage safe disposal of waste materials

♦ Develop nuclear power for aerospace or naval industries to use on spacecraft and ships

♦ Find medical uses for radioactive materials to help treat diseases

The reason for only 7 percent growth in nuclear engineering stems from the fact that new commercial nuclear power plants have not been built in the United States for many years. Still, nuclear engineers are needed to manage existing plants. It's a small field with a small number of graduates each year that roughly matches the number of career openings annually. Most of the best jobs will be in nuclear medical technology, defense areas, and nuclear waste management. We've covered the education requirements for engineers extensively in this chapter, so I won't repeat them here. Let's instead move on to discuss nuclear power reactor operators, the field with the most growth of all the nuclear engineering specialties.

### Another Path

If you have a passion for nuclear energy but don't want to go the nuclear engineer or power reactor route, consider becoming a nuclear technician. You'll still get to work with engineers and scientists in both energy production and laboratory testing. However, the educational requirements are lighter. Now that's a fast track to a nuclear energy career.

According to the U.S. Department of Labor, there are approximately 3,800 nuclear power reactor operators in the United States. The field is expected to grow to over 4,200 operators by 2016 and the average annual salary is between $62,000 and $78,000. So this career makes less than nuclear engineers who have achieved higher educational levels, but the growth projections are much better. The basic responsibilities of a nuclear power reactor operator includes the following:

♦ Practice standard procedures to adjust nuclear controls, including temperature and rate of flow

♦ React to any nuclear system abnormalities to identify the cause and take corrective action

♦ Manage start-up and shut-down procedures to ensure plant safety

◆ Record operational data on nuclear facilities to track plant performance and note inconsistencies

◆ Conduct regular plant inspections and partner with plant personnel on maintenance procedures

As you can see, the main focus is on operation, maintenance, and inspection. You can land a nuclear power reactor operator position with one or two years of postsecondary education plus on-the-job experience. This means you can fast-track your way into the field without committing four years to college. Plus, you can always work toward an engineering degree if you decide you want to stay in the field. Furthering your education is always a solid recession-proof strategy.

## The Least You Need to Know

◆ Environmental engineers are on the cutting edge of finding solutions to Earth's biggest hazards, including air pollution, water contamination, and global warming.

◆ Civil engineers make sure new construction complies with the latest environmental regulations and policies.

◆ Agricultural engineers work to improve food production through conservation techniques, biological research, and natural resource management.

◆ Wind and solar energy are constantly in the news, but nuclear energy just might be the fastest growing of the alternative energy career choices.

# Chapter 13

# Hazardous Materials, Sewage, and Green Utilities

## In This Chapter

- How to remove hazardous materials from homes and commercial sites while building a recession-proof career

- Why septic tank servicers and sewer pipe cleaners are the most stable plumbing specialty around

- How to repackage your utilities skills to transition to a job working with renewable energy

- Why both wind and solar energy are two of the most promising career fields when it comes to green utilities

This is a chapter about waste and renewal. How can two seemingly different topics go together? Well, waste is all about removing what we don't need. Renewal is about repeatedly using something to avoid waste. Both waste and renewal share something else in common. They both can lead to recession-proof careers if you know where to look.

We start with two career choices that involve hazardous material and waste removal. First, we cover hazardous materials removal workers who rid buildings of contaminants including asbestos, lead, and mold. This is dangerous work, but with the proper safety precautions, you can avoid unnecessary exposure to harmful toxins. Next, we review septic tank servicers and sewer pipe cleaners. This is a recession-proof career built around keeping waste flowing smoothly out of homes, offices, and commercial buildings.

After finishing with waste, we switch to renewal. While many utility careers are in decline, this is not the case for renewable energy. Everything from wind to solar power is in growth mode, and employees are needed to make this industry flourish. Whether you want to install solar panels, inspect wind turbines, or work in energy sales, there's something for you. In fact, many utility workers already have skills to transfer to green utilities. Talk about repackaging yourself to move from a declining industry to a recession-proof one. Now that's how you keep your career stable without stepping out of the workforce for years of training. By the end of this section, you'll be ready to help save the world and put money in your pocket every week.

# Hazardous Materials Removal Workers

What exactly constitutes a hazardous material? Anything that can catch fire easily, erode, corrode, or that contains toxic materials counts as a hazardous material. Increasingly, state and federal regulations are requiring removal of these hazardous materials from our homes, buildings, factories, and the environment. The job of a hazardous materials removal worker is to find, remove, and dispose of these materials. The most common include asbestos, mercury, lead, and radioactive materials.

## Outlook for Hazardous Materials Removal Workers

| | |
|---|---|
| Current Number of Employees | 39,000 |
| New Jobs Created by 2016 | 4,400 |
| Expected Job Growth by 2016 | 11% |
| Geographical Hotspots | Tennessee, Utah |
| Average Hourly Earnings | $13–$23 per hour |

*Sources: U.S. Bureau of Labor Statistics National Employment Matrix, State Occupational Projections*

Often called decontamination or remediation workers, this career category is broken into several specialties, including the following:

- **Asbestos and lead abatement workers:** Remove asbestos, lead, and similar hazardous materials when structures are renovated or demolished

- **Emergency and disaster response workers:** Travel to accident scenes, such as truck accidents, to clean up hazardous material spills

- **Decommissioning workers:** Treat and remove radioactive materials created by nuclear power plants and facilities

- **Treatment, storage, and disposal workers:** Transport hazardous materials to facilities either for cleaning or for disposal

- **Mold remediators:** Clean interior walls, showers, and other damp spots to eliminate moldy conditions, particularly for people suffering allergic reactions

As you might guess, safety is the name of the game in this career. The last thing you want is exposure to these harmful and hazardous contaminants. That's why safety precautions, guidelines, and proper procedures are in place for anyone entering this field. Companies in this industry know that unintended exposure for even one worker could open up a big enough lawsuit to bankrupt the organization.

Of all the specialties mentioned in this section, the fastest growing is decommissioning workers. Employment prospects for this group benefit from two main factors. First, U.S. government and local regulations call for safer and cleaner nuclear energy generation. Second, nuclear power is still one of the fastest-growing and most viable alternative forms of energy. These two factors combined add up to great recession-proof prospects for decommissioning workers. With experience, decommissioning workers can even advance to become radiation protection technicians. Now your job is to use survey meters and other remote devices to evaluate potentially radioactive materials and recommend cleaning and disposal procedures.

Breaking into a hazardous materials removal career requires little more than a high school diploma. However, local, state, and federal government regulations require specific on-the-job training for each specialty. For example, almost all hazardous materials removal workers need a minimum of 40 hours of formal on-the-job training. The specific training for each specialty is dictated by the Occupational Safety and Health Administration (OSHA). Asbestos

### Another Path

Hazardous material removal workers—particularly those workers dealing with radioactive materials—learn many skills that are transferrable to other fields. Radioactive material removal can translate to working as a power plant operator at a nuclear facility.

and lead abatement workers, two of the most common contaminant cleaners, have an OSHA-sponsored training program. It's typically performed on-site with the employer or at an OSHA-approved training center.

Emergency and disaster response workers must earn a federal license through an OSHA program specifically for this field. The program covers everything from protective equipment to hazard identification to health hazards on the job. Many hazardous materials removal workers choose to get licensed in multiple contaminants. This way, if they're removing one hazardous material and come across another, they can continue working without calling in someone else.

If you want to go the decommissioning route—the most recession proof of the careers in this section—the training will be the most extensive. Beyond the OSHA-sponsored 40 hours of hazardous materials training, you'll also be subject to additional training through the Nuclear Regulatory Commission. Over the course of three months, you learn everything from radiation safety to nuclear materials. You don't have to take the three months of training consecutively, but you will be required to take refresher courses yearly to maintain your license.

Beyond the qualifications and licensing for the job, there are some skills that also lead to success on the job. Three of the most important include these:

1. **Mathematical calculation skills**
   Many of the neutralizing solutions for hazardous materials require pinpoint mixing. You'll have to analyze the level of contamination and determine just the right mix of neutralizing solution to get the job done.

2. **Physical strength**
   This is a job involving manual labor. From sweeping to cleaning to knocking down walls, you have to have the strength to work long hours on your feet.

3. **Construction knowledge**
   Treating hazardous materials often starts with some detective work to find the source of the problem. Knowledge of pipes, dry walls, and construction techniques will help you find the most likely hiding places for hazardous materials.

Ultimately, if you're willing to deal with those materials most folks would rather never see, then you can find a recession-proof career as a hazardous materials removal worker. Just take those safety precautions you learn from OSHA and you'll get to work without fear of inadvertent contamination.

# Septic Tank Servicers and Sewer Pipe Cleaners

Very few of us think about waste beyond flushing the toilet. Probably the only time waste is more than a passing thought occurs when a toilet or sink is plugged. But there's a whole recession-proof industry based on servicing and cleaning septic tanks and sewer pipes. Known as septic tank servicers and sewer pipe cleaners, these workers clean and repair septic tanks, sewer lines, and drains.

## Outlook for Septic Tank Servicers and Sewer Pipe Cleaners

| | |
|---|---|
| Current Number of Employees | 24,000 |
| New Jobs Created by 2016 | 7,000 |
| Annual Job Growth through 2016 | 7%–13% |
| Geographical Hotspots | Nevada, South Dakota |
| Median Annual Earnings | $34,000 |

*Sources: Occupational Information Network, U.S. Bureau of Labor Statistics National Employment Matrix, State Occupational Projections*

Basic responsibilities of the job include all of the following:

◆ Clean and repair septic tanks, sewer lines, and similar structures such as manholes

◆ Keep records of maintenance and repair actions taken on septic tanks and sewer lines

◆ Operate machinery that cleans septic tanks and sewer lines, including sewer flushers, water jets, and power rodders

◆ Mark and measure excavation sites for digging out pipelines to prep for repair jobs

◆ Inspect septic tanks and sewer lines for clogs, deposits, and other blockages that prevent proper functioning

This is clearly a hands-on profession, one where you're going to be digging, cleaning, checking, inspecting, and fixing septic tanks and sewer lines. Similar to hazardous materials removal workers, you're often going to be dealing with contaminated or toxic materials. Therefore, safety precautions and procedures are equally important in this profession.

**Another Path**

If you're already working as a plumber and customers are drying up, consider spe-cializing as a septic tank servicer and sewer pipe cleaner. You'll have learned many of the necessary skills from your plumbing days, which will make the transition to this recession-proof career that much easier.

Similar to hazardous materials removal workers, septic tank servicers and sewer pipe cleaners need little to no formal education beyond a high school diploma. Most of the training and safety precautions are taught on the job. This means you can break into the field sooner than later, work under an experienced professional, and quickly get up to speed. There are, of course, some additional skills that will help you succeed on the job. Three of the most important competencies include the following:

1. **Manual dexterity**
   This is a hands-on profession in which you're tightening, loosening, and maneu-vering things all day. One minute you'll be raising a manhole, the next you're flushing out a septic system. Manual dexterity is key to getting the job done.

2. **Investigative skills**
   When a customer calls with a clog, it can be anywhere along the pipeline. The last thing you want to do is open walls and pipes unrelated to the problem. Your experience and investigative skills will help you identify the problem and mini-mize destruction of structures that don't need to be touched.

3. **Attention to detail**
   Regular maintenance on hundreds or thousands of septic tanks and sewer lines requires keeping track of what's been cleaned and what's been fixed. Your cus-tomers will depend on you to know when their system needs various procedures.

If you choose to run your own business, then customer service skills will be para-mount. You won't be cleaning anything if customers don't trust you to do the job right. As your business grows, you may want to hire an employee devoted to handling customer inquiries and scheduling appointments. This will free you up to focus on doing what you do best. Of course, if you don't have the entrepreneurial spirit, you can always work for one of the larger septic tank and sewer pipe cleaning companies. Getting on board with an established company may be your ticket to learning the ropes in this field.

# Green Utilities

The last time you used the bathroom in your home, you likely triggered four different utilities. First, you turned on the lights, which required electricity. Second, you flushed the toilet, which created the need for waste removal. Then you washed your hands, which required clean water plus natural gas (or maybe electricity) to heat the water. Imagine, one simple daily act in your home bringing together electricity, waste removal, water, and heat. Multiply this act by the millions of people in the United States and it's hard to imagine utilities would be anything but a recession-proof career. However, the fact is that most utility professions are either stagnant or declining. Consider these statistics for some of the most common utility professions:

| Utility Profession | Projected Employment Growth by 2016 |
|---|---|
| Top executives | –16% |
| Administrative service managers | –10% |
| Dispatchers | –19% |
| Meter readers | –17% |
| Electricians | –5% |
| Maintenance and repair workers | –5% |
| Pipelayers, plumbers, pipefitters, and steamfitters | –8% |

*Source: U.S. Bureau of Labor Statistics National Employment Matrix*

Overall, the utility industry is expected to see a 6 percent employment drop by 2016, according to the U.S. Department of Labor. So why the big drop when electric power, water, and gas are so essential to our daily existence? Well, much of the workforce is aging and headed toward retirement. When jobs are open, many technical workers are choosing other professions. This leaves utility companies having to automate jobs that used to be done manually or to contract with retirees to continue working part-time. Either way, the decline means certain areas of utility work are anything but recession proof.

Let's get clear on the type of work that falls in the utility category. From there, we're going to discover how you can reapply the utility skills you already have to a recession-proof green utility career. Overall, the traditional utility profession includes three broad career categories.

1. **Electric power generation, transmission, and distribution**
   Any company involved in the generation, transmission, and distribution of electric power falls under this category. Much of this power is generated today from coal, followed by nuclear power, petroleum, and other energy sources. Renewable sources of energy, such as wind and solar, are growing rapidly but make up a small percentage of today's energy generation.

> **Career Caveat**
>
> Anytime you work in utilities, you must be aware of harmful and toxic elements in water, sewage, and waste. According to the Environmental Working Group (EWG), this kind of work can expose you to asbestos, lead, and other contaminants. If you're going to work hands-on in the utility profession, take the necessary precautions to avoid exposure.

2. **Natural gas distribution**
   After natural gas is discovered and brought to the surface by oil and gas extraction companies, it is transported across the United States by gas transmission companies using pipelines. Local distribution companies then take the natural gas from pipelines and deliver it to industrial, commercial, and residential customers. People who work in construction, installation, maintenance, and repair of the pipelines, as well as end-customer delivery of the gas, make up most of these occupations.

3. **Water, sewage, and other systems**
   More than 34 billion gallons of water are delivered each day to customers in the United States. Water is collected from rivers and lakes, then treated and sold for public and private company use. In small towns and rural areas, a single plant operator may monitor the water system. In major urban areas, an enormous system of dams, pipelines, and water treatment plants requires the coordinated work of hundreds of staff. Though septic tank servicers and sewer pipe cleaners are recession proof, the rest of the occupations involved in sewage are not in growth mode. Finally, other systems in this category include steam and air-conditioning suppliers who produce and distribute steam, heated air, and cooled air.

Put these three broad utility career categories together, and two themes emerge. First, thousands of people are needed to operate and maintain the distribution of the utilities we rely on every day. Second, if these careers are in decline while renewable sources of energy continue to explode, then migrating your skill set to green utilities is the perfect recession-proof strategy. So let's talk about how you can repackage your skills to be on the utilities cutting edge.

Do you remember our discussion of math and science teachers? We talked about how federal government investment was driving the explosive growth for these teaching professions. Well, the same holds true for careers in renewable energy. The U.S. Department of Energy (DOE) and the National Science Foundation are co-sponsoring a joint initiative to encourage thousands of workers to enter fields

> ## In Their Own Words
>
> We have a great opportunity in our nation's history to advance the green movement by solving our energy needs in an economically sustainable and environmentally friendly way.
>
> —The Honorable Dr. Stephen L. Johnson, former Administrator of the U.S. Environmental Protection Agency

related to clean energy. Among the goals of this joint initiative include reducing our dependence on foreign oil, developing new energy technologies, and reducing energy-related emissions. The U.S. government's strong monetary commitment to this field is your ticket to finding a recession-proof career in green utilities. Remember, we already covered environmentally friendly science and engineering jobs in the previous two chapters. Now let's focus on green utility careers, specifically involving wind and solar energy.

# Renewable Wind Energy

According to the DOE, wind could be responsible for more than 20 percent of the nation's energy by 2030. With more than 16,000 jobs already in wind turbine construction and maintenance, you can only imagine how many more will be needed by 2030. Consider the fact that wind farms now operate in 34 states around the country. That means you can find a wind-related renewable energy job in nearly 70 percent of the states, with more wind farms opening every year. So what kind of jobs can you strive for in wind energy? There's a great resource for finding open jobs on the website of the American Wind Energy Association (AWEA). Go to www.awea.org and click on the career center to find open jobs and qualifications. You'll likely see jobs such as these:

- ◆ **Wind technician:** Responsible for the operations and maintenance of wind turbine generators, including troubleshooting mechanical and electrical problems

- ◆ **Wind energy specialists:** Coordinate with wind developers, regulators, and operators to oversee business development and strategic planning operations for wind-based renewable energy sites

◆ **Wind power analyst:** Oversee data collection to provide accurate and real-time information on power plant usage and supply availability

From technicians to specialists and analysts, this is just a taste of the jobs you could go for in wind energy. What you can see right away is that technician-type jobs are similar to those in traditional utility companies. The only difference is you're repairing wind turbine blades. The specialist and analyst roles are similar to many of the desk jobs in traditional utility companies. In other words, there's a great opportunity to transfer your skills to wind energy whether you work hands-on or in front of a computer. You can even decide to do one of these jobs for a private company or with the government.

## Renewable Solar Energy

According to the American Solar Energy Society (ASES), there are nearly 8,000 people employed in the solar energy industry. Though this is less than are employed in wind energy, the U.S. government has enhanced incentives for residential and commercial property owners to install solar energy panels. This will lead to an increased demand for workers in the industry. The most likely kind of work will be installing solar panels on residential properties.

Because this work typically involves installing solar panels on roofs, it is a highly transferrable job for people with either construction or electrical experience. So if you've been working in construction or for an electric utility company and got laid off, this could be a great way to reinvent your career. This is also a feel-good career choice; you know you're helping the environment every time you switch a customer to solar energy.

Visit the ASES website at www.ases.org to see job listings in solar energy. A quick scan of the site shows jobs such as these:

◆ **Outside sales representative:** Work in a specific U.S. region looking for new solar energy customers and managing existing customer relationships

◆ **Facilities maintenance technician:** Responsible for overseeing the factory that produces solar energy products and troubleshooting production issues

◆ **Construction services manager:** Oversee the project planning and physical labor on solar panel installations

You can easily see how workers could transfer skills from other industries. If you have sales, technical, or construction experience, you can roll those skills into a new solar energy job. Also, keep in mind we've covered only wind and solar energy in these sections. You can also transfer your skills to other renewable energy industries, including hydroelectric, geothermal, biomass, and biofuels. The opportunities really are endless as you consider repackaging your skill set into a recession-proof renewable energy career.

## The Least You Need to Know

- If you're willing to remove hazardous materials from homes, offices, and other commercial properties, you can build a recession-proof career.

- Septic tank servicers and sewer pipe cleaners keep waste flowing out of homes and offices smoothly while building stable careers for themselves.

- Though American usage of basic utilities continues to climb, the associated professions are, for the most part, in decline.

- Many of the skills you learn in traditional utilities are transferable to renewable energy jobs connected to wind and solar energy.

# Part 5

# Honor and Defend Your Country

In the entire history of our country, governing it effectively and defending it from global threats has been critical. It's no wonder that careers in government and defense are recession proof. In good times and bad, our country still needs to be led and protected. If you've thought about public service, homeland security, law enforcement, and community service, then this is the part for you.

We begin with a look at the most recession-proof careers available in government, including public sector agencies and support staff. From there, we talk defense, including careers in aerospace, homeland security, and correctional facilities. Finally, it's time to give back to your community. We review community service manager, social and human service assistant, and regional planner roles that are sure to stand the test of time.

# Chapter 14

# Careers In and Around the Law

## In This Chapter

- ◆ How private investigators help solve tough computer, people, and corporate cases

- ◆ Why paralegals are taking on more of what lawyers used to do and building recession-proof careers along the way

- ◆ How litigants' inability to reach compromises will keep arbitrators in business for years to come

- ◆ Why correctional officers will always be needed as long as people continue to commit crimes

- ◆ What security guards protect for a living and how our nation's continued safety frenzy is propelling this career

The law has an impact on us in more ways than we might realize. It's not just about breaking or following the rules. A host of jobs touch the law from many different angles. There are people who investigate crimes, research laws, resolve legal disputes, watch over lawbreakers, and even prevent crimes from happening. This chapter is all about recession-proof careers in and around the law.

We start with private detectives and investigators. From spying on cheating spouses to recovering deleted e-mails, these folks solve mysteries and piece together evidence for a living. Next we talk about paralegals and legal assistants who make the lives of lawyers that much easier. Lawyers would be nowhere near as prepared for court without the diligent, behind-the-scenes work of paralegals. From there, we cover arbitrators who step in to resolve disputes when two sides can't seem to meet in the middle. Next we review why correctional officers will always find work as long as people get convicted of crimes. Finally, we end with security guards who know how to protect their careers by protecting people, places, and valuables.

By the end of this chapter you'll be ready to jump into five of the most recession-proof careers related to the laws that govern us. So whether you want to investigate crimes or help rehabilitate those who commit crimes, there's a stable job waiting for you.

# Private Detectives and Investigators

Do you ever watch your favorite detective show on television and think, "I could do that!" Does the thought of surreptitiously tracking suspects, scanning deleted e-mails for clues, and helping law enforcement officers crack cases excite you? If so, then private detective and investigator just might be the right recession-proof career for you. You'll be helping individuals, businesses, attorneys, and the police solve cases, uncover facts, and analyze information.

## Outlook for Private Detectives and Investigators

| | |
|---|---|
| Current Number of Employees | 52,000 |
| New Jobs Created by 2016 | 9,400 |
| Expected Job Growth by 2016 | 18% |
| Geographical Hotspots | Colorado, Nevada |
| Average Annual Earnings | $24,000–$48,000 |

*Sources: U.S. Bureau of Labor Statistics National Employment Matrix, State Occupational Projections*

Your basic responsibilities might include the following:

◆ Investigate computer-based crimes, including identity theft and child pornography

◆ Conduct background investigations and pre-employment screenings to check the viability of job candidates

♦ Follow suspected adulterers to collect visual evidence of cheating

♦ Examine dubious insurance claims for evidence of lying and fraud

♦ Interview suspects and family members in connection with a missing person case

This is one field where no two days will be the same. That's because your work encompasses office time, travel, and on-site investigative work. For example, you might spend your morning combing through case files behind your desk. By midday you're catching a flight to Phoenix to interview a case lead. Later that day you're on the phone with your case supervisor reviewing evidence. Just before dinner you're parked on a street corner secretly watching a suspect for clues. This variety will keep your job interesting, but it also means irregular hours. You can't exactly expect suspects to operate only between 9 and 5 on weekdays.

If this kind of work excites you, the good news is you'll be working in a profession expected to grow 18 percent by 2016. Much of this increased demand stems from the heightened security concerns since the attacks on the World Trade Center on September 11, 2001. Individuals and companies simply want to spend more to protect what they value most. Additionally, computer-based crime continues to get more and more sophisticated. Investigators who can stay one step ahead of the perpetrators will be in high demand. Finally, with the financial meltdown of 2008, many people will spend more to protect themselves and their companies from financial losses, particularly from fraudulent investors.

**Career Caveat**

Let's get one thing straight about private detective and investigative work. You're watching people who may not be pleased to have you on their trail. This means the job can be dangerous; suspects may be armed and dangerous. You'll have to take precautions to protect your safety and avoid bodily harm.

This variety of demand has spurred growth in multiple sub-specialties for private detectives and investigators. Here are some of the most common:

1. **Legal investigators**
   Legal investigators help prepare and assemble evidence for trials. This may include locating witnesses, serving legal documents, and gathering information on litigation parties.

2. **Corporate investigators**

   Corporations hire corporate investigators to examine both internal and external company problems. Examples might include expense report abuse, merchandise theft, or even fraudulent billing by a company supplier.

3. **Computer forensic investigator**

   Deleted e-mails are not necessarily gone for good. Computer forensic investigators recover erased files, restore e-mails, and tackle various computer system intrusions. What's recovered can become evidence in civil and defense cases.

4. **Store detectives**

   Those metal detectors aren't always enough to dissuade shoppers from stealing merchandise. Store detectives are on the lookout for customers attempting to leave the store without paying.

5. **Financial investigators**

   If a big merger is imminent, a financial investigator might be hired by one company to build a financial profile of the other. In this case, you'll be working closely with accountants and bankers to create the profile.

This is clearly a field in which your investigative prowess is the single most important factor in your career progression. That's why nearly 30 percent go the self-employment route after gaining experience and building a reputation. There are plenty of opportunities to gain experience at one of the larger investigative or security firms. Another alternative, one followed by nearly 100,000 detectives, is to focus on investigations related to suspected federal, state, or local law violations. That's right, the U.S. government, as well as local and state governments, employs thousands of detectives and investigators to help enforce the laws that protect us all.

Whether you want to go it alone, work for a private security firm, or land employment with the government, be aware of the educational and training requirements to break into the field. The good news is that many jobs require only a high school degree and on-the-job training. If you want to go the corporate investigator route, then employers prefer a college degree in a business-related field. If computer investigation is your calling, you'll benefit from a computer-related college degree. Getting some form of postsecondary training—perhaps an Associate's degree in political science or criminal justice—will improve your chances of landing that first gig, no matter how you specialize.

Most states require you to be licensed to become a private investigator or detective. In most cases, the requirements include some form of schooling, work experience, and passing grades on a licensing exam. Beyond state licensing, you can also earn certification from a professional organization. As an example, the National Association of Legal Investigators offers the Certified Legal Investigator designation to those who qualify. It certainly won't hurt your chances in a job interview.

# Paralegals and Legal Assistants

When you see a shiny-suited lawyer arguing a case in court, he or she often looks polished, prepared, and ready to do battle. What you probably didn't realize is there's a team of paralegals and legal assistants behind the scenes making sure that lawyer looks good in court. While lawyers have the ultimate responsibility for legal work performed, they delegate many tasks to paralegals.

## Outlook for Paralegals and Legal Assistants

| | |
|---|---|
| Current Number of Employees | 238,000 |
| New Jobs Created by 2016 | 53,000 |
| Expected Job Growth by 2016 | 22% |
| Geographical Hotspots | Florida, Utah |
| Average Annual Earnings | $34,000–$55,000 |

*Sources: U.S. Bureau of Labor Statistics National Employment Matrix, State Occupational Projections*

Also called legal assistants, these professionals are not permitted to give legal advice or present cases in court. However, they carry out many important responsibilities, including these:

- Help a lawyer prepare for a hearing, trial, or corporate meeting

- Research the facts of a case to provide a lawyer with all relevant case materials and background

- Identify relevant case precedents, laws, or legal materials to help argue the current case

- Prepare written reports lawyers use to file with judges or submit to clients

◆ Draft legal documents including contracts, mortgages, wills, and divorce agreements

◆ Act as an informal office manager to keep a team of lawyers organized and prepared for cases

There are many different kinds of lawyers, and therefore paralegals, to match all the different career choices. Though most paralegals work for law firms, the government, and corporate legal departments, they can work in many different areas of the law. Some of the most common include personal injury law, criminal law, intellectual property, family law, and real estate. The bigger the firm you work for, the more likely it is you'll specialize in a particular brand of the law. At smaller firms, paralegals tend to be generalists who can handle multiple legal categories.

A primary driver of the forecasted 22 percent growth for paralegals by 2016 is the desire to reduce costs by delegating more and more tasks to paralegals. The more that a relatively low-paid paralegal can do, the fewer high-paid lawyers a firm needs to keep on staff. What makes paralegals recession proof is the fact that they're needed in both good times and bad. When business is booming, they're helping to complete business contracts, mortgages, and other documents. When the economy flounders, other areas of the law such as bankruptcy flourish.

**Another Path**

Working as a paralegal is not the only way to assist lawyers and judges in court. You can also go the law clerk route. You'll still get to research and prepare legal documents, and you may even meet with clients to gather case facts. The qualifications for both paralegals and law clerks are somewhat similar, so you can consider transferring from one role to the other over the course of your career.

There are four primary training paths to becoming a paralegal. The one that's right for you depends on where you are currently in your career.

1. **Community college paralegal program**
   The American Bar Association (ABA) sponsors more than 250 paralegal programs. These programs combine paralegal training with courses in relevant academic subjects.

2. **Certificate in paralegal studies**
   Many certificate programs take as little as three months to complete. However, they may require postsecondary education as a prerequisite for acceptance.

3. **Bachelor's or Master's degree in paralegal studies**
   If you're willing to commit to four or five years of schooling, you can earn either a Bachelor's or Master's degree in paralegal studies. Many colleges across the country offer this degree program.

4. **On-the-job paralegal training**
   Some employers will train paralegals on the job. This opportunity is usually reserved for experienced legal secretaries or applicants from relevant and needed fields such as tax preparation.

Assuming you follow one of these four paths to your first paralegal position, the next question is how you advance over the course of your career. The biggest sign your career is moving in the right direction is if you're given bigger cases to handle with less supervision. That means your employer is gaining trust in your expertise. You may even earn the right to lead a team of paralegals on more complex cases. There's also the option of attending law school on nights and weekends to earn your degree. Then you can officially go from helping lawyers get the job done to asking paralegals to help you do the same.

# Arbitrators, Mediators, and Conciliators

Court is not the only place where disputes are resolved. Sometimes two people, companies, or organizations seek an objective third party to help resolve their differences. This is where the work of arbitrators, mediators, and conciliators comes into play. Their job is to oversee disputes outside of court and help two parties reach a just and fair settlement.

## Outlook for Arbitrators, Mediators, and Conciliators

| | |
|---|---|
| Current Number of Employees | 8,500 |
| New Jobs Created by 2016 | 900 |
| Expected Job Growth by 2016 | 11% |
| Geographical Hotspots | Florida, Virginia |
| Average Annual Earnings | $49,000 |

*Sources: U.S. Bureau of Labor Statistics National Employment Matrix, State Occupational Projections*

The roles of arbitrators, mediators, and conciliators are somewhat different:

- Arbitrators are typically lawyers or business people with a specific and relevant expertise who oversee a dispute and then provide either a binding or voluntary decision.

- Mediators are most commonly used when opposing parties are interested in preserving their relationship but need help working through their differences.

- Conciliators are best thought of as facilitators who help guide two parties to a settlement. Parties have the right to pursue legal action if not satisfied with the outcome.

The biggest factor driving the growth prospects for arbitrators, mediators, and conciliators is the desire by companies and litigants to avoid, or at least reduce, court costs. Everyone knows court cases may come with everything from lengthy delays to unwanted publicity. Arbitration, mediation, and conciliation are often viewed as faster, less expensive, and clearer ways to resolve a dispute. Many states recognize the value of alternative dispute resolution programs to lighten the load of court cases on the docket. Some states are even now requiring litigants to go through some form of mediation before filing official papers with the court.

Life as an arbitrator, mediator, or conciliator typically includes both office work and travel time. You'll spend time behind the desk reviewing cases and preparing for hearings. However, you'll also travel to predetermined negotiation sites where parties are making their case. Though workweeks are usually 35 to 40 hours, deadlines might require long nights of work as well.

### Another Path

The two previous careers covered in this chapter, private detectives and paralegals, both build transferrable skills that can land you in an arbitration role. After all, much of this role is about uncovering the truth and understanding the law. It's nice to know you can bounce from one recession-proof career to another and take your skill set along with you.

There are three primary educational paths to breaking into this field. You can attend an independent mediation program, gain training through a mediation membership organization, or seek a postsecondary training program. Many mediation programs are state funded and have training requirements specific to the state. For example, you might be required to complete a 20- or 40-hour training course followed by mediation on-the-job experience. This may come from volunteer work at the local mediation center or from working with an experienced mediator to build your skills. If you want to go the formal training path, a Bachelor's degree focused in conflict resolution or public policy will pave the way for entry into the field. Going on for your law degree won't hurt your chances either.

Though there are no national credentials or licensing requirements to become an arbitrator, mediator, or conciliator, each state has its own guidelines. In some states, you'll need a law degree to oversee cases. Other states require credentials available through professional organizations such as the American Arbitration Association.

Ultimately, your best bet for recession proofing your career is building a reputation as the go-to person for a specialized field. For example, imagine lines of professional athletes clamoring for you to hear their salary arbitration cases. The more you become known for a particular expertise, the more in demand you'll be every time a relevant dispute arises.

# Correctional Officers

If only our nation's citizens could just follow the laws. There would be no need for jails and no need for correctional officers. Unfortunately, more than 1.5 million people are incarcerated in our federal and state prisons at any given time. Another 700,000 are sitting in local jails. All together, more than 12 million people are admitted and processed through the jail system every year. The sheer number of lawbreakers is enough to make correctional officers recession proof. Their job is to oversee individuals who have been arrested, convicted of a crime, or are simply awaiting trial.

## Outlook for Correctional Officers

| | |
|---|---|
| Current Number of Employees | 500,000 |
| New Jobs Created by 2016 | 82,000 |
| Expected Job Growth by 2016 | 16% |
| Geographical Hotspots | Arkansas, Mississippi |
| Average Annual Earnings | $28,000–$47,000 |

*Sources: U.S. Bureau of Labor Statistics National Employment Matrix, State Occupational Projections*

Primary responsibilities of a correctional officer include the following:

◆ Maintain jail security to prevent disturbances, riots, and escapes

◆ Monitor work assignment of inmates and keep them on a schedule throughout the day

◆ Inspect inmate living quarters for illegal contraband and other banned substances

◆ Settle disputes among inmates to keep the peace in prison and prevent fights

◆ Report on inmate conduct and behavior; contribute to reports for parole hearings

With more than 500,000 correctional officers around the country, the jobs are plentiful. More than 60 percent of correctional officers are employed in state prisons and youth correctional facilities. Just less than 10 percent work in federal prisons or privately owned facilities. Most of the rest of the jobs are in city and county jails. Finally, a small percentage of correctional officers work for the U.S. Immigration and Naturalization Service, supervising people pending deportation or release.

### Another Path

Supervising inmates can be hazardous work. Remember, these folks are behind bars because they already disregarded one or more laws. If you want to deal with convicts on a somewhat safer basis, you can consider working as a probation officer. You'll still help rehabilitate convicts, but not in a jail setting.

Breaking into the correctional officer field requires a combination of basic qualifications and training. For starters, you must be at least 18 years of age, be a U.S. citizen or permanent resident, and have no felony convictions. You'll also need to meet minimum standards of physical health, eyesight, and hearing. After all, this job is all about watching and listening for trouble and potentially physically dealing with inmates.

From an educational standpoint, you'll need at least a high school degree or the equivalent. Further educational requirements depend on where you want to work. Some prison systems require either previous experience in law enforcement or relevant college credits. Other systems look for at least two years of work experience in any field to demonstrate working stability. If you want to work for the Federal Bureau of Prisons, you'll need at least a Bachelor's degree, plus at least three years of full-time experience in a relevant field. Examples include counseling or supervising individuals in a prior role. At the state and local level, military or law enforcement experience may be enough to waive the college credits requirements.

The American Correctional Association and the American Jail Association have created official guidelines for correctional officers in training. Instruction programs include these:

◆ Interpersonal communication and relations skills

◆ Firearm training and self-defense instruction

◆ Prison regulations, policies, and operations

◆ Security and custody guidelines

If you go the federal prison route, you're required to complete 120 hours of formal training at the U.S. Federal Bureau of Prisons residential training center in Georgia. From there, you'll receive annual ongoing training to stay on top of the latest tools and tips for correctional officers.

Whether you choose to work at the local, state, or federal level, or even through a private prison system, advancement is possible. The most likely promotion is to oversee and supervise a team of correctional officers. The ultimate achievement for correctional officers is to advance to become the warden. The person in this role is responsible for overseeing all security operations at a given prison.

# Security Guards

From stores to airports to office complexes, security guards are everywhere. Unfortunately, the world we live in requires more than a million security guards to watch over our valuables and us. That's what keeps this career choice going strong. Security guards are responsible for patrolling property, protecting against fire and theft, and warding off illegal activities.

## Outlook for Security Guards

| | |
|---|---|
| Current Number of Employees | 1,040,000 |
| New Jobs Created by 2016 | 175,000 |
| Expected Job Growth by 2016 | 17% |
| Geographical Hotspots | Colorado, Utah |
| Average Annual Earnings | $18,000–$27,000 |

*Sources: U.S. Bureau of Labor Statistics National Employment Matrix, State Occupational Projections*

Some of the most common responsibilities for security guards include the following:

◆ Prevent criminal activity and trespassing on an employer's property

◆ Guard a celebrity or high-profile person to prevent mishaps during public outings

◆ Contact police and emergency personnel when assistance is required after a security breach

◆ Keep logs of security observations and activities during shifts to track events

◆ Maintain workplace safety by overseeing admittance of employees and guests at a company

◆ Testify in court accurately to share eyewitness accounts of events that transpired

The nature of the work for security guards varies by the role performed. For example, many security guards spend considerable hours on their feet, patrolling a building or store. Others may have static positions behind a guard desk inside a building where they watch closed-circuit televisions. Still others work at facility gates, admitting or denying entry to those requesting entrance to a gated community or office complex. Regardless of where security guards work, the most important quality is to be ready for anything. While most days will be routine, you never know when a security breach or emergency will occur.

### Another Path

If you've worked as a correctional officer in the prison system, but desire a less hazardous job, then transferring to a security guard position may be the right move. Instead of guarding convicts, you'll protect valuables, office complexes, and gated communities. You'll still use the same vigilance skills, just in a less stressful setting.

Think about all of the places that need security guards. It's easy to see why the career is recession proof. In good times and bad, these spots still need protection. Some of the most common places to land employment include stadiums, malls, gated communities, office complexes, museums, parks, hospitals, government agencies, military bases, universities, and even parking lots. That's just a short list. Pay attention to how many security guards you encounter in a given day. You might be surprised at how many you come across in the course of your daily routine.

Let's take a quick snapshot of a day in the life of the average citizen to see all the security guards we meet. You leave the house in the morning and pass a security guard working at the gate of your condominium complex. Arriving at work, another security guard checks your badge before allowing you to enter. During your lunch hour, you see two security guards. The first is working at the restaurant where you dine. The second is guarding valuables and preventing shoplifting when you stop at a store for a quick errand. After work, you attend a concert with friends where security guards ensure that the crowd is orderly. Finally, on the ride home, you pass one last security guard helping pedestrians cross the street. One typical day and you've come across six security guards. This sure is a profession in high demand.

Landing a security guard position requires education, training, and licensing as follows:

1. **High school education**
   In most states, a high school degree is required to land a security position.

2. **Formal and on-the-job training**
   The American Society for Industrial Security International has written a voluntary training protocol to provide minimum standards for the quality of security services. Most employers also have their own training guidelines specific to the job. For armed security professionals, the training will be more extensive, as the handling of firearms would dictate.

3. **Licensing**
   Most states require licenses for security guards. Typical requirements include that you're at least 18 years of age, have passed a security background check, and complete classroom training in relevant subjects such as emergency protocol. Drug testing is also common for security guards.

Assuming you have the education, training, and licensing to enter the profession, opportunities for advancement exist. If you're willing to go from unarmed to armed security guard, you'll typically earn more money. Of course, this also means you're more likely to encounter riskier or more dangerous situations. If you work in a large security organization, you can move up the ranks to oversee a team of security guards and earn higher pay.

## The Least You Need to Know

◆ If you know how to solve mysteries, you'll find work as a private detective or investigator.

◆ The more you can make a lawyer's life easier, the more valuable you'll be as a paralegal or legal assistant.

◆ If you're good at objectively hearing two sides of an issue and reaching a fair conclusion, then consider becoming an arbitrator.

◆ Correctional officers have a tough job watching over convicted lawbreakers, but their jobs are by no means in jeopardy.

◆ Public venues, private companies, shopping malls, and many more locations continue to require security guards to ensure the safety and security of people and goods.

# Chapter 15

# Govern Your Career in the Government

## In This Chapter

◆ Why the federal government is the single largest employer in the United States

◆ How to land a federal job in 1 of 400 occupational categories

◆ Why the U.S. Department of Homeland Security continues to be one of the hottest government jobs around

◆ How you can join the U.S. Armed Forces in combat or noncombat roles and build a recession-proof life

All of our tax dollars have to go somewhere. In fact, much of that money pulled from your paycheck supports the more than 1.7 million federal government workers in our country. From health, energy, and labor agencies to the Department of Homeland Security, and even the armed forces, recession-proof careers abound in your government.

This chapter begins with a snapshot of the more than 400 occupational career categories available for qualified workers. You'll be amazed at the vast array of industries, specialties, and expertise called for in government jobs. From there, we delve into three specific government career categories. First, we review the largest category—government jobs in general. From there we focus on the Department of Homeland Security. Created after the attacks of September 11, 2001, this department continues to protect our homeland from terrorist attacks and other threats. Finally, we end with the armed forces. We're not just talking about combat duty. You can make a nice living without ever seeing a day in the battlefield.

By the end of this chapter, you'll see why U.S. government jobs are stable, secure, and expected to be around for years to come. So if you ever wanted to work directly for the very organization that governs the land where you live, then this is the chapter for you. Let's dive right into a quick review of the diverse career opportunities available for those who desire federal employment.

# Working for the Nation's Largest Employer

According to USAJobs.com, the official job site of the federal government, approximately 50,000 jobs are open at any one time. That's a clear indicator that the federal government is the nation's largest employer. These jobs fall roughly into 25 main federal agencies, as defined by the *Occupational Outlook Quarterly*. This list shows these 25 agencies, starting with the largest employer and continuing down the line:

1. Department of Veteran Affairs

2. Army

3. Navy

4. Department of Homeland Security

5. Air Force

6. Department of the Treasury

7. Department of Agriculture

8. Department of Justice

9. Department of Defense

10. Department of the Interior

11. Social Security Administration

12. Department of Health and Human Services

13. Department of Transportation

14. Department of Commerce

15. Department of State

16. National Aeronautics and Space Administration

17. Environmental Protection Agency

18. Department of Labor

19. Department of Energy

20. General Services Administration

21. Department of Housing and Urban Development

22. Federal Deposit Insurance Corporation

23. Smithsonian Institution

24. Department of Education

25. Securities and Exchange Commission

A quick scan of USAJobs.com can give you a great sense of the wealth of career opportunities available in the federal government. The 25 agencies just listed identify broad career categories for employment. Right now, let's get more specific. Here's a list of the occupation categories covered on the USAJobs website. You can see that many of the careers we covered previously in this book as private sector opportunities are also available as government positions. Here's the list:

**Career Caveat**

Many federal government jobs are administration proof. This means you won't get your walking papers just because a new president from a different political party takes the oath of office. However, leadership positions in some U.S. government agencies are subject to turnover after an election.

- ◆ Accounting, budget, and finance

- ◆ Biological sciences

- ◆ Business, industry, and procurement

- ◆ Education

- ◆ Engineering and architecture

- ◆ Equipment, facilities, and services

- Human resources

- Information technology

- Information, arts, and public affairs

- Inspection, investigation, enforcement, and compliance

- Legal and claims examining

- Library and archives

- Management, administration, clerical, and office services

- Mathematics and statistics

- Medical, dental, and public health

- Physical sciences

- Quality assurance and grading

- Safety, health, and physical and resource protection

- Social science, psychology, and welfare

- Supply

- Trades and labor

- Transportation

- Veterinary medical science

Now that's a list! Talk about some recession-proof career opportunities. Practically every career under the sun is available through the U.S. federal government. Check out www.usajobs.com for the current list of open jobs under each career category.

Clearly, each of the opportunities on this list requires completely different training and certifications. Some need little more than a high school degree. Other careers may require advanced degrees and official licensing. Your best bet is to home in on the career category of interest, then check websites, organizations, and career guides to understand the specific requirements. If you review enough job listings in your desired career area, you'll also get a sense of the typical training, qualifications, and work experience required, not to mention advancement opportunities.

Now that we know the general career categories available within the federal government, let's take a closer look at two major federal employers. First we'll tackle

Homeland Security, the very people who keep our country and borders safe, and then the U.S. military. You'll soon see that this area offers tremendous recession-proof career opportunities.

# Careers in Homeland Security

Problem solving is a tough challenge for many people. Now imagine trying to solve problems before they happen. That's the job for those who work in the Department of Homeland Security.

Since the attacks on the World Trade Center in New York City, our country has been squarely focused on protection from future terrorist threats. In fact, that is why the Department of Homeland Security was created. However, the department extends beyond just terrorist activity prevention. Pandemics and natural disasters also fall under this department's jurisdiction. Broadly, here are the main areas of responsibility that fall under the Department of Homeland Security:

- **Customs and border protection:** Agents are positioned along U.S. physical borders to prevent illegal entry into the country.

- **Citizenship and immigration services:** Agents process paperwork and make decisions on granting citizenship for immigrants.

- **Federal Emergency Management Agency (FEMA):** Staff helps prepare for and react to natural, technological, and other disasters.

- **Transportation and Security Administration (TSA):** Agents are positioned mostly at airports to screen passengers before boarding planes.

- **U.S. Coast Guard:** Personnel trained in watercraft operation and/or diving respond to sinking boats, drowning swimmers, and other water-based emergencies.

- **U.S. Secret Service:** Agents protect public figures and investigate federal criminal activity.

The beauty of working for the Department of Homeland Security is that you can find employment in the air, at sea, or on land. As one of the largest federal employers, jobs are available in every state and even abroad. Created back in 2001, the agency employs nearly 200,000 workers. If keeping our country safe sounds fulfilling to you, then this just might be the most rewarding recession-proof work you can find. After all, it's not as if hurricanes and terrorist threats strike only when the stock market is at an all-time high. Homeland security workers need to be ready at a moment's notice to handle the next emergency.

The *Occupational Outlook Quarterly* breaks homeland security work into roughly nine career categories. Keep in mind that many of these positions are available with the U.S. Department of Homeland Security. However, several of these positions can also be found in private industry. So to recession proof your career, you can actually jump between government-based positions and those with private companies. Here are the nine broad categories:

1. **Business continuity**
   When a disaster such as Hurricane Katrina hits, how do you get local businesses up and running again? This is the job of a business continuity expert or emergency response manager.

2. **Emergency management**
   FEMA is often the first on the scene after a natural disaster. From coordinating search-and-rescue efforts to taking emergency calls in call centers, this agency is always on call when disaster strikes.

3. **Information security**
   Did you ever wonder how our government ensures that highly classified documents and e-mails don't end up in the wrong hands? Information security experts protect information behind the scenes to make sure documents and e-mails get where they're supposed to go. Professionals in this arena may also focus on stopping cyber-security threats such as computer hackers.

4. **Infrastructure protection**
   Transportation, public health systems, and utilities all need to be kept running smoothly. While much of this infrastructure is set up by private industry, there are plenty of jobs in both the private and public sectors making sure community infrastructures are safe and secure.

5. **Intelligence analysis**
   If solving mysteries and piecing clues together sounds like interesting work, you just may enjoy life as an intelligence analyst. Here your job is to pull together information from a variety of sources to detect, and therefore prevent, homeland security threats.

6. **Law enforcement**
   More than 80 federal organizations around the country employ law enforcement agents and officers. Their job is to make the country safer by investigating and preventing crimes as well as by apprehending criminals.

7. **Physical security**
   From transportation security agents at airports to private security guards, there are people keeping an eye on everything from stores to personal property.

8. **Scientific study**
   Preventing threats from weapons of mass destruction is a big part of this job, including chemical and nuclear weapons. Stopping the spread of disease also falls under scientific study jurisdiction.

9. **Other homeland security positions**
   Many other fields touch on homeland security. For example, translators fluent in Middle Eastern languages are in high demand.

The opportunities in homeland security are both plentiful and varied. Practically every educational level, geographic location, and career specialty can be found within the confines of homeland security. Your best bet for working in homeland security is to gain the education, training, and experience necessary for your chosen specialty. You can always gain initial experience in private industry and then transfer those skills to a government-based position. Wherever you choose to work, rest assured the continued threat of natural and terrorist disasters will make homeland security positions recession proof for years to come.

# Opportunities in the Armed Forces

National defense is a top priority for our country. From manning the battlefield to manufacturing defense equipment and working in army hospitals, more than 2.6 million people work for the U.S. Armed Forces. More than 1.4 million of these people work in the active army, navy, marine corps, and air force. The remaining 1.2 million work in the armed forces Reserves or National Guard. The U.S. military further distinguishes armed forces occupations into two categories:

- ◆ Enlisted personnel carry out military operations including combat, engineering, human services, and other areas. Enlisted personnel account for nearly 85 percent of the armed forces.

- ◆ Officers lead the military by supervising activities in every conceivable armed forces arena. Officers account for the remaining 15 percent of military professionals.

Within both enlisted and officer occupations, there are several career specialties. In the next two sections we review these specialties to help you understand the wealth of career options for those who work for the U.S. military.

# Enlisted Occupations

According to the U.S. Department of Labor, there are 13 specific career categories for enlisted personnel.

1. **Administrative careers**
   As in any business, someone needs to maintain files, prepare reports, and record information in the military. Administrative positions are all about keeping information, meetings, and reports organized.

2. **Combat specialty occupations**
   Operating tanks, assault vehicles, missiles, and guns requires weapon specialists who know how to use this combat equipment. Many combat specialists go on secret and special missions where specific expertise is required.

3. **Construction occupations**
   Bunkers, buildings, and airfields all need maintenance, repair, and construction work. Partnering with engineers and building specialists, construction workers build and maintain the structures used by the military.

4. **Electronic and electrical equipment repair personnel**
   Communication is critical in the armed forces, so much so that an entire military career focuses on repairing and maintaining electronic equipment. From weapons systems to telephone connections, repair personnel keep systems running smoothly.

5. **Engineering, science, and technical personnel**
   Everything from information systems to spacecraft operations requires technical experts who know how to operate and fix the most complex military equipment. Some personnel in this category work to interpret aerial photos taken by military aircraft to uncover intelligence.

## Another Path

When it comes to engineering careers, there's one that crosses over well between both military and nonmilitary careers. Working as an aerospace engineer can lead to recession-proof opportunities designing both armed forces aircraft; nonmilitary aircraft, such as NASA spacecraft; and even private sector aircraft. It's reassuring to know you can find work in the public, private, and military sectors.

6. **Health-care personnel**

   There's no question that military duty can be dangerous. As such, an entire team of medical professionals is needed to care for the wounded and respond to medical emergencies.

7. **Human resources development specialists**

   When there's no military draft, a team of recruiting specialists work to attract men and women into military service. Stationed around the country, these individuals also track pay, benefits, and personal data on enlisted military members.

8. **Machine operator and production personnel**

   Ships, submarines, parachutes, and even nuclear reactors need people trained to operate and fix the equipment. Most folks in this line of work specialize in a particular type of equipment.

9. **Media and public affairs personnel**

   The military has an image it wants to portray, just like a company develops an image with its logo and with its products and advertisements. Media and public affairs personnel run press conferences and public presentations and write talking points for military personnel who are quoted in the media.

10. **Protective service personnel**

    Crimes are sometimes committed within the military company community. Protective service personnel investigate those crimes. They may also provide emergency response services when disasters occur.

11. **Support service personnel**

    From cafeteria workers to grief counselors and even chaplains, support service personnel support the well-being and mental state of those who serve in the military.

12. **Transportation and material handling specialists**

    People and cargo need to be transported safely in the military. Whether by land, sea, or air, transportation and material handling specialists move military personnel, combat equipment, and supplies from one destination to another.

13. **Vehicle and machinery mechanics**

    Preventive maintenance needs to be completed on everything from military aircraft to combat equipment. Most mechanics specialize in a particular group of military equipment.

# Officer Occupations

There are nine specific career specialties that make up officer occupations. You'll recognize some overlapping career choices from the previous section. In these cases, it's the officers who are likely to be leading a team of enlisted workers in the given career category:

1. **Combat specialty officers**
   Planning and directing a team of combat specialists is challenging work. These officers lead military offensives, combat operations, and intelligence-gathering operations.

2. **Engineering, science, and technical officers**
   From running communication centers to overseeing the development of complex computer systems, these officers are the brains behind the technical operations of the military.

3. **Executive, administrative, and managerial officers**
   Officers who specialize in finance, accounting, or purchasing, for example, keep the backoffice operations of the military running smoothly. The military purchases billions of dollars of equipment each year, and this crew keeps those orders in check.

4. **Health-care officers**
   Health-care officers include doctors, dentists, and registered nurses. Most of these officers work on-site at military facilities where health-related needs are met.

5. **Human resources development officers**
   Human resources development officers put together the recruitment and selection strategy for the military. Main responsibilities also include career counseling, training, and education for enlisted professionals.

6. **Media and public affairs officers**
   This group oversees public dissemination of information about the military. From commercials to public seminars, media and public affairs officers strategize on how best to communicate the goals and mission of the armed forces.

7. **Protective service officers**
   Putting together safety, evacuation, and emergency response plans falls on the shoulders of protective service officers. They're doing their job well when military personnel are both safe and prepared for unexpected events.

8. **Support services officers**

   Overseeing food preparation and morale-boosting activities falls under the domain of the support services officers. Managing cafeteria operations and counseling military personnel on drugs and alcohol abuse are two of the most common jobs.

9. **Transportation officers**

   Managing transportation teams is important work when it comes to ensuring the safe conveyance of military people, equipment, and supplies.

# Training and Advancement in the Military

Whether you go the enlisted or officer occupation route, there are some basic training requirements. The first big distinction is that enlisted personnel typically need only a high school degree; officer occupations usually require at least a Bachelor's degree or higher.

Most armed forces personnel enter the military after high school graduation. One of the bigger draws is the opportunity for tuition reimbursement. It's a win-win for the military and enlistees. The military keeps its ranks full with new recruits, and newly enlisted military members can learn valuable skills on the military's dime.

Upon enrollment, most recruits go through basic training, commonly referred to as boot camp. Here you learn military skills while getting in the best physical shape of your life. The basic training program is designed to build camaraderie among new recruits because teamwork and trust are critical to surviving the battlefield. After 6 to 12 weeks of basic training, you'll be ready for an additional 10 to 20 weeks of specialized training. Here's where you begin on the path of one of the enlisted occupations. It's also the time when you can begin tuition-reimbursed training in exchange for the military time of service contract you signed upon enrollment. If you prove your merit through basic and advanced training, you can even go on to earn specialized and advanced degrees with continued tuition reimbursement.

As you might expect, advancement within the military is based on structured and competitive processes. Time in service, performance on the job, fitness level, and even written examination scores play into who moves up in the military. One of the biggest benefits of military enlistment is the likely opportunity to earn a pension after 20 years of service. If you enroll right out of high school, you may qualify for retirement benefits before your fortieth birthday. That means you could begin a civilian career while collecting military pension benefits. It's not a bad way to protect your net worth for the golden years of your life.

## The Least You Need to Know

♦ The federal government is the single largest employer in the United States, providing jobs for more than 1.7 million people.

♦ Whether you want to help control infectious diseases, litigate on federal cases, or work toward renewable energy, there's a government agency in your area of expertise.

♦ The Department of Homeland Security offers recession-proof employment for those who want to protect our borders from invasion, disasters, and terrorist threats.

♦ The U.S. Armed Forces are not just about combat training and action; you can also earn a living without ever seeing the battlefield.

# **16**

# Give Back to Your Community

## In This Chapter

- ◆ How community service managers organize the very programs and activities that keep your local community running strong

- ◆ Why social and human services assistants are expected to experience more job growth than almost every other career covered in this book

- ◆ How urban and regional planners maximize land potential and revitalize towns and cities

Towns don't run themselves. There's an infrastructure in place to keep a town humming along for years and years. This infrastructure includes everything from community outreach programs to health and human services to the very layout and design of the town itself.

This chapter is all about the people most responsible for maintaining the infrastructure of your community. We start with community service managers. The community outreach programs you may rely on over the course of your lifetime are likely organized by such a professional. Next we talk about social and human services assistants. A whole host of programs is managed by this type of job, including welfare, food stamps, addiction counseling, and rehabilitation services. In fact, this is one of the fastest-growing recession-proof careers around. We close the chapter with a look at urban and regional planners. These are the folks who can look at a town in ruins and visualize a complete revitalization.

The beauty of the careers covered in this chapter is that they all fall under the umbrella of giving back to your community. You're giving back to those you live near and stabilizing your career at the same time. That's not a bad way to make a living. Let's get started on some community-based recession-proof careers. I have a feeling that by the end of this chapter you'll be checking the want ads in your own local newspaper.

# Community Service Managers

When is the last time you walked into your local community center? You likely picked up a few brochures for the town services and programs offered. What you probably didn't realize is that the person who gave you the brochure works in a recession-proof career. That's right—community service managers are on solid ground. Their job is to organize many of the community outreach programs we all benefit from.

## Outlook for Community Service Managers

| | |
|---|---|
| Current Number of Employees | 130,000 |
| New Jobs Created by 2016 | 32,500 |
| Expected Job Growth by 2016 | 25% |
| Geographical Hotspots | Louisiana, North Carolina |
| Average Annual Earnings | Approximately $52,000 |

*Sources: U.S. Bureau of Labor Statistics National Employment Matrix, State Occupational Projections*

Some of the most common responsibilities of a community service manager include the following:

◆ Partner with other community agencies and organizations to coordinate community services and avoid duplication of effort

◆ Analyze community needs and develop programs that would most benefit the needs of residents

◆ Speak to community groups to explain services offered and how residents can take advantage of the programs

♦ Organize and track community budgets and other key data for a town

♦ Oversee administrative procedures for effectively rolling out new programs and services to community residents

Where does a community service manager work? The local community center is one option. You are also likely to find work at religious institutions, grant-making groups, civic organizations, and government offices. Wherever you choose to work, you'll be on the front lines of delivering much-needed community services to those in need.

### Another Path

If you find community service work rewarding, the local community center is not the only viable place of employment. Educational institutions in your town, such as elementary, middle, and high schools, need educational administrators. Many of the skills required to succeed in this career are similar to those of a community service manager. It's something to keep in mind if you want to transfer your skills from a community to academic setting.

If you're ready to give back to your community as a community service manager, here's what it takes to break into the field. Many mid-level positions require a Bachelor's degree in a relevant subject, such as public administration, human services, and organizational management. You may not need the Bachelor's degree to get started in the field, but it's something to work toward as you work your way up in the field.

Here's a hypothetical look at what might keep you busy as a community service manager. At the office, you scan the Internet and newspaper for important headlines. You're looking for any news on proposed or passed legislation, regulations, or rule changes that might impact your work. By 10 A.M., you're in a budget meeting with your director to review results and expenditures for programs that you run or oversee. After the meeting, it's back to your desk to hit the phones. You're looking for 50 volunteers to pitch in at the local homeless shelter to cook and deliver meals. Your address book is full of residents who have volunteered in the past, and you hope to convince them again to give up their time and volunteer.

Lunchtime arrives and you meet an agency counterpart to discuss a joint community initiative. Combining your budgets might allow you to accomplish the project. By 2 P.M., you're back at your office to oversee the first meeting of a new after-school community program. The smiling faces of 50 kids assure you that the program is successful. Your day ends with a Board of Directors meeting. Many of the biggest donors to your community agency attend. They want a full report on all the good that has been accomplished through their generous donations. You wow the crowd with all the wonderful programs and initiatives getting off the ground thanks to the money and support provided by those in the room.

So what do you think? Quite a busy day but also highly rewarding. Not a bad recession-proof way to spend your days. If this sounds fun and rewarding to you, then a career as a community service manager may be right for you.

Of course, you may desire to move up the ladder over time. Earning that Bachelor's degree is certainly an important step. The next move is advancing from an individual contributor to a people leader. If you can prove capable of leading a team of community service managers, you'll ultimately take on greater responsibility and earn more income for yourself. If leading people is not your thing, you can also prove your merit by taking on increasingly more complex projects. For example, you can advance from organizing a small walk-a-thon to putting on a major fundraising event with thousands of attendees. The more responsibility you can handle, the more recession proof you'll become over time.

# Social and Human Services Assistants

This is a section you're going to want to read closely. You're about to learn about one of the fastest-growing recession-proof careers covered in this entire book. How's 34 percent growth by 2016 sound to you? Plus, this career is a versatile one. That's right, as a social and human services assistant, you can work with everyone from social workers to health-care workers to physical therapists. Your primary job is to assist these and other professionals in providing various services to people.

## Outlook for Social and Human Services Assistants

| | |
|---|---|
| Current Number of Employees | 339,000 |
| New Jobs Created by 2016 | 114,000 |
| Expected Job Growth by 2016 | 34% |
| Geographical Hotspots | Idaho, North Carolina |
| Average Annual Earnings | $20,000–$32,000 |

*Sources: U.S. Bureau of Labor Statistics National Employment Matrix, State Occupational Projections*

Here are some examples of the key responsibilities of social and human services assistants:

♦ Research eligibility for people to receive benefits and services such as food stamps and welfare

♦ Maintain case records on clients and report progress to supervisors and case workers

♦ Assist clients in need of emergency counseling or crisis intervention

♦ Arrange for transportation and escorts for clients who need assistance getting to appointments

♦ Partner with medical personnel and caregivers to monitor client medications and overall care

It's important to understand that social and human services assistants are a catchall category for a bunch of different roles. Some of the most common job titles that fall under social and human services assistants include human services worker, social work assistant, life skills counselor, and case management aid. The title depends on where you choose to work. Let's look at the most common places you can find employment as a social and human services assistant.

There's a 60 percent chance you'll find a job working in the health-care and social assistance industries. Examples include working in psychiatric hospitals, rehabilitation programs, and clinics. You'll help clients master life skills such as communication, socializing, and physical capabilities. You may even assist clients in group counseling programs to overcome addictions and emotional problems.

The next most likely employment option is to work for a local or state agency. Here you'll help administer government-sponsored programs to those in need. You'll be involved in programs such as Medicaid, food stamps, and welfare. You also may support developmentally challenged or mentally disabled clients enrolled in government improvement programs.

## Reasons for Growth

We said before that social and human services assistant jobs are poised for 34 percent growth by 2016 according to the U.S. Department of Labor. The big question is why this industry is expected to see such tremendous growth in the coming years. It boils down to six key trends.

1. **Rising elderly population**

   It can't be emphasized enough that the growing elderly population is going to need all kinds of help, aid, and support that falls under the social and human services assistant domain. The sheer volume of folks getting older is enough to guarantee job opportunities for years to come.

2. **Increasing need for job training programs**

   Many government programs are about helping people get back to work and off government assistance programs. Social and human services assistants who can lead job training programs will be in huge demand.

3. **Growing residential care facility needs**

   People living with disabilities are on the rise. Many live in residential care facilities where they need daily help with basic tasks and life skills. To meet this increased need, many residential care establishments will turn to social and human services assistants.

4. **Changing from prison to treatment**

   There's a continued push for drug abusers to land in counseling programs instead of behind bars. Helping people with drug problems instead of locking them up means more social and human services assistants will be needed to counsel the offenders.

5. **Outsourcing to the private sector**

   The government can only take on so many projects. To accomplish everything on the government's agenda, the need to outsource projects to the private sector grows.

6. **Growing trend toward cost efficiency**

   If an employer can train talented employees willing to work at a lower amount to perform more complex tasks, then it's a cost-saving initiative for the employer and a recession-proof opportunity for you.

# Training

As you can see, social and human services assistants *are* in a recession-proof position. How do you break into the field? The good news is most employers will not require a Bachelor's degree to land a job. With a high school degree alone, you can likely land an entry-level position. You'll likely receive extensive on-the-job training while beginning with the most basic of services. Examples might include helping clients complete paperwork or arranging appointments.

If your goal is to advance beyond entry-level work, you'll need some form of education beyond high school. For starters, you can seek a certificate or associate degree in a relevant field, such as human services or behavioral sciences. Degree programs typically include a core curriculum plus field experience. You'll learn everything from crisis intervention techniques to treatment plan implementation and even patient referral procedures. You can also specialize your degree in a particular social and human services assistant field such as addiction or child welfare.

If you really want to move up the ranks, then consider earning a Bachelor's degree. This is your ticket to moving up from administrative duties to counseling and program coordination. You may even earn the opportunity to oversee a group of assistants and learn valuable leadership skills. Now that's a competency you can take anywhere.

Remember, one of the biggest benefits of this field is the variety of places you can work. From health-care facilities to government agencies, there are many employers looking for people like you. That's a great way to build some seriously transferable skills to recession proof your career. You can even branch out to related fields, such as physical or occupational therapist assistant, or even home health aide.

# Urban and Regional Planners

There's a street in my town that used to be deserted. Three years later, that same street had two restaurants, two banks, a health club, a children's learning center, and a café serving the most delicious homemade gelato. Urban and regional planners are to thank for the metamorphosis. Their job is to develop plans for the use of land to revitalize urban, suburban, and rural communities.

## Outlook for Urban and Regional Planners

| | |
|---|---|
| Current Number of Employees | 34,000 |
| New Jobs Created by 2016 | 4,900 |
| Expected Job Growth by 2016 | 15% |
| Geographical Hotspots | Louisiana, Nevada |
| Average Annual Earnings | $44,000–$71,000 |

*Sources: U.S. Bureau of Labor Statistics National Employment Matrix, State Occupational Projections*

Basic responsibilities include all of the following:

◆ Forecast the future needs of a given population to determine the infrastructure required

- Recommend locations for schools, businesses, and roads to make the best use of land

- Determine the right mix of residential, commercial, and recreational building within a town or city

- Protect ecologically sensitive regions such as wetlands or forests by building around them

- Report on current usage of land to understand what needs to be improved as the population changes over time

Imagine that someone gave you a map of a given town and wanted you to figure out the perfect mix of schools, roads, parks, airports, libraries, community shelters, and everything else that goes into a thriving community. This hypothetical challenge sums up the job of an urban and regional planner.

As you might expect, about two thirds of urban and regional planners work for local governments. A handful of planners work for federal and state government agencies. In the private sector, you can also land a job working for companies involved in architecture, engineering, and technical consulting services.

The driving force behind the recession-proof nature of this line of work is the expanding population. Governments, from the smallest towns to the largest cities, need to plan for the changing demographics and growing population. Urban and regional planners will be needed to address the many challenges that arise from more people inhabiting a given zip code. Adding one housing development in a city opens the door to the need for access roadways, schools, libraries, sewer systems, and recreation facilities.

So what might a day in the life of an urban and regional planner look like? Let's say you are revitalizing a particular strip of land in the center of town. You might start with a visit to the spot to survey the area. You'll take measurements, record what you see, and begin visualizing the potential of the area. You might then head back to the office to review the budget available for the project and run some analytics to weigh the pros and cons of different development options. From there you might meet with local land developers and public officials to weigh the development choices and jointly arrive at a future game plan.

If this sounds like an exciting way to spend your day, you'll want to know what it takes to break into the business. Let's begin with the educational requirements. You're looking at a Master's degree in urban or regional planning or a related field. Around 70 programs in the United States offer accredited Master's programs. There are 15 additional undergraduate programs, which could land you an entry-level position. But if you want your career to go upward, you'll eventually need to earn that Master's degree.

While many undergraduate degrees are possible for entry into the right Master's program, certain undergraduate programs improve your chances. Undergraduate degrees in economics, environmental design, and geography are particularly relevant in improving your acceptance chances in a Master's program in urban or regional planning.

During your two years of graduate studies, you'll have the opportunity to specialize. Potential avenues include community development, urban design, environmental resource planning, and code enforcement. Regardless of specialty, computer skills are a must, particularly statistical techniques and computer modeling. Many geographic modeling programs will be used as you practice building cities and towns in an academic setting.

As your graduate studies progress, you'll shift from academic work to workshop and laboratory courses. The intention of these courses is to give you practice at analyzing and solving realistic planning problems. The practice will get even more real when you are required to work part-time or during the summer months in a planning office. Here you'll get some quality experience under the watchful eye of experienced urban and regional planners.

Beyond the academic requirements, five personality characteristics tend to make for a solid urban and regional planner:

1. **Written and oral communication skills**
   As an urban and regional planner, you write planning reports and present recommendations to development partners and at public town meetings. You have to be able to articulate ideas clearly in both written and oral forms.

2. **Spatial relationship abilities**
   Laying out entire towns is a visual exercise. You're taking land that looks one way and developing a completely new land usage plan. You must be able to see the big picture and visualize what's needed to lay out the land effectively.

3. **Consensus-building and negotiation skills**
   You meet often with architects, government officials, and town residents. These folks have differing opinions on how best to use the land. You are responsible for building consensus, negotiating the differences, and ultimately arriving at one plan that all key stakeholders approve.

4. **Mathematical and computer modeling capabilities**

   A person can't just look at 20 acres of land and simply visualize how to transform an entire town. Sophisticated mathematical and computer modeling programs are required to determine space requirements.

5. **Predictive and forecasting knowledge**

   You get loads of data to review on everything from anticipated population growth to environmental challenges. Your job requires taking in this information to make predictive forecasts about how best to use the land given anticipated future change.

Let's say you earn that graduate degree with flying colors and have the characteristics just described to succeed as an urban or regional planner. Now you've scored that first job at an urban or regional planning office. How might you move up the ladder and truly recession proof your career? The first option is to seek official certification. The American Institute of Certified Planners grants certification to planners who have achieved the right mix of professional and educational experience and who have passed an exam. Scoring an official certification can help make your case for a promotion.

Beyond certification, you can let your work do all the talking. Do well on simpler projects and you are likely to land more complex projects. For example, you can work your way up to designing larger developments or commercial properties. Over time, you may work up to managing a greater jurisdiction, say entire cities instead of just one town. Designing and laying out the city of the future sure sounds like a rewarding way to recession proof your career.

## The Least You Need to Know

- If community outreach sounds rewarding to you, consider finding recession-proof work as a community service manager.

- Social and human services assistants will be in such great demand that you'll easily be able to find work with government agencies, residential care facilities, and counseling programs.

- If you would enjoy mapping out the residential, commercial, and recreational land usage for a town, then an urban and regional planner might be the right career for you.

# Part 6

## Scratch Your Career Itch with a Niche

Not every recession-proof career falls under a major industry label such as health care, education, government, or defense. Some recession-proof niche careers are worth covering, too. This is the part in which to learn more about some career paths you may not have considered.

We begin Part 6 with a look at chefs, bill collectors, and funeral directors. After all, in good times and bad, people still need to eat, settle their debts, and plan memorial services. From there we cover the need to keep things clean and tidy, with the help of recession-proof workers who maintain our homes, offices, automobiles, and lawns. Finally, we review the trends that keep entire industries afloat, specifically gambling and adult entertainment.

# Chapter 17

# Food, Collections, and Funerals

## In This Chapter

- ◆ How food preparation workers, bill collectors, and funeral directors are all bound together by common human needs and problems

- ◆ Why America's appetite doesn't go away during economic down cycles, particularly for budget-conscious dining

- ◆ How bill collectors track down overdue balances and why this job skyrockets in trying times

- ◆ Why funeral director jobs are not for everyone, but will continue to thrive for years to come

You're probably wondering how food preparers, bill collectors, and funeral directors ended up in the same chapter. On the surface, they seem like unrelated fields. There is, however, one common bond that links these three careers. In good times and in bad, people need to eat, pay their bills, and memorialize loved ones. This chapter is all about three facts of life that stay steady even in recessions.

We start with a look at chefs, cooks, and food preparation workers. Granted, you probably see some local restaurants go under when the economy sours. But many types of restaurants and food preparation occupations still thrive in trying times. We concentrate on the thriving ones in this chapter. Next, we turn to bill and account collectors. These are the folks who follow up on past-due balances. There are always people behind on their bills, but this profession absolutely explodes when the job market hits a down cycle. Finally, we review funeral directors. Responsible for managing the details and logistics of funerals, funeral directors are always in need, regardless of the state of the economy.

By the end of this chapter you'll have learned three completely separate career paths all bound for growth in the coming years. Whether the stock market goes up or down, you'll always find work feeding Americans, helping collect their debts, or handling logistics when a loved one passes away. So read on to learn the nature of the work, training required, and advancement opportunities for all three recession-proof careers.

# Chefs, Cooks, and Food Preparation Workers

Let's get one thing straight from the start: not everyone who cooks and prepares food for a living is in a recession-proof career. Some cooks and food preparers are poised for double-digit job growth, while others are stagnant at five percent or less. In this section, we closely review the cooking occupations on the rise and highlight the ones to steer clear of in coming years. This way, we can cover how the entire industry is set for 11 percent growth, but some subcareers are really the ones driving the growth.

## Outlook for Chefs, Cooks, and Food Preparation Workers

| | |
|---|---|
| Current Number of Employees | 3,113,000 |
| New Jobs Created by 2016 | 351,000 |
| Expected Job Growth by 2016 | 11% |
| Geographical Hotspots | Varies by job |
| Average Annual Earnings | Varies by job |

*Sources: U.S. Bureau of Labor Statistics National Employment Matrix, State Occupational Projections*

We cover three types of workers: head chefs, mid-level cooks, and other food preparation workers. Within these categories, nearly two thirds of the workers are in restaurants and other food service establishments. Another 15 percent work in school cafeterias, hospitals, and nursing facilities. The remaining food professionals earn their money primarily at hotels and grocery stores with food buffets.

# Executive Chefs and Head Cooks

Let's begin with a look at chefs and head cooks. These are the folks most responsible for putting quality food on the table. The job description for chefs and head cooks includes the following:

♦ Measure and mix ingredients to prepare recipes

♦ Use a variety of kitchen equipment including pans, pots, grills, ovens, and strainers

♦ Lead the cooking team in the kitchen to organize and prepare all of the dishes for restaurant patrons

♦ Estimate food requirements and order food supplies while maintaining a budget

♦ Plan upcoming menus to create new dishes and keep the restaurant menu fresh and interesting

As an executive chef or head cook, you may be overseeing multiple kitchens. For example, if you work in a hotel with three restaurants on site, your job may be overall coordination of all food-related services for the three restaurants. This will include leading the other cooks in each of the restaurants, managing revenue and expenses in all three restaurants, and ordering supplies and food for the entire hotel.

What does it take to break into a career as an executive or head chef and how do you truly recession proof your career? This is the most advanced of all the food specialties in this section; it requires the most academic and on-the-job training. For starters, you'll need a high school degree to get accepted into a vocational cooking school program.

Now the big question becomes where you want to work after graduation. If your goal is an upscale restaurant, you'll likely need a two- or four-year cooking school degree.

**Another Path**

Rather than work as a head chef in a restaurant, consider becoming a private chef for a family. If you can find work with a wealthy family, you may be set for life as the family chef. You'll plan meals to the family's tastes, shop for groceries, and cook breakfast, lunch, and dinner. You may even get to prep food for banquets, parties, and other social gatherings at the house.

In addition, many years of experience will be required to master various cooking techniques and specialty cuisines. Mid-level restaurants will likely accept three months to two years of vocational cooking training. You'll have learned the basics of slicing, dicing, baking, and broiling. This training, combined with on-the-job training, should be enough to get you on the right track. Again, executive chefs and head cooks are not hired right out of school to these senior positions. You'll need to work your way up through mid-level cooking positions until you reach this top level of the profession.

Advancement opportunities ultimately are driven by the quality and creativeness of your food preparation, as well as by your ability to gain a following. If restaurant patrons come to love your distinct brand of cooking, you'll earn customers for life. Now that's a great strategy for recession proofing your executive chef or head cook career. You may even land a book deal someday to spill your cooking secrets. Then you'll have some passive income through book royalties to supplement your cooking salary.

## Mid-Level Cooks

Within the mid-level cook category is where we find the greatest discrepancy between stagnating career choices and those on the rise. Mid-level cooks in restaurants, hospitals, and cafeterias are all expected to grow 11 percent or more by 2016. However, short-order and fast-food cooks are seeing growth under 10 percent, and some are as low as 5 percent or less. You might think fast food and short order would perform well in recessions as diners try to cut costs. That may prove true during the recession dip, but remember your overall job security relies more on long-term job growth in both good times and bad.

Let's focus on the types of cooks with double-digit growth. Whether you work in a restaurant, hospital, or cafeteria, you are running the nuts and bolts of the kitchen operation. Your job includes the following:

◆ Prepare menus under the supervision of a head cook

◆ Notify those responsible for ordering food ingredients and supplies when inventories run low

◆ Cook in bulk for meals served buffet style to large groups of students or patients

◆ Help plan menus in advance to make the most efficient use of ingredients and save food preparation costs

Mid-level cooks are often on the way to becoming executive chefs or head cooks. Or you can stay as a mid-level cook your entire career and carve out a niche. As we covered in the last section, training requirements are less for mid-level cooks compared with those for head chefs. Vocational programs lasting less than two years—or even as short as three months—can get you in the door as a cook. In school, you'll learn everything from food safety and handling procedures to specific grilling, baking, and cooking techniques.

The American Culinary Federation accredits more than 200 cooking school programs around the country. Many of these programs link to two-year apprentice programs where you can learn under the supervision of an experienced cook. It's a great way to get real-life cooking experience while working toward your degree.

Many mid-level cooks work part-time, on nights and weekends, as a means to supplement income from other careers. It's nice to know you can land yourself in a recession-proof supplemental career while earning money elsewhere.

Keep in mind that the earning potential is lower for mid-level cooks compared with that of executive chefs and head cooks. Average annual earnings for mid-level cooks range from $17,000 to $31,000. Executive chefs earn anywhere from $26,000 to $46,000 per year. Income can become significantly higher for executive chefs who find a following and make a name for themselves. This earning mobility is more limited for mid-level cooking positions.

## Food Preparation Workers

Food preparation workers have the highest anticipated job growth of any position covered in this section. Expected to grow 15 percent by 2016, food preparation workers perform the routine and repetitive tasks under the direction of higher-level cooks. Typical responsibilities include the following:

- Prepare ingredients for complex dishes by slicing, dicing, and precooking various components

- Weigh and measure ingredients accurately and according to recipes or instructions

- Stir pots and pans and keep an eye on simmering dishes to keep food preparation moving along smoothly

- Prepare and sanitize cooking areas, then clean up after the day or night of cooking is complete

The beauty of a food preparation career is that little formal training is required. Most skills are learned on the job and employers are willing to take a chance on employees and gauge their performance. This explains why it's a popular choice for students and young adults. It's also a great career choice for those seeking seasonal employment, perhaps during the summer months at a resort or vacation spot. From day one, you'll get training on workplace safety, food sanitation, and food preparation and cooking procedures. This will help you hit the ground running.

If you show a knack for these basic skills, over time you can move up to a mid-level cook. At this point, you'll want to think about formal cooking school training to learn the rest of the tricks of the trade. If earning more money is your goal, go for the training. As a food preparation worker, your annual salary will fall between $15,000 and $20,000. This is much lower than the earning potential for mid-level cooks and significantly less than that of executive chefs.

The bottom line on all three cooking professions covered in this section is that each offers different levels of income, requires different training, and presents different job growth potential. It comes down to how far you want to go with your food-related career. The call is yours, but the good news is you're on a recession-proof path any direction you choose.

# Bill and Account Collectors

Have you ever gone past due on a credit card, department store account, or utility bill? Do you remember that call or letter informing you that your unpaid bill had gone to collections? The person behind that call or letter was likely a bill or account collector. This recession-proof career is a steady choice that spikes upward in the worst of economic times. Account and bill collectors keep track of overdue accounts and attempt to collect payments.

## Outlook for Bill and Account Collectors

| | |
|---|---|
| Current Number of Employees | 434,000 |
| New Jobs Created by 2016 | 99,000 |
| Expected Job Growth by 2016 | 23% |
| Geographical Hotspots | Idaho, South Dakota |
| Average Hourly Earnings | $11–$17 per hour |

*Sources: U.S. Bureau of Labor Statistics National Employment Matrix, State Occupational Projections*

Basic responsibilities include the following:

◆ Locate and notify delinquent customers of past-due account balances

◆ Track down new addresses for customers who have moved

◆ Review account balances with past-due customers to explain charges and resolve disputes

◆ Contact past-due customers to remind them about payments or to establish alternative payment plans, and then track whether or not the payment is made

◆ Negotiate payment extensions or debt reductions to recover a percentage of unpaid balances

Bill and account collectors work across multiple industries. After all, anyone who charges for a service may have customers with unpaid balances. Some of the most common industries requiring bill and account collectors include hospitals, physician offices, retail stores, banks, and credit card companies. Many bill and account collectors also work for third-party collection agencies. These are companies hired by businesses to collect debts on their behalf.

Let's talk a little about a day in the life of a bill and account collector. Chances are you'll be working in a call-center environment. You have to be comfortable talking on the phone most of the day and entering information in the computer. Some customers will be defensive or confrontational when pressed to settle up their debts. Hang-ups, raised voices, and unhelpful responses are

> **Career Caveat**
>
> In addition to bill and account collectors, bankruptcy lawyers and foreclosure specialists also see more business when times are tough. Remember, this is a book about finding jobs that thrive in both good times and bad, not just bad. Ultimately, you want a stable career regardless of economic fluctuations. That's what a recession-proof career is all about.

quite common. On the flip side, some customers will appreciate your willingness to help them resolve their financial difficulties. Offering payment plans and reduced settlements can actually remove stress from a customer, and that's a good thing.

Why is this career likely to flourish for years to come? For starters, companies are increasingly focused on cash flow management. The sooner debts are settled, the better. Second, tracking down delinquent customers is never easy, so companies are increasingly willing to shell out the money to recover more money. Rising health-care costs and increased sick and preventive care visits also contribute to the recession-proof aspects of a bill and account collector career. As more unpaid medical balances stack up, bill and account collectors are increasingly necessary.

Keep in mind that economic downturns are a double-edged sword for bill and account collectors. On one hand, more accounts go delinquent during recessions, so the sheer number of unpaid accounts will keep bill and account collectors busy. However, people are more willing and able to pay these balances when times are good. So the ratio of calls made to debts settled will actually improve in an upward economy.

### Another Path

Bill and account collectors are not the only careers focused on reviewing and collecting account information. Your skills are transferrable to related careers such as loan officers and credit authorizers. Considering multiple fields is a great way to open doors to alternative career options should your bill and account collector career stagnate for any reason.

Breaking into a bill and account collector career is relatively easy. Typically the only requirements are a high school degree, some customer service experience, and on-the-job training. Of course, many employers prefer workers with at least some college training, particularly in relevant courses. On-the-job training usually includes learning phone call procedures, computer systems, and customer negotiation techniques. You'll likely also learn all about laws governing debt collection as mandated by the Fair Debt Collection Practices Act, which applies to all third-party collection agencies and many in-house debt collection departments.

Before we talk about advancement opportunities, let's cover the required competencies to excel as a bill and account collector. It comes down to five key skills to be successful:

1. **Communication skills**
   You must be able to articulate the past-due situation calmly to customers who may be uncooperative or distressed.

2. **Computer savvy**
   Bill and account collectors use computer systems to pull up customer call lists, enter account information, and follow up on debt settlement agreements. Employers expect computer literacy or provide brief training programs.

3. **Patience and perseverance**
   Customers are likely to be upset, but you can't take it personally. In many cases, customers are simply venting over an unfortunate situation they know they brought on themselves. Your job is to hear them out and sympathize, but then stay on task and collect the unpaid debt.

4. **Negotiation skills**

   In many collection agencies and in-house collection departments, you'll have the authority to negotiate extended payments and lower debt settlements. Negotiation is an art form that requires practice to reach settlements that are fair to both the customer and the company.

5. **Attention to detail**

   You may be on the phone all day talking to hundreds of customers. The ability to keep accounts current and accurate is of utmost importance. Computers help keep track, but you have to enter the information correctly for computers to do their jobs.

How can you move up the ladder as a bill and account collector? Taking on more complex cases over time is one way. The bigger the unpaid balances, the more money at stake—and the more experienced account collectors need to be to recover the money. If you can prove yourself on smaller cases, you can eventually take on bigger cases and earn more income yourself. You can also move up from debt collector to supervisor of a team of collectors. Now your job changes from making calls yourself to leading and motivating a team of collectors and monitoring their progress against goals.

This is a job that often requires night and weekend work. After all, you want to call customers when they're most likely to be home. Some collection companies do offer flexible hours and even telecommuting setups given the irregular working hours required for the job. Still other collection agencies seek employees to work traditional 40-hour workweeks.

# Funeral Directors

Death is not a pleasant topic, and the career we are about to discuss is certainly not for everyone. But if you take pride in providing comfort and good service in a time of need, then the funeral director profession may be for you. Plus, death rates do not fluctuate in conjunction with economic cycles, so you're clearly working in a recession-proof career.

## Outlook for Funeral Directors

| | |
|---|---|
| Current Number of Employees | 32,000 |
| New Jobs Created by 2016 | 3,600 |
| Expected Job Growth by 2016 | 12% |
| Geographical Hotspots | Louisiana, Utah |
| Average Annual Earnings | $37,000–$65,000 |

*Sources: U.S. Bureau of Labor Statistics National Employment Matrix, State Occupational Projections*

Also known as morticians or undertakers, funeral directors are responsible for managing all of the logistics and details of funerals. Basic responsibilities include all of the following:

◆ Communicate with the family to understand their wishes about the funeral

◆ Manage dates, times, and location for wakes, memorial services, and burials

◆ Coordinate with the person who will officiate the ceremony and proceedings

◆ Arrange for a hearse to transport the deceased to a funeral home or mortuary

◆ Handle logistics at the burial place for the deceased, or handle cremation details

Funeral directors may also provide many other services related to funerals. Some of the most common include arranging for pallbearers, coordinating the opening and closing of the grave with a cemetery, decorating the memorial and grave site with flowers, and even coordinating shipment of a body for an out-of-state burial.

Many funeral directors are also trained and licensed embalmers. Embalming involves washing the body of a deceased person with germicidal soap and replacing the blood with embalming fluid to preserve the tissues. Cosmetic procedures may also be done to make the body look more presentable for the funeral. This can include simple make-up or reconstructive procedures, usually on facial features. Embalming is definitely another aspect of the funeral director profession that may not be for everyone.

> **Career Caveat** _____
>
> In your lifetime, you've probably attended a handful of funerals. The emotions, pain, and suffering can take a toll. Imagine feeling this grief every day as you watch families memorialize loved ones. If you find it fulfilling to comfort people who are grieving, then you may find this career rewarding. However, be very aware of the long-term emotional toll of working around grieving people.

## Working Conditions

Most funeral homes are family-run businesses and the funeral director is often either the owner-operator of the facility or an employee with management responsibilities. This means comforting grieving families and arranging funeral logistics is not your only role. You must also take an interest in the overall profitability of the business. Some of the skills you'll need include recording income and expenses, generating invoices, and applying for death certificates. Marketing skills also come in handy because you have to advertise your services and present an image that will appeal to prospective clients.

If you're going to go the funeral director route, be aware of three additional challenges that you may encounter:

1. **Religious customs**

    As a funeral director, you come into contact with families of every religious faith imaginable. Each religion has its own set of customs, traditions, and funeral proceedings. You need to be well versed in religion-specific guidelines to ensure funeral services run smoothly and meet the needs of each family.

2. **Contagious diseases**

    In some cases, you'll be working with the bodies of people who have died from infectious or dangerous diseases. Because you'll be coming into contact with these bodies, especially if you provide embalming services, you must follow strict health regulations to maintain sanitary conditions.

3. **Irregular hours**

    The call concerning the passing of a loved one can come any hour of any day, including nights, weekends, and holidays. As a funeral director, you work long, irregular hours, which can be stressful over time. Similar to doctors, funeral directors have to be on call at all times to manage funeral proceedings at a moment's notice.

# Training to Be a Funeral Director

Funeral directors must be licensed in the state in which they work. While licensing requirements vary, most states require you to be at least 21 years of age, have at least two years of formal education, complete a one-year apprentice program, and pass a state exam.

Let's start with the educational requirements. Funeral directors typically complete a program in mortuary science. The American Board of Funeral Service Education accredits more than 50 mortuary science programs around the country. Lasting anywhere from two to four years, the program typically includes coursework in anatomy, physiology, embalming techniques, management, and computer skills. You'll also take courses in the softer side of funeral direction, such as grief counseling, communication skills, and business ethics.

With degree in hand, you'll need to complete a one-year apprentice program under the supervision of a licensed funeral director. Your degree plus apprenticeship open the door to taking the state exam to earn your license. With license in hand, you'll want to complete continuing education classes to keep the license in good standing. In fact, more than 30 states require continuing education credits to maintain a funeral director license. Continuing education classes are typically in relevant fields such as family counseling, business management, and communication.

## Advancement Opportunities

If you work in the family funeral home, your best bet for advancement is eventually taking over the family business. Many parents seek to leave family funeral homes to their children to carry on the family tradition. If your parents do not own a funeral home, then working for a larger funeral home company may be your ticket to increased responsibility. Over time you can earn a promotion to a higher-paying position, say as a branch manager overseeing multiple funeral homes. You can also work toward buying your own funeral home and taking the entrepreneurial route.

Prospects for funeral directors also remain good due to the aging of current funeral directors. With an older population compared to most other occupations, retiring funeral directors will open the door for new ones to enter the profession. If you land a funeral director position, performing many services related to funerals (i.e., embalming) is a solid strategy to diversify your offerings and recession proof your career.

## The Least You Need to Know

- Food preparers, bill collectors, and funeral directors all work in recession-proof careers related to human needs.
- Budget-conscious dining establishments thrive in bad times, opening the door for food preparation careers.
- Good communication skills, the ability to stay calm, and computer skills will suit a bill and account collector well.
- Funeral directors provide comfort, emotional support, and logistical support in an industry that never falters.

# Chapter 18

# Home, Auto, and Facility Management Services

## In This Chapter

◆ Why cleaning buildings, hospitals, and residences is a career choice with stability

◆ How to make money renovating rooms, houses, or entire offices and keep the clients rolling in

◆ Why a tough economy causes people to put money into maintaining their cars

◆ Why maintaining lawns, gardens, and grounds is a no-brainer recession-proof career choice

People will always care about certain things, no matter how the economy sizzles or sours. This chapter is all about recession-proof areas of our lives that continue, even in recessions. We talk about taking care of your home, your car, and your yard. You might think that people stop keeping up on these categories when dollars are tight. In fact, as you read this chapter, you'll see there are opposing trends that make these careers flourish in the worst of times.

In this chapter, we start with a look at building cleaning workers who keep our offices, apartments, hospitals, and other buildings clean and safe. From there, we review interior designers who can transform anything from a single room to an entire building. Next, we cover automotive service technicians and mechanics. These are the folks who inspect, maintain, and repair our vehicles to keep them running smoothly for years to come. Finally, we end the chapter with grounds maintenance workers who keep our lawns, gardens, and grounds looking good year-round.

# Building Cleaning Workers

Building cleaning workers is a broad category that encompasses a few different careers. Let's get clear on the different career choices before reviewing the training, education, and other qualifications needed for success.

## Outlook for Building Cleaning Workers

| | |
|---|---|
| Current Number of Employees | 4,154,000 |
| New Jobs Created by 2016 | 569,000 |
| Expected Job Growth by 2016 | 14% |
| Geographical Hotspots | Varies by specialty |
| Average Annual Earnings | Varies by specialty |

*Sources: U.S. Bureau of Labor Statistics National Employment Matrix, State Occupational Projections*

Following are the main careers under the building cleaning workers category:

- **Janitors and cleaners:** Perform heavy-duty cleaning services such as cleaning floors, emptying trash, and making minor repairs

- **Maids and housekeeping cleaners:** Focus on light cleaning duties such as cleaning homes, offices, hotels, restaurants, and hospitals

- **Private household cleaners:** Work in clients' homes and take on both cleaning duties and household tasks such as folding laundry, buying groceries, and running errands

- **Cleaning supervisors:** Assign janitorial and cleaning tasks to a team of workers and then ensure the job gets done to meet specifications

These jobs sound different, but all of them have one thing in common. They help clean and maintain buildings. The time of day you work depends on the job you take.

For example, many offices are cleaned after hours when workers go home. So in this profession, you're more than likely working a night shift. If you take a janitorial position in a school, much of your work can take place throughout the day. Finally, the hours for home-based positions will be driven by client needs.

## Another Path

General janitorial and cleaning positions keep homes and offices neat and tidy. You can also think about repackaging your skills to work for a pest control company. This job, too, is all about keeping a building clean—in this case, that means "pest-free." With continued new construction as the population grows, particularly in remote areas where pests reign, the need for pest control services will remain strong.

Building cleaning workers can break into the business with a high school degree or less. Much of the training will be on-the-job. Your most important skill will be an ability to listen to directions and master routine tasks. The more proficiency you demonstrate, the more complex tasks you'll get to work on over time.

Of course, where you choose to work dictates the skill sets needed. If you go the private home route, then building a relationship with the homeowner is important to keeping your gig. This is less important if you clean offices after hours when workers are out of the building.

You may think cleaning services are luxuries when times are tough. After all, can't you just clean your own home? Remember, many of the home cleaning positions will be with more affluent customers who are less affected by recessions. Further, many homeowners will be working longer hours in tough times to keep their jobs. This means they have even less time to handle routine cleaning tasks at home.

Building cleaning worker is not a job for everyone. In fact, there are a few important traits you'll need to succeed. Here are the three most important ones:

1. **A love of routine work**

   Let's say you work in a hotel cleaning rooms. You may be responsible for cleaning an entire floor of rooms in a given day. That's a lot of vacuuming, mopping, and changing sheets. This is a job where routine work is the nature of the role.

2. **The desire to clean**

   Take a look around your home. Do you like to keep it tidy, or does a big mess reign supreme? If you don't feel the urge to clean your own surroundings, you may not have the passion for this profession. On the flip side, if you get satisfaction from cleaning, then you may find this work extremely rewarding.

3. **Listening skills**
   Cleaning and janitorial projects need to follow guidelines and instructions from supervisors and clients. You have to be able to take in instructions and get the job done accordingly.

One of the best ways to recession proof your building cleaning career is to latch on to a job in the health-care field. Remember from earlier chapters in this book that the health-care industry is one of the fastest growing around. If you can land a gig cleaning a hospital, doctor's office, nursing home, or other health facility, you'll minimize your odds of losing your job over time. Working as a cleaner in a recession-proof industry is a great way to recession proof your career.

# Interior Designers

You might view interior designing as a luxury. If that's your point of view, then you probably think the field would suffer during a recession. In fact, an opposing trend keeps interior designers working hard even in bad times. You see, many folks would like to buy a bigger house or a newer house. But when times are tough, those moving plans often go on hold. Instead, people stay in their existing homes, but they act on the desire to make improvements. Enter the interior designer. Even a small living room makeover can revamp a home's entire look. This section is all about the role interior designers play in improving the function and aesthetics of interior spaces.

## Outlook for Interior Designers

| | |
|---|---|
| Current Number of Employees | 72,000 |
| New Jobs Created by 2016 | 14,000 |
| Expected Job Growth by 2016 | 19% |
| Geographical Hotspots | Nevada, Utah |
| Average Annual Earnings | $32,000–$57,000 |

*Sources: U.S. Bureau of Labor Statistics National Employment Matrix, State Occupational Projections*

The basic responsibilities for an interior designer include the following:

◆ Work with various colors and textures to identify the right mix for a room or office

◆ Select the appropriate furniture to maximize space and functionality in a given design space

◆ Choose lighting, window treatments, and even artwork to accent overall room design

◆ Partner with architects on room details such as crown molding, built-in bookshelves, and ledges

◆ Oversee a small or large redesign of anything from a small room to an entire office or residential building

More than 25 percent of interior designers are self-employed. In fact, Entrepeneur. com offers some good advice on building your own practice. For starters, the site recommends thinking about how you specialize. For example, you can focus on designing specific types of properties, such as hotels or restaurants. Or you can specialize by the type of work you do. Examples include complete renovations, single-room makeovers, or even shoestring budget designs. Entrepreneur.com goes on to offer some valuable tips on building your client network. You can create an inexpensive brochure and mail it to architects and contractors in your town. They're always looking for interior designers to partner with on renovation projects. Networking through local professional organizations, appearances on local radio and TV shows, and speaking appearances at your local Chamber of Commerce can also get your name out there.

Most of the remaining 75 percent of interior designers work for large design corporations and smaller boutique firms. Here there's less pressure on making a name for yourself and scoring new clients. Instead, you're banking on the reputation of your employer to keep the clients lined up. Still, there will be pressure in meeting tight deadlines driven by the customer. It's not uncommon for clients to need work done by a specific date to accommodate an upcoming event.

Let's take a look inside the life of an interior designer to see whether it might be the right career choice for you. From there we'll delve into the training and qualifications needed to succeed. Whether you're self-employed or whether you work for a large firm, the general approach to projects is quite similar. It generally comes down to five steps.

**Career Caveat**

It's hard to turn on the TV without seeing a do-it-yourself home improvement show. Also, many discount stores play up the do-it-yourself angle to help customers save money. Your best bet is either to offer initial consultations to help clients get do-it-yourself projects off the ground or to focus on the more complex design projects not likely to be undertaken by clients.

1. **Client needs**

   You can't dive into an interior design project without understanding client needs first. This typically means a face-to-face visit with the client and a tour of the design space. Talking to the client and seeing the starting design point gives you the basis to begin planning your design.

2. **Design plan**

   The design involves sketching the proposed redesigned space and estimating project costs. The days of the hand sketch are long gone. You'll likely use computer-aided design (CAD) to formulate the design plan. Then you gain client buy-in for the proposal.

3. **Material specification**

   Once you and the client have agreed on the final design and projected costs, it's time to order materials for the job. This might include furniture, flooring, lighting, artwork, or anything else involved in the new look.

4. **Project timeline**

   As with any project, there's a deadline. It's not always easy to coordinate material deliveries and work by subcontractors. So you have to lay out the project from start to finish and coordinate all of the interconnected project parts.

5. **Execution**

   Planning and design are important but, ultimately, interior designers need to execute flawlessly to earn repeat business and build a positive reputation. Your ability to deliver what you say, when you say, and exactly how it was supposed to look is the most important and final step in the interior design process.

If this work excites you, let's talk about the educational and training requirements to break into the field. For starters, you'll need some form of postsecondary education. You can go the two- or three-year route if you want to work as an interior design assistant. Or you can go the four-year Bachelor's degree route if you want to become a full-fledged interior designer.

There are two national associations that accredit degree programs in interior design. The National Association of Schools of Art and Design accredits more than 250 postsecondary programs in art and design. The National Council for Interior Design Accreditation also accredits nearly 150 Bachelor's degree programs in interior design. All of these programs cover the basics that you'll need for interior design success. Classes will include spatial planning, ergonomics, drawing, colors and fabrics, and even furniture design.

With degree in hand, you're likely to enter a multiyear apprenticeship program to gain enough experience to pass the required licensing exam. Lasting anywhere from one to three years, your apprenticeship will probably be at either a design or architecture firm where you can work under the supervision of an experienced designer. Another route is to work at a furniture store that employs interior designers.

With degree and apprenticeship behind you, it's time to take the licensing exam. Depending on your state, passing the exam grants you the title of Certified, Registered, or Licensed Interior Designer. To be eligible to take the exam, you'll need a combined six years of academic training and work experience. A four-year degree program plus a two-year apprenticeship or three years of each will fit the bill. You'll also need to attend continuing education classes to maintain your license.

Finally, you have the degree, the apprenticeship, and the license. Now you're in an amazing recession-proof spot to build your career. As previously mentioned, most interior designers will ultimately specialize. Becoming known as the kitchen and bathroom guru or the home office specialist is a great way to build a client base and get known in the industry.

# Automotive Service Technicians and Mechanics

Many of us take our cars for granted until we hear an unexpected clunk. Suddenly the only thing that matters is getting an estimate and understanding what it will take to restore the car to peak performance. You might think that folks would put off maintenance and repair in a down economy to avoid expenses. However, an opposite trend actually occurs, particularly for car owners. People choose smaller cost repairs and maintenance procedures over the potential larger cost of buying a new automobile. If you can keep your car running smoothly through regular maintenance, you'll reduce the odds of a complete auto breakdown requiring an expensive new car.

It is this trend that makes automotive service a recession-proof career choice. A technician's or mechanic's job is to inspect, maintain, and repair the automobiles we all depend on to get to work, to take us on vacations, and to run everyday errands.

## Outlook for Automotive Service Technicians and Mechanics

| | |
|---|---|
| Current Number of Employees | 773,000 |
| New Jobs Created by 2016 | 110,000 |
| Expected Job Growth by 2016 | 14% |
| Geographical Hotspots | Nevada, Utah |
| Average Hourly Earnings | $12–$22 per hour |

*Sources: U.S. Bureau of Labor Statistics National Employment Matrix, State Occupational Projections*

The basic role of an automotive service technician and mechanic includes the following:

◆ Conduct diagnostic tests on cars and trucks to identify performance problems

◆ Lubricate car parts and replenish fluids to keep cars and trucks running smoothly

◆ Compare computerized test results against manufacturer standards to identify mechanical or electrical problems

◆ Use simple manual tools such as screwdrivers all the way up to complex, automated power tools to perform repairs

◆ Fix technology-based car add-ons such as driving navigation systems and built-in TV/DVD combos

As you might expect, the vast majority of job opportunities lie in repair shops, either independently owned or operated by car dealerships. While the standard 40-hour workweek is common, many repair shops offer evening and weekend appointments to satisfy customer demand. So working periodically in the evening or on a weekend is quite common.

While some automotive service technicians and mechanics are generalists, many choose to specialize in a certain type of repair. For example, transmission technicians focus on testing and fixing all aspects of a vehicle's transmission. Air-conditioning repairers service air-conditioning components such as compressors and condensers. Front-end mechanics focus on wheel alignment and steering mechanisms. Brake specialists work mainly on adjusting and replacing car and truck brake systems.

**Career Caveat** _____

This is a career choice in which you're going to get your hands dirty. You'll be dealing with greasy parts, oil, and other fluids. There's also the risk of injury when working with manual and automated tools. You have to follow recommended safety procedures in the repair shop to minimize the risk of injury. You're also going to be bending, stretching, and working in awkward positions to fix hard-to-reach parts. Keep your back limber to avoid unnecessary injuries.

If rolling up your sleeves and making America's cars and trucks run smoothly sounds like satisfying work, then you're probably wondering how you break into the field. There are three basic paths to launching your career:

1. **On-the-job training**

   Unless you're planning to work in a large, urban area where certification is required, on-the-job training may be all you need to start working. Simply watching an experienced technician or mechanic and repeating what you learn can teach you the tricks of the trade.

2. **Targeted high school degree**

   The Automotive Youth Education Service runs a partnership among high school automotive repair programs, automobile manufacturers, and car dealers. Graduates from this program qualify for entry-level technician or mechanic positions.

3. **Vocational postsecondary training**

   Many dealers and larger repair shops sponsor two-year associate degree programs. These programs typically alternate between classroom training and full-time work in service departments. This combination of theoretical and practical training is considered the best preparation among the three options to launch your career.

As mentioned earlier, if you want to work in a large urban area, you'll likely need an official certification from the National Institute for Automotive Service Excellence (ASE). This certification is not typically required for basic automotive service positions. However, many advanced, non-entry-level technician positions require the ASE certification. There are eight automotive service areas available for certification, such as engine repair, brake systems, and electrical systems. To earn your certification, you'll need to pass an exam after completing at least two years of work experience. You can substitute one of the two years with academic training instead of on-the-job experience.

If you really want to go for the gusto, you can strive for the Master Automobile Technician certification. This requires passing grades in all eight automotive service areas. This is also a great way to recession proof your job and advance your career. The more parts of a car you can fix, the more valuable you'll become to your employer. You can even become a supervisor with your vast knowledge and oversee less-experienced mechanics and technicians.

# Grounds Maintenance Workers

Lawns, gardens, and grounds don't maintain themselves. Someone has to cut, prune, rake, shovel, and trim the grass, bushes, trees, and plants. Though you can make a case that extravagant landscaping gets scaled back in recessions, basic grounds maintenance still marches on. That's what makes grounds maintenance a recession-proof career choice. Grounds maintenance workers maintain all of the greenery and plants that surround buildings and make up gardens and yards.

## Outlook for Grounds Maintenance Workers

| Current Number of Employees | 1,521,000 |
| --- | --- |
| New Jobs Created by 2016 | 270,000 |
| Expected Job Growth by 2016 | 18% |
| Geographical Hotspots | Varies by specialty |
| Average Annual Earnings | Varies by specialty |

*Sources: U.S. Bureau of Labor Statistics National Employment Matrix, State Occupational Projections*

Basic responsibilities of grounds maintenance workers include all of the following:

◆ Mow lawns, blow leaves, and distribute fertilizer to maintain landscapes

◆ Trim trees, branches, bushes, and plants to maintain a well-manicured look to properties

◆ Take on landscaping projects to design outdoor areas and residential properties

◆ Spray natural or commercial pesticides and other treatments to prevent weeds and other influences damaging to the landscape

◆ Care for indoor plants and gardens in large office buildings, malls, and other public areas

The grounds maintenance field in general is made up of many different specialties. Some workers focus on just one area; others learn multiple specialties. For example, landscaping workers typically install and maintain plants and other shrubbery for a manicured area. Groundskeepers work on existing grounds such as golf courses, university campuses, and community or public parks. Pesticide handlers are responsible for applying weed killers, insect repellants, and fungicides. Tree trimmers remove dead wood from trees and trim branches to keep trees and shrubs healthy. Finally, landscape architects design areas from scratch incorporating a mix of lawn, flowers, shrubs, and trees to achieve the desired look.

**Career Caveat** _____

Grounds maintenance work may be recession proof, but keep in mind that it tends to be seasonal, particularly in colder climates. Lawns don't need much in the way of care when there are 6 inches of snow on the ground. Many grounds maintenance workers shift to snow plowing and shoveling jobs in the winter to keep income flowing throughout the year.

Most grounds maintenance workers can learn on the job, with little to no formal classroom training. Of course, the big question is whether you want to simply do the hands-on work or advance to more complex positions. This is the point when training and certification come into play.

For example, most states require licensing or certification for workers who apply pesticides. While requirements vary, many states require passing a test on how to dispose of harmful pesticides and lawn chemicals properly.

The Professional Landscape Network offers six different certifications for grounds maintenance workers who want to demonstrate specific expertise in a particular area of landscaping. The Tree Care Industry Association also offers four levels of certification including Tree Care Apprentice, Ground Operations Specialist, Tree Climber Specialist, and Tree Care Specialist. These certifications can help advance your career or land more business if you ultimately open your own landscaping business.

So where are the jobs when it comes to working as a grounds maintenance worker? According to the Department of Labor, the top employment options include:

- Building and residential landscape companies
- Amusement and recreation facilities
- Golf courses
- Racetracks
- Educational institutions
- Real estate development firms
- Parks and zoos
- Hospitals and health-care facilities
- Government jobs for local or state parks

Because so much of your work will be outside, you can always think about translating your skills to a related field. For example, working on a ranch, farm, or at a state forest would require many of the same skills as a grounds maintenance worker. It's nice to know you can find new work outside should one career stall for any reason.

## The Least You Need to Know

- There are careers related to homes, offices, and cars that still flourish when times are tough.

- Interior designers are needed in tough times as many people will choose to renovate rooms and homes over an expensive move to a new home.

- When the economy sours, many people will look to extend the life span of their car through enhanced maintenance to avoid buying a new car.

- Lawns, gardens, and grounds still need to be cut, manicured, and cared for regardless of how the stock market performs.

# Chapter 19

# People Pay Big Prices for Their Vices

## In This Chapter

- How gambling continues to gain approval in new states and creates employment opportunities for gaming services occupations

- Why gambling jobs are no longer limited to Las Vegas and Atlantic City

- How to land one of the many recession-proof gambling occupations, including dealers, supervisors, and sports book writers

- Why the $13 billion adult entertainment industry needs workers for magazine, Internet, and novelty sales

You don't need me to tell you gambling and adult entertainment are big business. The two industries together account for more than $45 billion in revenue annually. So even if you personally view gambling and adult entertainment as bad habits or unnecessary vices, there is no arguing against the business viability of these industries. In fact, an economic downturn can be a boon to these industries.

In this chapter, we're going to cover what makes gambling and adult entertainment recession proof. We begin with the gambling industry, and we cover a multitude of occupations, including dealers, supervisors, slot key persons, and gaming and sports book writers and runners. From there we focus on gaming surveillance officers. We're treating this subspecialty separately from the others because the job and training are somewhat different. We close this chapter with an inside look at the adult entertainment industry. There's no doubt that adult magazines, Internet sites, novelty stores, and clubs continue to show robust sales.

Again, this chapter is not about whether you agree or disagree with the act of gambling or sampling adult entertainment. Instead, the goal here is to show the recession-proof occupations you can explore.

# Gaming Services Occupations

Casinos are big business, and many different recession-proof occupations keep casinos running smoothly. The purpose of this section is to review those positions with the biggest growth prospects in the coming years.

These career choices are grouped under the heading of gaming service occupations, but each is different in terms of the nature of the role and skills required. One thing they all have in common is their ability to withstand market ups and downs. Let's review each to understand the roles and responsibilities:

1. **Gaming supervisors and managers**
   Someone has to make sure the gamblers and workers are following casino protocol. That job falls on gaming supervisors and managers. Your job is to work in an assigned gambling area and make sure casino patrons understand and follow the rules of the games. You're also the first point of contact for any complaints about games or customer service at the tables.

2. **Slot key persons**
   If you want to supervise the slot machine department and its workers, then this is the field for you. Job responsibilities include paying out lucky winners, resetting slot machines, and refilling machines with money when they run out. You're also expected to be a bit of a do-it-yourselfer in this job because minor adjustments often need to be made to slot machines.

## Outlook for Gaming Services Occupations

| Occupation | Current Employees | New Jobs by 2016 | Job Growth by 2016 | Geographic Hotspots | Average Annual Earnings |
|---|---|---|---|---|---|
| Gaming managers | 4,000 | 1,000 | 24% | Illinois, Oregon | $63,000 |
| First-line supervisors | 54,000 | 10,000 | 19% | n/a | n/a |
| Gaming supervisors | 34,000 | 7,900 | 23% | Oregon, Louisiana | $41,000 |
| Slot key persons | 20,000 | 2,200 | 11% | Nevada, Oregon | $23,000 |
| Gaming dealers | 84,000 | 20,000 | 24% | Nevada, Oregon | $15,000 |
| Gaming and sports book writers and runners | 18,000 | 5,200 | 28% | Illinois, Maine | $19,000 |

*Sources: U.S. Bureau of Labor Statistics National Employment Matrix, State Occupational Projections*

3. **Gaming dealers**

    Craps, roulette, and blackjack are run by gaming dealers. From dice to cards, you're running the show as casino patrons gamble for big bucks. This job is about both technical expertise in running the games and interpersonal skills as you deal directly with the gamblers. You have to be quick in playing the games, determining winners, and making payouts.

4. **Gaming and sports book writers and runners**

    From bingo to keno, and even sporting event bets, sports book writers and runners handle the action. Main jobs include scanning bettor tickets, calculating winnings, and making payouts. You may even get to work the bingo machine calling out numbers and waiting for that moment when someone yells "Bingo!"

So what's your day like working for a casino? If you've ever gambled late into the night, then you know casinos are open all hours of the day and night. For this reason, most casino workers work during one of three eight-hour shifts. You'll likely rotate among daytime, nighttime, early morning, and weekend work. In some casinos, seniority will get you preferential treatment on shifts.

**Career Caveat**

Working in casinos can be a high-stress gig. First, you have cameras tracking your every move and surveillance officers waiting to crack down on the slightest infraction. Second, you're surrounded by people winning and losing everything from small sums to lifetime savings. It's not uncommon for an irate gambler to blame the dealer for a bad hand.

Remember, gambling is a business, but it's also entertainment for casino patrons. If you're going to be dealing directly with gamblers, say as a dealer, then strong customer service skills are essential. When a player gets on a roll, they often become chatty and want the dealer to share in the fun. On the flip side, you've got to be skilled in calming down cold gamblers who can't seem to catch a break. If you want to work up to a casino manager or supervisor position, your leadership skills will come in handy. You'll be overseeing a team of casino workers, and that will require strong communication and organizational skills. Ultimately, you can continue to advance if you learn new casino roles. For example, a dealer who can handle both craps and blackjack has more value than a one-game specialist.

When it comes to education, each casino determines its own training requirements. At a minimum, you'll need a high school degree or equivalent. From there, many of the larger casinos run their own in-house training programs. Here you'll learn the ins and outs of the games you'll be managing. There are even vocational schools that specialize in teaching dealing skills. Graduation from one of these programs will help you land a job interview, but you'll still need to show your stuff in front of casino personnel to get the gig. They'll be looking for both your technical skills and your ability to entertain casino patrons.

If you want to go the manager or supervisor route, then training in customer service and hospitality is as important as your casino-based experience. Earning an Associate's degree or certification from a hospitality-based program will help your chances.

Regardless of the gaming services occupation you choose, you'll be required to earn a license from the state where you're employed. State casino control boards and commissions dole out the licenses. Typical requirements include passing a background check, meeting minimum age standards, and being drug free. You can even earn a license to work on cruise ship casinos. Here you'll travel the world rather than be limited to one casino on dry land. Not a bad recession-proof way to make a living.

# Gaming Surveillance Officers

Have you ever been sitting at a blackjack table thinking, "big brother is watching"? Well, he probably is—in the form of a gaming surveillance officer. All of those black globes you see above the betting tables have cameras inside. Those cameras are linked to a security room where gaming surveillance officers keep an eye on the action. Their job is to act as the security agents for casinos and look for any irregular betting activity, theft, or cheating.

## Outlook for Gaming Surveillance Officers

| | |
|---|---|
| Current Number of Employees | 8,700 |
| New Jobs Created by 2016 | 2,900 |
| Expected Job Growth by 2016 | 34% |
| Geographical Hotspots | Illinois, Iowa |
| Average Annual Earnings | $22,000–$36,000 |

*Sources: U.S. Bureau of Labor Statistics National Employment Matrix, State Occupational Projections*

Main responsibilities of the role include the following:

- Monitor audio and video surveillance equipment from a central observation room

- Review recordings from security cameras to identify any suspicious activity

- Walk the catwalk above casino floors where one-way mirrors have been installed to keep an eye on the action

- Stroll the casino floor to watch the betting action firsthand

- Provide video security evidence in cases where patrons are accused of any wrong-doing

Because most casinos are open 24 hours a day, seven days a week, gaming surveillance officer shifts run at all times. You'll typically work 8-hour shifts for 35 to 40 hours per week. However, you can expect some night and weekend shifts, especially when you're new on the job. Much of your work will be in the computer room monitoring a bank of video cameras.

So what's driving the anticipated 34 percent growth for gaming surveillance officers by 2016? You might be thinking that gambling revenues would be down during recessionary times. That may be true for existing casinos. However, many states, seeking additional revenue sources, are legalizing gambling. The continued expansion of casinos beyond Atlantic City, Las Vegas, and Indian reservations means more jobs in good times and bad.

### Another Path

Many gaming surveillance officers work part-time, and that leads to a need for supplemental income. One of the most popular secondary jobs for a gaming surveillance officer is a security guard. Most of the skills are transferable, and the flexible shifts in each profession make the two careers complimentary.

Before we get to the training and education required to become a gaming surveillance officer, let's look at the skill set necessary to succeed. First, your observation skills are critical. You must be able to scan multiple video screens and quickly see signs of suspicious activity. Staying in good shape won't hurt, either. There are times when you have to spring into action to detain a suspect while waiting for authorities to arrive. Finally, your attention to detail and organizational skills will be important. Gaming surveillance officers are expected to track and record everything. So accurately logging the activity you witness will be a big part of the job.

Now, let's tackle the training and education required for this field. Unlike the typical security guard, you'll need to go for secondary training beyond high school. While you won't necessarily need a college degree, you'll need to earn an official certification from an educational institution that offers a program in surveillance. You'll undergo classroom training, video surveillance practice, and even casino-like dry runs, which serve as dress rehearsals for a real gig. After earning your certificate, you still may not land a position right away. Many casinos look for individuals with casino experience or a law enforcement background. As such, gaming surveillance officers typically start as other types of guards or in alternative law enforcement positions to gain the necessary experience.

As you work yourself up the ranks as a gaming surveillance officer, you can advance your career. The first way is to move up to a supervisory level, in which you'll oversee a team of officers. Another mode of advancement is to be given more important shifts to work. For example, watching the casino floor on Saturday at 9 P.M. is a much busier and more challenging shift than say Tuesday morning at 5:30 A.M. You can even work your way up to middle- or high-level management, where you get involved in more critical security decisions at the casino. One example would be helping decide on a new video camera system to install.

# Adult Entertainment

Putting moral questions aside, there's no arguing that the $13 billion adult entertainment industry is here to stay. There's simply too much interest, too many customers, and too many companies catering to sexual desires to see this industry go away. In fact, adult entertainment sales actually outpace traditional Hollywood entertainment. That means strip clubs, adult entertainment Internet sites, DVD sales, and magazines bring in more dollars than all of those Hollywood movie blockbusters combined.

## Adult Entertainment Industry Revenue Statistics

|  | Revenue (in billions) |
| --- | --- |
| Video | $3.62 |
| Internet | $2.84 |
| Exotic Dance | $2.00 |
| Cable and Pay-Per-View | $2.19 |
| Novelties | $1.73 |
| Magazines | $0.95 |
| Total | $13.33 |

*Sources: TopTenReviews.com;* Journal of Economic Perspectives, *Volume 23, Number 1*

Driving much of the growth of the adult entertainment industry has been evolving technology. Consider the following.

◆ Before the invention of television, adult entertainment was limited to strip clubs, movie theaters, and magazines.

◆ The invention of the VCR and DVD player brought adult entertainment into households for the first time.

◆ Pay-per-view services and Internet subsequently opened the door to eroticism on demand.

◆ Adult entertainment delivered directly to wireless devices is expected to become a $1.5 billion industry by 2012, according to Hoovers.

The amazing technological evolution in the distribution channels available for adult entertainment explains the rapid growth of the industry in the last half century. It's also clear that as technology continues to advance and erotica can increasingly get delivered right to a cell phone or other wireless device, revenues will only climb.

According to Lawrence G. Walters, First Amendment Attorney and Partner at Weston, Garrou, Walters, and Mooney, the first hotspot for the adult film and video industry was the state of California. That's because a key court ruling in the 1980s determined that the state's prostitution and pandering laws did not apply to the creation of adult films. From there, other geographical hotspots such as South Florida, Arizona, New York, and Chicago became hotbeds of adult video creation and distribution. Today, however, digital cameras and the Internet enable people across the country to produce sexually explicit material on a commercial basis.

## In Their Own Words

The adult industry relies on a basic human instinct for its continued viability—sex drive. Like industries such as farming, medicine, and energy, a reduction in disposable income does not impact one's basic needs for food, shelter, and intimacy. While the profitability of commercial erotica has been impacted by external factors like piracy, criminal prosecutions and the availability of free material online, the economy will have little effect, as individuals will not hesitate to spend scarce dollars satisfying the need for sexual experiences.

—Lawrence G. Walters, First Amendment Attorney and President, First Amendment Lawyers Association (www.firstamendment.com)

The purpose of this section is not to cover acting, modeling, and dancing careers in the adult entertainment industry. Rather, we're going to review the recession-proof careers that support the adult entertainment industry. Let's consider each of the distribution channels to understand the jobs available:

1. **Adult videos**

   Each video needs a camera crew to shoot the scenes, followed by an editing team, and sound coordinators. The video covers need to be designed, and then the finished product needs a distribution team and, potentially, a sales force to get the videos in the hands of consumers. So adult videos offer work for cameramen, editors, sound mixers, designers, distributors, and salespeople.

2. **Adult entertainment Internet sites**

   Despite the racy content of these Internet sites, the backbone of the operation is much like any e-commerce site. You need site designers, technical programmers, e-commerce specialists, search engine optimization experts, and pay-per-click advertising specialists. If you have the technical know-how and are willing to work on adult entertainment sites, the job opportunities are bountiful.

3. **Exotic dance clubs**

   It's not just dancers that keep an exotic dance club running. In many ways, these clubs need the same staff as typical restaurants and nightclubs. There need to be waiters, bouncers, managers, disc jockeys, cooks, and announcers.

4. **Cable and pay-per-view programming**

   Putting together cable and pay-per-view programming is a team effort. Players needed include camera crews, editors, set designers, scriptwriters, distribution managers, salespeople, and programmers.

5. **Novelty stores**

   Adult novelty stores sell everything from videos to sexual enhancers. These stores can't operate without cashiers, sales managers, security guards, and product buyers. Additionally, an entire industry of product creators comes up with the very goods you see on novelty store shelves.

6. **Adult entertainment magazines**

   If you've worked for a magazine, you know it takes writers, photographers, editors, circulation specialists, advertising executives, and a dedicated sales force to stay afloat. Adult entertainment magazines require the same team to keep the revenue flowing in.

The bottom line is that many of the jobs found in less racy industries also apply to the adult entertainment field. Whether you have advertising experience or computer technical skills, if you're willing to work in this field, recession-proof opportunities await.

**In Their Own Words** _____

The global demand for adult entertainment products and services is enormous; and companies that can bring innovative offerings to market and are able to compete at the highest levels should be able to profit regardless cf the broader economic outlook. Far from being the stereotypical province of "back-room thugs," the brain trust behind the top tier adult companies could be the envy of any industry, and will always need personnel of the highest caliber.

—Stephen Yagielowicz, Managing Editor, *XBIZ World*

According to Hoovers, there are more than 89,000 adult entertainment industry companies in the United States. The average employee earns almost $32,000 per year, and the average company employs nine people. Of course, there are much larger conglomerates, such as Playboy and major adult entertainment media companies, which employ thousands.

Your best bet for breaking into the industry is to gain experience in the particular job you want. For example, if your goal is to work on adult video production, gaining production experience in another industry will help open doors. Or if you want to work in magazine sales, you can gain that experience at a cooking or fitness magazine. Then you can transfer the skills to the adult entertainment field.

## The Least You Need to Know

♦ Gambling and adult entertainment are big business, pulling in over $45 billion in annual revenues.

♦ If you want to work in the gaming industry, employment opportunities now extend beyond just Atlantic City and Las Vegas.

♦ You can make money in the gambling industry in many ways, including as a dealer, supervisor, or surveillance officer.

♦ The adult entertainment industry offers employment opportunities through magazines, Internet sites, novelty stores, and exotic clubs.

# Part  7

# Corporate Support, at Home and Abroad

You may think that business careers tank when the economy sours. While you certainly do read a lot about corporate layoffs during stock market plunges, many business-related jobs hold tough. This is particularly true for corporate support roles, both at home and abroad.

Part 7 is all about roles in human resources, insurance, sales, and management that remain steady when the economy falters. We also cover computer-based careers not likely to be outsourced anytime soon. So if you want to stay in business when times are tough, this is the part for you.

# Chapter 20

# Human Resources and Back Office Support

## In This Chapter

- ◆ Why human resources professionals become even more critical when companies restructure or downsize

- ◆ How to recession proof your career by helping companies minimize insurance risks

- ◆ How accountants and auditors work in stable careers by helping companies and clients report financial results and pay taxes

- ◆ The critical role executive secretaries play in making managers successful every day on the job

Don't let the title of this chapter fool you. Just because we call them back office jobs doesn't mean they're not recession proof. Have you ever heard an actor accept an award or a professional athlete speak after winning the big game? Invariably they thank the supporting cast that made everything possible.

This chapter is all about the critical support people who help make decisions, run organizations, and just get the work done. We start with a look at human resources and labor relations professionals. These folks become so important during layoffs. After all, someone has to help process all the severance packages and help work through corporate restructurings. Next we learn about actuaries who primarily help insurance companies minimize risk by determining the statistical probabilities of events that result in claims. From there, we read about accountants and auditors. From filing personal taxes to double-checking company financial reports, individuals and companies alike always need these professionals. Finally, we cover executive secretaries who support high-level company executives. Without their correspondence preparation, travel planning, and other duties, executive days would likely grind to a halt.

Think of this chapter as your recession-proof opportunity to support someone who needs you. Whether it's a displaced employee, an auto insurance company, a tax filer, or a senior executive, you can make someone else's life easier and recession proof your career at the same time. So read on and learn how back office support can be front and center in building a stable career.

# Human Resources, Training, and Labor Relations

Human resources, training, and labor relations is a big career category that encompasses many career choices. Some are more recession proof than others. Though the sum of all jobs in this category is expected to grow 17 percent by 2016, we're going to focus on two specific career choices that are most needed when times are tough. First are the human resources (HR) generalists who guide executives through restructurings and employee displacement decisions. Second are labor relations specialists. These are the professionals who represent companies, employees, or unions in labor disputes. As you can imagine, both professions become absolutely critical in economic uncertainty.

## Outlook for Human Resources, Training, and Labor Relations

| | |
|---|---|
| Current Number of Employees | 868,000 |
| New Jobs Created by 2016 | 147,000 |
| Expected Job Growth by 2016 | 17% |
| Geographical Hotspots | Varies by specialty |
| Average Annual Earnings | Varies by specialty |

*Sources: U.S. Bureau of Labor Statistics National Employment Matrix, State Occupational Projections*

Before we learn more about HR generalists and labor relations specialists, let's quickly review why other related HR professions may not be quite as recession proof in tough times. First, many companies scale back employee training during recessions. This means the training and development department has less to do and therefore may experience layoffs. Similarly, recruitment specialists who bring in top talent during economic booms may see hiring freezes during downturns. This dries up work pretty quickly and can lead to layoffs in staffing departments. Finally, compensation and benefits professionals may or may not see job reductions during recessions. Certainly companies need to keep paying their employees and providing medical benefits, but this will clearly not be a growth area when companies are losing money and/or laying off employees. Still, it's worth providing overall numbers for this entire field so you know it's expected to grow significantly as a whole.

## In Their Own Words

There are critically important support functions in any organization including human resources, finance, and technologies. For companies of any size in any economic climate, talent, financial reporting, and technological infrastructure keep the organization running. While there may be some rightsizing of these departments at times, the important nature of their role cannot be underplayed.

—Todd Stottlemyer, former President and CEO, National Federation of Independent Business

Now that we have the basics out of the way, let's delve deeper into what HR generalists and labor relations specialists do for a living, determine why they're so critical in tough economic times, and review the required training for each position.

# Human Resource Generalists

The HR generalist is the bridge between an HR department and business executives. Success in this career requires a keen understanding of HR policies plus business knowledge to earn a seat at the table with executives. Examples of primary roles for an HR generalist might include the following:

- Partnering with the talent management group to conduct a talent assessment for an executive's department

- Working with the training department to roll out a new training program to up-skill departmental workers

◆ Matching high-potential employees with executive coaches to improve leadership performance

A college education is typically required to perform the HR generalist role. On the work experience front, you'll likely need a rotation of jobs in HR process areas, including compensation, benefits, training, and compliance. At some point, if you really want to advance, a Master's degree in an HR-related field is quite common.

The time when HR generalists earn their recession-proof merit badges is in tough times. This is when layoffs and restructurings take over the job. Executives need an expert guide to handle the inner workings of reducing a department by 10 percent, 20 percent, or more. They also need help in administering severance packages for those employees laid off during downsizing periods. If you have an understanding of the business, you'll also help guide discussions on how the same amount of work can still get done with fewer employees. This includes recalibrating workloads and redefining job descriptions. If you can prove your merit during these tough stretches, executives will want you on their team when the good times come back again. By the way, if you're in the HR field, consider an ongoing membership with the Society of Human Resource Management (www.shrm.org) to stay on top of the latest developments in HR and job openings.

## Labor Relations Specialists

Collective bargaining agreements, grievance procedures, and union complaints are complex issues. They become particularly complex when times are tough. This is when grievances and complaints most commonly arise. It's not surprising that labor relations specialists become so critical when companies are looking to lay off employees, cut back benefits, and renegotiate labor contracts.

Labor relations specialists typically represent either companies or the union employees that work for companies. The job is still the same, you're just on opposing teams. When working for companies, your job is to help negotiate a deal that motivates workers but is profitable for the company, too. When working for unions, your job switches to negotiating the most lucrative deal possible for the employees.

Many issues can arise when companies and employees negotiate. You'll need to understand a wide range of issues, including salaries, benefits, employee welfare, pensions, union policies, and, of course, federal and state labor laws. At times, you'll be working with mediators and arbitrators who help decide disputes between employers and unions.

This is not the kind of career you can break into with limited experience. Many labor relations specialists have advanced degrees in industrial or labor relations. Several go for law degrees because many disputes have legal implications. Beyond educational requirements, this is a job that's all about experience. The more disputes you resolve and the more negotiations you lead, the better you'll get at reaching win-win scenarios that benefit both companies and employees or unions. The better you get at resolving disputes, the more valuable you'll become, and the more recession proof your career will be.

# Actuaries

How would you like to assess risk for a living? How about putting in place policies that minimize risk and its financial impact on companies and clients? If this sounds like rewarding work, then an actuarial career may be the choice for you. Actuaries put together and analyze data to estimate the probability and financial costs of events such as death, disability, sickness, injury, or property loss.

## Outlook for Actuaries

| | |
|---|---|
| Current Number of Employees | 18,000 |
| New Jobs Created by 2016 | 4,300 |
| Expected Job Growth by 2016 | 24% |
| Geographical Hotspots | Indiana, Pennsylvania |
| Average Annual Earnings | $59,000–$115,000 |

*Sources: U.S. Bureau of Labor Statistics National Employment Matrix, State Occupational Projections*

Basic responsibilities for an actuary include the following:

◆ Assess the risk of a particular event occurring and then formulate policies to minimize that risk

◆ Design insurance policies and pension plans in such a way that they remain on solid financial ground

◆ Generate probability tables to determine the likelihood that potential events will generate insurance claims

◆ Estimate the amount a company can expect to pay in claims when an event occurs

◆ Evaluate pension plans to help estimate retirement payouts based on ages of workers and other relevant factors

Let's bring the actuarial career to life with a simple example. Pretend you're an actuary for a car insurance company. A potential client walks in the door looking for car insurance on his or her new Honda Accord. As an actuary, you can help determine the right premium to charge the prospective client. How exactly do you determine the right premium? Through sophisticated modeling programs, you enter data about the client into a program that assesses risk. Factors such as the driver's age, gender, driving record, and type of car all help determine the likelihood of an accident. Enter all of this information in the computer and it will tell you a fair and competitive premium based on the probability of one or more accidents for the driver. This way, you can help the insurance agent charge a fair premium that will cover costs and turn a profit. Sure, you might ultimately lose money on this particular client if he or she has more accidents than predicted. However, if you sign enough clients who fit this same profile, probability says you'll make money on most of them.

**Another Path**

The sophisticated modeling capabilities you'll learn as an actuary are transferrable to other recession-proof careers. Personal financial advisors, accountants, auditors, and even market researchers all use statistics in their professions. While you may need some additional training to break into these fields, it's nice to know many of your learned skills are relatively easily transferable.

Where might you work as an actuary? Not surprisingly, more than half of all actuaries work for insurance carriers. Another 21 percent work for scientific, professional, and technical consulting services. The rest work for insurance agents, brokers, and even for the U.S. government. As you can imagine, this is a desk job with your typical 40-hour workweek or longer. If you go the actuarial consulting route, you'll also travel to client sites.

Breaking into the field requires a Bachelor's degree, typically in a field such as business, statistics, or mathematics. You can also major in actuarial science if you attend one of the hundred colleges around the country offering such a program. If you know, as a college student, that you want to be an actuary, it would be wise to take classes in economics, applied statistics, and corporate finance. This coursework will be required for certification, so you might as well get it out of the way during your undergraduate years.

At the entry level it's common to rotate among company departments to learn key phases of insurance work and actuarial operations. You'll gain valuable experience preparing data reports for licensed actuaries while you learn the ropes. If you decide this is the career for you, then it's time to get licensed. This is a major studying commitment, so don't take it lightly. Your employer may even help sponsor your licensing attempt by paying exam fees and allowing free time for studying. You're going to want to learn two acronyms at this point. The first is SOA, which stands for the Society of Actuaries. The second is CAS, which stands for the Casualty Actuarial Society. These are the two professional societies that sponsor programs that lead to full actuarial licensing. Three of the first four exams required for either license are actually the same. This means you don't have to choose a licensing path or commit to a specialty early on. However, after you pass the first three exams, you'll need to choose either the SOA or CAS path. Let's take these one at a time to understand the requirements for each.

## Society of Actuaries Certification

SOA certifies actuaries in the fields of life insurance, retirement systems, benefits systems, and finance and investment. There are two levels of certification you can achieve. First is the associate level. To earn this certification, you'll need to complete all of the following:

- Four total exams, including the initial three that are required by both the SOA and CAS

- Coursework in applied statistics, corporate finance, and economics (unless already completed in college)

- Eight computer-learning modules that come along with two corresponding assessments

- Selection of one of the SOA specialties (e.g., benefits systems, life insurance)

Completing all of these steps will take anywhere from four to six years after college graduation. You'll likely be working during most of this time, gaining actuarial experience. If you're willing to commit another two or three years to training, you can strive for the fellowship level. You'll need to pass an additional two exams and complete another three computer-learning modules. The extra years of training will likely lead to more responsibility, greater income, and increased odds of recession proofing your career.

## Casualty Actuarial Society (CAS) Certification

CAS certifies actuaries in the property and casualty field, which includes personal injury liability, workers' compensation, medical malpractice, and car/homeowner insurance. Similar to the SOA certification, there are two levels you can achieve with the CAS. The first is the associate level, which requires completion of these requirements:

- Completion of seven total exams, including the initial three that are required by both the SOA and CAS

- Coursework in applied statistics, corporate finance, and economics (unless already completed in college)

- Attendance in one professionalism course

Similar to the SOA certification, reaching Associate status in the CAS likely will take four to six years. You can also go for the fellowship level. Now you'll need to pass an additional two exams in more advanced financial and investment topics. FCAS certification will likely require another two or three years after achieving Associate status.

Similar to the SOA certification, your ticket to promotion and greater income is passing exams and earning certifications. The more exams you pass and the more years you work on the job, the more rewards you'll earn and the more secure your job will become.

# Accountants and Auditors

Unless you work as an accountant, you probably think about this profession around early spring when your taxes are due. As for auditors, you hope never to hear from one because you know it means your tax paperwork is in question. What you may not realize is that according to *Forbes*, accountants and auditors are among the top 10 most recession-proof jobs around. That's right, the very people who collect, analyze, and submit financial information for companies and individuals are working on extremely steady ground.

## Outlook for Accountants and Auditors

| | |
|---|---|
| Current Number of Employees | 1,274,000 |
| New Jobs Created by 2016 | 226,000 |
| Expected Job Growth by 2016 | 18% |
| Geographical Hotspots | Nevada, Utah |
| Average Annual Earnings | $43,000–$72,000 |

*Sources: U.S. Bureau of Labor Statistics National Employment Matrix, State Occupational Projections*

The category of accountants and auditors is actually an umbrella category that encompasses multiple career choices. In fact, this category is typically broken out into four main careers:

1. **Public accountants**

   This is the accounting profession with which you are probably most familiar. Public accountants offer a broad range of services for individuals, companies, and the government, including accounting, auditing, tax, and consulting support. Public accountants are the ones you turn to for filing your taxes or seeking tax advice on business decisions such as write-offs or small business legal structuring.

2. **Management accountants**

   Management accountants are responsible for financial reporting for their employers. Typically, management accountants are part of an executive team and help business leaders make sound financial decisions. For example, a management accountant might provide financial reporting on a new product or service to help the business leader determine the success rate. Another important part of the job is preparing financial reports for external groups such as stockholders, regulatory agencies, and tax authorities.

3. **Government accountants and auditors**

   Government accountants and auditors work in the public sector. Many are responsible for maintaining and reviewing government agency records to ensure proper accounting. Many also focus on auditing private businesses and individuals to ensure proper taxes are paid based on revenue and income. One of the most prevalent jobs for government accountants and auditors is a position with the Internal Revenue Service (IRS).

4. **Internal auditors**

   Internal auditors check for any mistakes, mismanagement, or fraud in company financial reports. This job is all about accuracy and control. Internal auditors need to make sure a firm's information systems, management procedures, and internal controls are all on target. Ultimately, internal auditors are there to verify the integrity of the financial data reported by firms, particularly public companies.

**Career Caveat**

With all the accounting scandals and misreported financial information from companies, there is tremendous pressure on accountants and auditors to get the numbers right. When an executive knows jail time is possible for errant reporting, accountants and auditors are going to feel the crunch to do a great job. This is not the job for you if attention to detail, tight deadlines, and pressure from the top don't suit you.

You can see from the four types of accountants and auditors where job opportunities lie. First, many accountants choose to work for large accounting companies. You can also land work with bookkeeping and payroll service firms. Around 10 percent of accountants are self-employed; they complete tax reports for individuals and small businesses. Finally, the government employs many accountants and auditors through the IRS. If your focus is tax preparation, don't plan any vacations leading up to mid-April. With annual income taxes due on April 15, this will be your busy season, and long nights and weekends are common.

Breaking into the accounting field is going to require at least a Bachelor's degree in accounting or a related field. If you're hoping to file financial and tax reports with the Securities and Exchange Commission (SEC), you'll need to become a Certified Public Accountant (CPA). Every state uses the four-part Uniform CPA Examination run by the American Institute of Certified Public Accountants (AICPA). This is no easy test; less than 50 percent of those who take the test pass every part attempted on the first try. The good news is you're not required to take all four parts in one sitting. Most states allow you to spread the exams over 18 months. This takes the pressure off cramming for everything at once. Assuming you ultimately pass the four-part exam and earn CPA status, you'll need to take continuing education classes to keep your certification current.

Beyond earning CPA status, there are many other certifications available from professional societies that can further your career and improve your job-seeking status with employers. These certifications also give you a sense of where accountants and auditors can specialize over time. Here are some of the most common certifications:

- The Association of Government Accountants offers the Certified Government Financial Manager (CGFM) certification for local, state, and federal government financial employees. Candidates must earn a Bachelor's degree, complete at least 24 hours of financial management study, pass three exams, and work at least two years for the government before CGFM certification is possible.

- The Association of Certified Fraud Examiners offers the Certified Fraud Examiner (CFE) designation for accountants involved in fraud detection and investigation. Requirements include a Bachelor's degree, two years of relevant work experience, and passing grades on a four-part exam.

- The Accreditation Council for Accountancy and Taxation offers four specialist designations including Accredited Business Accountant (ABA), Accredited Tax Advisor (ATA), Accredited Tax Preparer (ATP), and Elder Care Specialist (ECS).

Candidates for these specialist certifications need to complete relevant coursework and pass an exam.

- ◆ The Information Systems Audit and Control Association (ISACA) provides certification for candidates who have audited information systems for five years and who get passing grades on an exam. Relevant college coursework can be substituted for a portion of the five-year experience requirement.

- ◆ The Institute of Internal Auditors offers the Certified Internal Auditor (CIA) designation for people with two years' experience as an internal auditor plus required college coursework.

- ◆ The Institute of Management Accountants offers the Certified Management Accountant (CMA) designation for candidates with a college degree, two years of experience as a management accountant, passing grades on a four-part exam, and the commitment to complete continuing educations classes in the future.

Clearly, the specialty options for accountants and auditors are plentiful. Your best game plan is to get an undergraduate degree in accounting or a related field, then choose one of the paths described in this section. From there, the experience, exams, and certification paths are pretty clear.

The beauty of going after a recession-proof accounting or auditing career is that many of your skills are transferable. Think about all the related careers that would utilize similar skills. Examples include budget analysts, loan officers, tax examiners, and even financial advisors. With so many opportunities to shift your skill set, it's no wonder accounting and auditing is a recession-proof career choice.

# Executive Secretaries and Administrative Assistants

Let's get one thing straight from the get-go in this section. Though there are more than four million secretaries and administrative assistants in our country, not all of them work in recession-proof careers. In fact, according to the U.S. Department of Labor, the entire profession will grow only 9 percent by 2016. That growth is only average compared to all professions in the United States.

In this chapter, we're talking specifically about *executive* secretaries and administrative assistants. These are the folks who provide support for top organizational executives. They're also the ones on track to grow 15 percent by 2016.

## Outlook for Executive Secretaries and Administrative Assistants

| | |
|---|---|
| Current Number of Employees | 1,618,000 |
| New Jobs Created by 2016 | 239,000 |
| Expected Job Growth by 2016 | 15% |
| Geographical Hotspots | Nevada, Utah |
| Average Annual Earnings | $30,000–$46,000 |

*Sources: U.S. Bureau of Labor Statistics National Employment Matrix, State Occupational Projections*

The general responsibilities of an executive secretary include the following:

◆ Plan and schedule meetings and appointments

◆ Answer phones, transcribe voice-mails, and communicate messages to the executive supported

◆ Organize travel arrangements, including transportation to and from airports, plane tickets, hotel reservations, and car rentals

◆ Take notes in staff meetings to track decisions, next steps, and accountabilities for action

◆ Act as a gatekeeper for employees and/or clients who want to set up time with a busy executive

Executive secretaries differ from the average administrative assistant by virtue of providing higher-level support. The job typically entails fewer clerical tasks because many senior executives also employ a junior assistant for routine matters. This frees up the executive secretary for more challenging work such as reviewing and editing memos, preparing agendas for staff meetings, and conducting research for executive presentations.

In previous generations, executive secretaries relied mostly on typewriters and standard telephones. The computer age and Internet have vastly changed the expectations for an executive secretary. Qualified candidates now need computer proficiency in word processing, spreadsheets, database management, and even desktop publishing.

While most administrative assistants can land positions with high school degrees and office skills, executive secretaries are increasingly asked to have college degrees. The daily interaction with top executives necessitates a greater understanding of high-level business challenges. Your best bet is to earn a degree in the industry you want to support, say health care or insurance.

### Another Path

There is one specific category of secretaries and administrative assistants expected to grow faster than executive secretaries. Medical secretaries are expected to grow 17 percent by 2016. If you've ever wanted to assist a physician or other medical professional, this could be the recession-proof choice for you. You'll arrange medical appointments, record patient histories, and help physicians with speeches, articles, and travel arrangements.

You can also improve your odds of landing a top job through one of two prominent designations. You can become a Certified Professional Secretary (CPS) or Certified Administrative Professional (CAP) by passing an exam and building the required work experience on your resume. Both designations can improve your odds in an interview because they clearly demonstrate your commitment to the profession.

Work experience and designations can help your cause, but there are definite personal skill sets that improve your odds of success in the profession. Here are the top five:

1. **Communication skills**
   From answering phones to typing e-mail, you are the voice of the executive you support. You're expected to represent your executive professionally to help maintain his or her reputation.

2. **Discretion and tact**
   You may learn about top-secret information before it's divulged to the public. You may hear about an employee firing before the employee does. You have to handle sensitive information appropriately.

3. **Attention to detail**
   Your busy executive is jumping from meeting to meeting and call to call. Your job is to keep the executive organized. You have to be good at the small details, so your executive can stay focused on the big picture.

4. **Anticipation abilities**
   A big part of your job is foreseeing problems and fixing them before they happen. Let's say there's a major development at your company; you may need to clear your executive's calendar before the day even starts to shift focus to the biggest issue.

5. **In touch with employees**
   Many senior executives expect their administrative assistant to act as their eyes and ears. When employees are complaining about a business decision, your job is to bubble it up to the executive to help anticipate and deal with problems.

Many senior executives choose to work with one or only a handful of executive secretaries over an entire career. They say good help is hard to find, so it's no wonder that executives try to retain great secretaries once they're on board. Impressing the executive you support every day is your best recession-proof strategy. Make your executive feel as if he or she couldn't get the job done without you. If that's how the executive feels, then a promotion is much more likely than a pink slip.

## The Least You Need to Know

- ◆ Human resource and labor relations jobs become critical in periods of restructuring and downsizing.

- ◆ If you like the idea of analyzing data and minimizing risk for a living, consider an actuarial career.

- ◆ With so many changing tax guidelines for individuals and companies, it's no wonder accountants and auditors are recession proof.

- ◆ If you can make yourself indispensable to a senior executive, you'll recession proof your career as an executive secretary or administrative assistant.

# 21

# Specialized Computer Careers Not Headed Offshore

## In This Chapter

- ◆ How computer and information systems managers effectively coordinate company-wide computer-related activities

- ◆ Why computer systems analysts are so important in maximizing technological efficiencies within organizations

- ◆ How computer software and systems would never work properly without the hard work of computer software engineers

- ◆ Why computer scientist could be the right job for you if you enjoy researching and investigating new technologies

- ◆ Why much of the data stored within companies owes its existence to database administrators

Let's get one thing straight about this chapter before we even begin. People hear the phrase "computer-related jobs" and they instantly think "outsourcing." They assume that any job involving computer programming, software, implementation, and information systems is headed offshore. You may recall from Chapter 1 that we covered the computer-based careers likely to be outsourced. Those included careers in phone-based technical support and basic computer programming. These two areas specifically should not be considered recession proof. Remember: you're really not in a stable job if it can be done cheaper overseas and your company is looking to cut costs.

This chapter is all about computer careers *not* headed offshore. Technology is still exploding in the United States and many U.S.–based positions will be on the front lines of the continuing technological revolution. In this chapter, we cover four of the most recession-proof, computer-based careers around. These include computer and information systems managers, computer systems analysts, computer software engineers, computer scientists, and database administrators.

If you work in a computer-related career or want to jump on the technological bandwagon, then this is your chapter. You learn all about the training requirements, advancement opportunities, salary ranges, and specialties that can help you find and keep a fast-growing computer career. Let's get started and I'll show you how making computers your best friends can help you land a stable job for life.

# Computer and Information Systems Managers

If you've ever held an office job, you may have taken technology for granted. You sit in your cubicle, fire up your computer, and for the most part everything works fine. Your firewalls are in place, you can access the Internet, and your computer software runs smoothly. What you may have overlooked is that computer and information systems managers implemented the very infrastructure that helps you get your job done. Their job is to plan, coordinate, and implement the computer-related activities of companies.

## Outlook for Computer and Information Systems Managers

| | |
|---|---|
| Current Number of Employees | 264,000 |
| New Jobs Created by 2016 | 43,000 |
| Expected Job Growth by 2016 | 16% |
| Geographical Hotspots | Nevada, Utah |
| Average Annual Earnings | $79,000–$129,000 |

*Sources: U.S. Bureau of Labor Statistics National Employment Matrix, State Occupational Projections*

Basic responsibilities include these:

◆ Partner with company management to align business and technological goals

◆ Plan and coordinate the upgrade and installation of new hardware and software programs

◆ Develop and roll out computer networks to link all computers within a company

◆ Plan and implement company Internet and intranet sites

◆ Stay on top of the latest technological developments to help a company stay ahead of the competition

Ultimately, computer and information systems managers are responsible for managing the short- and long-term computer and information needs of their employer. This requires both an operational and strategic approach to rolling out and maintaining company-wide technologies.

The basic duties of computer and information systems managers fall into three basic job categories. First, Chief Technology Officers (CTOs) are in the most strategic technological position. Your job is to evaluate the most innovative and useful technologies around. When you find something that could benefit your company, you become a salesperson. You've got to prove to management that the investment required to implement the new technology will be more than made up for by the efficiencies gained, costs saved, or competitive advantage achieved. At this most senior level, you're likely to be overseeing a team of junior computer and information systems managers, so leadership skills are a must.

Management information systems (MIS) directors or information technology (IT) directors focus on ensuring the reliability and security of computer programs, software, and networks. One of the most common responsibilities is to oversee a technology help desk, which may actually be a set of outsourced workers. Here you're guiding a team responsible for troubleshooting employee computer-related problems. You may also be in charge of the software and hardware upgrades and installations your company's chief technical officer has convinced management to implement.

The final category of computer and information systems managers is the actual project managers. This is the most junior of the positions. You're the detail person, the one responsible for managing computer projects from development through implementation. The more strategic-based positions in your company rely on you to get their ideas off the ground.

**In Their Own Words** _____

Success in the computer world comes down to three factors. First, you've got to understand the business problem your client is trying to solve with technology. Second, you need to be quick in responding to client issues and requirements. Finally, you need to be on top of the latest technologies to ensure your client implements the best available solution.

—Lawrence and Michael Heier, Decisive Solutions, Inc. (decisiveITsolutions.com)

## Training, Certification, and Qualifications

Computer and information systems managers work at the intersection of technology and business. This means you'll need the technical knowledge to get the job done, but also the business understanding to communicate with management. The key is gaining both a business-minded education plus experience in a variety of technical fields.

Entry-level positions often require a Bachelor's degree. One of the most popular degrees is in management information systems. Here you'll learn foundational technical subjects as well as business concepts such as accounting and management. You can sometimes score a first job with only an Associate's degree. However, you'll need to demonstrate some serious technical skills in an interview to overcome the absence of a Bachelor's degree. If you do get in the door, you'll likely want to earn that Bachelor's degree on nights and weekends while working to solidify your job prospects.

In more senior positions, employers are likely to prefer or require an MBA focused in technology. This program is slightly different from the traditional MBA. While you'll still learn the core business curriculum, a heavy emphasis on information technology is included, too. This is the kind of MBA that can demonstrate your dual understanding of business and technology.

Unlike many other careers covered in this book, nationwide or statewide certifications are generally not offered. Instead, certifications are product specific. You might get certified in a particular software or hardware from the very company that created the program. Your product-specific certification can be a great interview differentiator to get the gig over the competition.

## Getting Ahead

Let's say you're working at a large corporation as a computer and information systems manager. How exactly do you get ahead and advance your career? While requirements vary across companies, these four qualities will certainly help build your case for a promotion:

1. **Nontechnical experience**

   The higher you go in a company, the more you're expected to understand inner business workings. You have to know how revenue is earned, where the company is headed, and how technology can help make it happen. Taking a lateral move out of the technology department to learn broader business skills will help your career down the road.

2. **Layman communication skills**

   Have your eyes ever glossed over listening to someone explain a concept? It's important to have solid technical skills, but you must be able to translate what you know into language everyone can understand. Communication in layman's terms is critical to connecting with the business side of the company.

3. **Leadership competencies**

   With each promotion, you'll likely be expected to manage bigger and bigger teams. Now your job evolves. You go from an individual contributor rolling out technologies to a people leader overseeing a team of technology implementers. Your ability to motivate and lead large teams will help you succeed as you move into more senior positions.

4. **Broad-based education**

   As we mentioned in the previous section, learn the technology you need to succeed, but supplement it with business training, too. This is especially important if you want to change companies. Interviewers will specifically look for that combination of technology and business education.

Above all else, staying on top of the latest technology trends is the most important factor in recession proofing your career. Technology changes so fast. Today's hot product can quickly become tomorrow's outdated program. The more you understand the newest technologies desired by companies, the more in demand you'll be.

# Computer Systems Analysts

Suppose you have outdated computer systems at your company. You know it's time for an upgrade, but the marketplace options are simply overwhelming. Where can you turn when you want to make sense of the choices? The answer is to turn to a computer systems analyst. This person's job is to help companies integrate technologies into existing systems and use these technologies as efficiently as possible.

## Outlook for Computer Systems Analysts

| | |
|---|---|
| Current Number of Employees | 504,000 |
| New Jobs Created by 2016 | 146,000 |
| Expected Job Growth by 2016 | 29% |
| Geographical Hotspots | Arkansas, Utah |
| Average Annual Earnings | $54,000–$88,000 |

*Sources: U.S. Bureau of Labor Statistics National Employment Matrix, State Occupational Projections*

The basic responsibilities of a computer systems analyst include the following:

◆ Configure hardware and software programs after helping choose the right computer system

◆ Expand existing systems to perform additional tasks to maximize technology benefits

◆ Consult with business managers to understand the goals of a new computer system and then find the best option

◆ Perform tests on newly installed systems to uncover bugs and improve system performance before company roll-out

◆ Prepare process diagrams for computer programmers to help them understand the desired functionality of a new system

Computer systems analysts often have more specific titles within an organization. For example, system architects are responsible for helping companies choose the right computer infrastructure. Systems designers typically fine-tune installed systems to maximize production. Software quality assurance analysts complete the in-depth testing needed to debug a system. Finally, programmer analysts design and update the software that runs on computer systems. Some computer systems analysts even specialize by particular types of computer systems. It's not uncommon to focus solely on accounting or financial computer systems, for example.

Let's dig further into this career choice to see if it might be right for you. Pretend you work as a computer systems analyst and are implementing a new technology. Here's a breakdown of how you might approach the project. See if this sounds like rewarding work to you. First, you meet with management to make sure you understand the end-user requirements of the new system. With end-user goals in mind, you begin researching system options. You put together a cost-benefit analysis for each option. You even design flow charts that explain in layman's terms how the new system will function.

Now you're ready to set up a follow-up meeting with management. You share the pros and cons of each system option. You also offer your official recommendation. After much discussion, one option is chosen. Now your job shifts from research and presenting to implementing the new system. You guide a team of programmers in designing and rolling out the new system. You

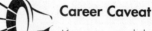

**Career Caveat**

Keep in mind that routine computer systems analyst work is the most likely to be outsourced. If you want to recession proof your career in this field, you have to learn new and more sophisticated computer systems. The more you stay ahead of the technology curve, the more desired you'll be at work and the more likely you'll build a career for life.

oversee testing on the system before leading a company-wide integration. Finally, you check back with management to see whether the new system is achieving its intended purpose. You make system tweaks to improve system performance. Now that's a job well done for a computer systems analyst.

Does it seem like the right gig for you? If so, you need some important educational credentials. Most employers seek at least a four-year college degree. We're not talking art history or English literature majors for this kind of job. Hiring decision-makers will look for technical undergraduate degrees in fields such as computer science, engineering, or mathematics. Don't worry if you've already graduated and your degree fits none of these categories. You can always take computer-specific courses to demonstrate expertise in a particular computer-based system. This alone can sometimes be enough to land an entry-level position.

The big question when it comes to advancement is whether you want to go down the business or technical path. The requirements for each are different. If you want to veer toward the business side of technology, at some point you'll want to consider an MBA. A broad-based business curriculum, coupled with technology-based work experience, will open doors to more senior computer systems analyst positions. On the flip side, you can choose to go the technical route. Now advancement may come from becoming the expert in a particular system or even earning a graduate degree in a technical field. Just make sure your technology field of choice is on the cutting edge. The last thing you want to do is invest months or years training for a computer system with limited shelf life.

Beyond the education and work experience required, three specific skill sets are important for your success:

1. **Analytical skills**
   Reviewing cost-benefit analyses on system options and designing process flows require problem-solving and analytical skills. You'll need to be comfortable working with spreadsheets and analyzing complex bits of data.

2. **Multi-tasking skills**
   Rolling out a new computer system requires keeping multiple miniprojects on track. You must be able to jump among all the interrelated tasks at a moment's notice to keep the overall project driving forward smoothly.

3. **Teamwork skills**
   Planning or implementing a company-wide system can rarely be accomplished by one person in a cubicle. Designers, programmers, testers, business contacts, and analysts all work together to make it happen. Communicating and relating with multiple stakeholders is important.

Ultimately, if you have a love for computers, the right education, experience with the latest technologies, and the right mix of personal skills, you'll find a solid recession-proof career as a computer systems analyst.

# Computer Software Engineers

When was the last time you used a really cool computer software program? Maybe it was a computer game or a business application. Perhaps it was a new operating system or word processing program. Did you ever wonder who was behind the very software program in front of you? The answer is likely a computer software engineer. A computer software engineer's job is to design, develop, test, and launch new computer software and systems.

## Outlook for Computer Software Engineers

| | |
|---|---|
| Current Number of Employees | 857,000 |
| New Jobs Created by 2016 | 324,000 |
| Expected Job Growth by 2016 | 38% |
| Geographical Hotspots | Illinois, Nevada |
| Average Annual Earnings | $63,000–$98,000 |

*Sources: U.S. Bureau of Labor Statistics National Employment Matrix, State Occupational Projections*

Basic responsibilities include the following:

◆ Analyze user needs to design the best possible computer software program to meet those needs

◆ Create the detailed set of instructions that tell a computer what to do in a given program

◆ Customize existing software or system to meet the unique needs of a company or client

◆ Oversee the expansion of a company's software programs to add more functionality

Computer software engineers are generally divided into two distinct roles. Computer applications software engineers focus on the computer applications software used within organizations. Computer systems software engineers instead focus on construction and expansion of company-wide computer systems.

Whichever direction you choose, the big choice is whether to work in-house or as a consultant with a variety of companies. If you work within a company, you have the traditional office structure or possibly a computer lab in which to work. If you go the software vendor or consulting route, then travel will be part of the equation. You can expect many overnight business trips to share the latest software programs with potential customers.

### Another Path

Many of the computer software skills you learn in this profession are transferable. We're not just talking other computer-industry jobs, such as programmers and database administrators. You can also package these skills and become a recession-proof actuary. Sure, you'll need some additional training, but many of the computer skills you've already learned will serve you well in the modeling actuaries require.

What does it take from an educational perspective to break into a computer software engineer career? Breaking into the field and establishing yourself comes down to three important factors:

1. **Bachelor's degree**
   Most employers want candidates with at least a Bachelor's degree. You'll want to earn that degree in a technical field such as computer science, software engineering, computer information systems, or mathematics.

2. **Computer system and technology experience**

   If you're looking to get hired by a company using a particular computer software program, you have to be familiar with it. Or if you want to work as a consultant or software vendor, then you'll likely need to demonstrate proficiency in multiple software programs.

3. **Continuing education**

   What you learn today may or may not be in use tomorrow. Continuing education and professional development seminars can keep you in tune with the latest software developments. These classes are often offered by local colleges, private training programs, and maybe even your employer.

Let's say you've got the Bachelor's degree, technology experience, and continuing education trifecta. How exactly do you package all of this to advance your computer software engineer career? At the entry level, you'll likely have your hands in testing new software. Prove that you're a sleuth when it comes to debugging new programs. This may open doors for you to get involved in the actual design and development of new software programs. From here you can continue to specialize and become an expert. Or you can go the management route, striving to become the leader of a technology department. If you want to go in the management direction, you'll want to supplement your technology expertise with sound business skills. You may even want to pursue an advanced degree in business to round out your background. Now that's a powerful way to recession proof your career.

# Computer Scientists and Database Administrators

This category is a catch-all for multiple computer and information technology positions.

## Outlook for Scientists and Database Administrators

| | |
|---|---|
| Current Number of Employees | 542,000 |
| New Jobs Created by 2016 | 200,000 |
| Expected Job Growth by 2016 | 37% |
| Geographical Hotspots | Kentucky, Virginia |
| Average Annual Earnings | Varies by specialty |

*Sources: U.S. Bureau of Labor Statistics National Employment Matrix, State Occupational Projections*

Computer and information technology generally includes the following three career positions:

1. **Computer scientists**

   Computer scientists are the innovators and inventors behind new technologies. They are the ones who tackle complex theoretical challenges and ultimately discover the new technologies to overcome these obstacles.

2. **Database administrators**

   Database administrators work with database management systems to figure out ways to organize and store data in the most efficient database possible.

3. **Network systems and data communications analysts**

   Network systems and data communications analysts design, test, debug, and roll out new systems including Internet, intranet, and other data communications systems.

The three careers just described differ in terms of roles and responsibilities, and the associated educational and training requirements are somewhat different, too. So let's examine the academic and work experience necessary to succeed in this field across all three career choices.

It's easier to break into a database administrator and data communications analyst position than it is to become a computer scientist. In fact, many employers consider hiring database administrators or data communications analysts with just two-year postsecondary training and relevant work experience. Of course, a four-year degree, in a relevant field such as computer science or management information systems, will open even more doors.

The more complex and research-based nature of computer scientist positions ultimately require a Ph.D. if you really want to advance. Sure you can break into the field with a Bachelor's degree alone, but your ability to move up in the organization will be stifled if you don't continue your education while working.

Regardless of the career choice you make, certifications are a great way to go if you want to prove your expertise beyond a shadow of a doubt. Many private institutions and even some employers sponsor certification programs in specific computer-related products. Waving that graduation certificate at a job interview is sure to squash any employer's doubts about your technology skills.

As your career progresses, there are four directions you can choose to go to further establish your career:

1. **Managerial positions**

   If you prove your skills as an individual contributor, you may advance to lead others. Here you'll oversee a team of scientists, database administrators, or data communications analysts. This direction makes sense if you're ultimately interested in the business side of technology.

2. **Academic jobs**

   If your expertise continues to grow, you can choose to leave behind the corporate gigs for an academic institution. Now your career changes from rolling out new technologies to teaching others how to do the same. If you gain satisfaction from inspiring and teaching others, then consider this route.

3. **Consulting opportunities**

   You can go it alone as an independent consultant, or work for a consulting firm that completes projects for clients. The independent route makes sense if you have a real name for yourself in the industry and a full address book. Working for a consulting firm could be the smarter recession-proof approach if you want less pressure on personally finding and keeping clients.

4. **Small business ownership**

   If you've got that entrepreneurial flare, then you can package everything you've learned and start your own technology company. Dreams of getting bought out for millions may motivate you in those early years. Of course, this is the riskiest of the career options and therefore the least likely to be recession proof.

The good news for this career category is that there are lots of different directions you can go. This diversity means you'll have lots of different ways you can recession proof your career over time. So consider all the skills you learn as transferable and keep an eye out for chances to jump among the career options described in this chapter.

## The Least You Need to Know

- If you want to coordinate computer-related activities, consider recession-proof work as a computer and information systems manager.

- Success as a computer systems analyst hinges on continuously learning the newest and most sophisticated technologies.

- Computer software engineers build and program many of the software programs we use every day.

- If you would enjoy researching new technologies on the horizon, then working as a computer scientist may be right for you.

- Database administrators play a vital company role by safely storing organizational data should systems fail.

# Chapter 22

# Sales Reps, Personal Financial Advisors, and PR Specialists

## In This Chapter

◆ How to recession proof your career selling ad space in magazines, newspapers, the Internet, and television

◆ Why insurance sales agents work in stable careers regardless of economic fluctuations

◆ How to help clients manage their investment portfolios in an industry that's growing more than 40 percent

◆ Why shaping public client images and reputations is a great way to shape up your own career prospects

This chapter is all about sales, advice, and images. We're going to cover advertising sales agents, insurance sales agents, financial advisors, and public relations specialists. Collectively, this group is responsible for everything from the advertising images you see on television to the celebrity images portrayed in the media. On the insurance and financial advice side, these are the professions that help clients protect their health and wealth.

We begin this chapter with a look at advertising sales agents. Without their ability to fill ad space between television segments and magazine stories, these programs and publications would not exist. Next, we cover insurance sales agents who offer the medical, disability, and property policies that protect our health and assets. From there, we talk about financial advisors who grow your portfolio in good times and protect your assets in downturns. Finally, we review public relations specialists who help shape the public image of people and companies.

By the end of this chapter you'll know all about four recession-proof careers (and even some related stable careers) that can keep you employed for years to come. So sit back and get ready to learn about everything from selling ad space to managing investment portfolios.

# Advertising Sales Agents

Television programs, newspapers, magazines, and Internet-based media companies all have something in common. Without advertising dollars coming in the door, their business doors would be closed. Those 30- and 60-second ads you see during your favorite programs pay employee salaries and keep the lights on at the station. That's why, even in down times, revenue-generating advertising sales agents are so important. They sell advertising space to companies who want to promote their products in the media. As *HR World* puts it, in an article on the top 25 professions to pursue in a recession, "anyone who is a source of income for a company will be safer in a recession."

## Outlook for Advertising Sales Agents

| | |
|---|---|
| Current Number of Employees | 170,000 |
| New Jobs Created by 2016 | 35,000 |
| Expected Job Growth by 2016 | 20% |
| Geographical Hotspots | Idaho, Utah |
| Average Annual Earnings | $29,000–$63,000 |

*Sources: U.S. Bureau of Labor Statistics National Employment Matrix, State Occupational Projections*

There are a few different kinds of advertising sales agents with varying roles, including the following:

◆ Local sales agents who are responsible for soliciting ads from companies in a particular region

- National sales agents who seek ads from companies who want to reach a nation-wide audience

- Media representation agents who work with media buyers at advertising agencies to buy ads on behalf of clients

- Inside sales agents who handle calls and e-mail from prospective buyers who contact the company offering advertising space

Regardless of your specific title, your job is to convince a potential ad buyer to purchase time or space in your media outlet. You accomplish this task by demonstrating the value and payback for advertising in your magazine, on your television station, and so on. To do your job well, you have to start with some research. What product does your client sell? Who are the customers? What geographic area is your client trying to reach? With research in hand, your job is to show clients how you can help them reach their target market effectively by advertising with you. In many cases, particularly at larger firms, you can sell an integrated advertising package including print, online, and television ads. When you have that initial buy-in, your job shifts to drawing up contracts, working through sample ads, and generating cost estimates.

After the contract is signed, your role is as a liaison between the client and the ad agency creating the ad. Ultimately, you need a great ad that makes your client happy, fits the budget, reaches the target audience, and converts to sales. So the final piece of your job is analyzing and reporting demographic audience reports and sales statistics. This is how you show the true value of your services to your client and to your employer.

Breaking into the advertising sales field will likely require a Bachelor's degree, particularly for the larger firms. In fact, more than 50 percent of people in the field have a Bachelor's degree. The most common and relevant degrees for advertising sales agents include communications, marketing, advertising, and even business degrees. Smaller advertising and telemarketing companies may accept high school degrees alone or some postsecondary education.

Ultimately, your success comes down to your ability to meet advertising sales goals

### Another Path

It's not uncommon for advertising sales agents to jump from selling to buying over the course of a career. So you can gain experience selling ad space to clients and then change paths and work for one of the clients as a buyer of ad space. Your experience selling will only help you when you're sitting on the other side of the negotiating table.

and monthly quotas. Following are the personality traits and skills that tend to translate well into advertising sales success:

1. **Persuasiveness**
   Selling advertising space is all about convincing someone to give you money to promote a product or service. You have to be persuasive to sway a client into choosing your media outlet over the competing companies.

2. **Communication skills**
   You have to be able to articulate the value your media outlet can provide. Whether sending e-mail, talking on the phone, or meeting in person, clear and concise communication skills are a must if you want to close the deal.

3. **Pleasant nature**
   There is something about human nature that makes us more likely to buy from someone we like than from someone we don't like. If you're rude, pushy, or demanding, clients simply don't want to send dollars your way.

4. **Persistence**
   You won't always close the deal on the first try. You'll have to handle ambivalence and rejection without giving up. The most persistent advertising sales agents are likely to close the most deals.

5. **Language skills**
   The more multicultural our country becomes, the greater the need for advertising sales agents who can conduct business in English and in other languages. The fastest-growing sector is Spanish-speaking, but any second language can help you reach new buyers.

Let's assume you have the educational skills and personality traits to succeed. How do you move up and advance your career? The first option is to take on bigger and more important clients. If you can prove the smaller clients want to buy from you, it's only a matter of time before your boss asks you to go after bigger, more profitable clients. The second option is to advance to a supervisory position, overseeing a team of advertising sales agents. This makes sense if you desire to advance from the individual contributor to the leadership level.

Keep in mind that this is a profession largely based on commissions. You'll earn a base salary, but your full income depends on closing deals. This can be stressful. On the flip side, it can be financially rewarding because your income can double or triple in a good year. Ultimately, if you can handle income fluctuations from good years and bad, then you might enjoy the excitement of a close link between pay and performance.

# Insurance Sales Agents

Insurance sales agents are one of those rare professions that people need in good times and need even more in bad times. When the economy is flying high, clients want to protect wealth accumulation through life insurance and other policies. When the market tumbles, people take a sobering look at their lives and want to make sure the proper protection is in place. Either way, insurance sales agents are recession proof. Their job is to help individuals, families, and companies choose policies to protect their property and health.

## Outlook for Insurance Sales Agents

| | |
|---|---|
| Current Number of Employees | 436,000 |
| New Jobs Created by 2016 | 56,000 |
| Expected Job Growth by 2016 | 13% |
| Geographical Hotspots | Idaho, Utah |
| Average Annual Earnings | $32,000–$69,000 |

*Sources: U.S. Bureau of Labor Statistics National Employment Matrix, State Occupational Projections*

Common responsibilities for insurance sales agents include the following:

◆ Sell policies to protect people and businesses from property losses resulting from fire, theft, or storms

◆ Offer life insurance policies to protect families in the event a primary income earner passes away

◆ Help protect businesses from malpractice, workers' compensation, or product liability claims

◆ Sell disability policies should an income earner be unable to work on a daily basis

◆ Provide medical and dental insurance for families and small business owners to cover health-related expenses

The role of an insurance sales agent falls into two broad categories. First, your job is building a clientele. This is especially important if you're starting your own insurance practice or joining a small firm. When clients are on board, or if you work for a larger insurance provider, your role is more about managing client relationships and renewing policies. That's why this job is really a hybrid of both sales and account management roles.

Before the Internet transformed the insurance and many other industries, it was not uncommon for sales agents to stand outside local grocery stores and malls to pitch to clients. You would be walking out of the supermarket with a bag of fresh fruit and frozen goods, and an insurance agent would approach you to ask, "Do you believe your kids are adequately covered should something happen to you?"

Those days are long gone. Now you can get five quotes in minutes from competing insurance companies on the Internet. So the sales process has migrated from face-to-face interaction to offering competitive quotes on the Internet. Many clients still prefer building longstanding relationships with insurance agents, so those client relationship skills are still important.

## In Their Own Words

The insurance business can provide diverse opportunities for a lifelong career. As with any sales job, you must enjoy working with people. Helping clients solve problems, plan for the future, and safeguard their families and property can be very rewarding.

Through good and bad economic times, as long as there are businesses and individuals who need insurance, there is a place for your services.

—Joel Konikow, CLTC, RFC, Principal, Konikow Associates, Inc., Old Tappan, New Jersey

Breaking into the field will likely require a college degree, especially at the larger firms. Degrees in business or related fields are most useful in landing entry-level insurance sales agent positions. Some companies will take on high school graduates and offer customer service positions while the employee completes additional training and education. Then you can think about advancing to the insurance sales agent level.

Where are you most likely to work as an insurance sales agent? According to insurance industry projections, about 50 percent of insurance sales agents work for insurance agencies. Another 25 percent work for insurance carriers. Most of the balance are self-employed. Starting your own practice is where those sales skills will be most needed to build a loyal clientele.

No matter what state you work in, every insurance sales agent must have a state-issued license to solicit clients and sell insurance products. So how exactly do you earn your license? Typically, you'll need to complete required coursework as defined by your state. From there, a state exam awaits you, covering insurance fundamentals and state insurance laws. You'll also be expected to complete continuing education classes to maintain your license in the years to come. Depending on the state where you work, separate licenses may be required to sell life and health insurance versus property and casualty insurance. Many states now have reciprocal agreements that allow you to earn a license in one state and practice in another.

As an insurance sales agent, one of the decisions you need to make is to specialize or be a generalist. For example, you can become the most trusted, most popular agent for clients seeking long-term disability insurance. If you go the specialty route, earning a professional designation in your specialty field helps build customer confidence. The National Alliance for Education and Research is one such professional organization offering specialty courses. You can also take the opposite approach and offer something for everyone. As a generalist, you'll try to bring in a client for one product and ultimately sell more insurance products over time to expand the relationship.

There's one more direction you can go if you want to advance as an insurance sales agent. It's also the perfect lead-in to our next section on personal financial advisors. Many clients are increasingly looking for one-stop shops to buy insurance products and get financial advice. This desire makes sense when you consider insurance and financial advice is all about protecting your wealth and health. You can go the route of partnering with a financial advisor and running your business together, or you can gain financial advisor expertise yourself. In the next section, we cover the educational requirements for financial advisors. Needless to say, mastering two recession-proof careers is quite a career-stabilizing strategy!

# Personal Financial Advisors

We touched on financial planners in the previous section, but now let's deep-dive into this recession-proof career. This is another career, similar to insurance agents, that flourishes in both up and down cycles. When the economy is roaring along, people expect financial advisors to maximize return on investment. When economic clouds appear, financial advisors help clients protect wealth and minimize stock market losses. The primary job of a financial advisor is to assess the financial needs of a client and to help manage an investment portfolio on behalf of the client.

## Outlook for Personal Financial Advisors

| | |
|---|---|
| Current Number of Employees | 176,000 |
| New Jobs Created by 2016 | 72,000 |
| Expected Job Growth by 2016 | 41% |
| Geographical Hotspots | New Hampshire, Rhode Island |
| Average Annual Earnings | $44,000–$114,000 |

*Sources: U.S. Bureau of Labor Statistics National Employment Matrix, State Occupational Projections*

Major responsibilities include all of the following:

◆ Help a client achieve short- and long-term investment goals

◆ Explain retirement and estate planning options to help a client plan for the golden years

◆ Guide clients through establishing a college education fund for offspring

◆ Offer tax advice in conjunction with an accountant to reduce tax liabilities

◆ Conduct quarterly, semi-annual, or yearly portfolio reviews to analyze investment performance and report to client

Financial advisors typically earn money in one of two ways. In scenario one, you're paid a management fee, which is a percentage of the total value of the portfolio. The other option is to earn transaction fees on the portfolio moves made. Of course, if you work for a large company, you may also earn a base salary. In fact, more than half of all financial advisors work for medium and large financial and insurance companies. Another 30 percent go the entrepreneurial path, building a small firm or working alone as a personal financial advisor.

Regardless of whether you go the big company or small firm route, prospects for financial advisors are excellent. The more than 40 percent growth comes down to three main factors. First, as baby boomers continue to retire in record numbers, financial advisors are increasingly needed to manage and guide retirement asset choices. Second, many companies are phasing out simple pension plans. This leaves the burden on individuals to manage their own retirement plan and many turn to financial advisors for assistance. Finally, the simple fact that folks are living longer means there is a greater need to manage finances over a longer life span.

> **Career Caveat**
>
> Money is an emotional topic for many clients. They've worked years to amass a nest egg and are depending on you to grow that portfolio. When the economy dips and investment accounts nose-dive, you can expect calls from irate customers challenging your investment advice. This is a career that requires patience to withstand market fluctuations and to gently soothe customers who expect big returns every year.

# Training

You'll need a Bachelor's degree to break into a financial advisory career. Coursework in accounting, finance, management, and other business skills will help your cause in that entry-level interview. Once on board, almost all financial advisors need to earn the Series 7 and Series 63 or 66 licenses. The Series 7 exam is required for anyone who wants to sell securities in the stock market. You'll need to answer 70 percent of the questions correctly on a wide range of investment topics, including stocks, bonds, and options. The Series 63 exam is required by most states to earn your state license as a securities agent. The Series 66 exam is your ticket to earning status as a Registered Investment Adviser Representative.

Beyond the licenses required by your state, you can obtain a Certified Financial Planner (CFP) credential. Awarded by the Certified Financial Planner Board of Standards, this credential requires four steps:

1. Three years of relevant work experience

2. A Bachelor's degree

3. Passing grades on a comprehensive exam

4. Adherence to a code of ethics

Step three, the comprehensive exam, covers a whole host of topics you'll need to know for career success. The subjects covered include insurance and risk management, financial planning, taxes and retirement planning, and even estate planning. It's no wonder the CFP credential is so trusted by clients seeking personal financial advice.

# Success and Advancement

Ultimate recession-proof success as a financial advisor comes down to advancing your career and building the right skill set. From an advancement perspective, you can accumulate more clients and manage larger assets. You can move into a managerial position and oversee a team of financial advisors. You can even go the entrepreneurial path and set up a branch office of a well-known financial firm. This is a business where referrals can mean the difference between a thriving branch practice and one that fails. Do a great job for Aunt Edna and you'll soon be managing portfolios for her sister, her fellow bridge club members, and close friends. That's why treating each and every client well is so important in this profession. That one client can easily help you build an entire practice.

There are also some personality traits and skill sets that lead to success as a financial advisor. First and foremost, you have to have good analytical skills. Reviewing stocks and making investment decisions means scanning computer spreadsheets and reviewing research reports on a daily basis. Second, your communication skills are critical. Investing can be overwhelming and confusing for clients. Your ability to translate complex financial topics into laymen's terms will help build client trust and grow the assets you manage. Finally, decision-making skills mean the difference between good and bad investment decisions. You need to take all the investment research and expert opinions available and make portfolio decisions based on this input. Ultimately, you're judged by how your decision making translates into investment returns for your clients.

# Public Relations Specialists

Can you remember the last time you turned on the television and watched a celebrity spin his way out of a damaging news story? Maybe he cheated on his wife, got caught using drugs, or assaulted an overzealous member of the press. Chances are, the person behind the press conference talking points was a pubic relations (PR) specialist. A PR specialist's job is to help build and maintain a positive relationship between their client and the media or the public at large.

## Outlook for Public Relations Specialists

| | |
|---|---|
| Current Number of Employees | 243,000 |
| New Jobs Created by 2016 | 43,000 |
| Expected Job Growth by 2016 | 18% |
| Geographical Hotspots | Idaho, Nevada |
| Average Annual Earnings | $36,000–$65,000 |

*Sources: U.S. Bureau of Labor Statistics National Employment Matrix, State Occupational Projections*

Basic responsibilities for a PR specialist include all of the following:

◆ Draft press releases and contact members of the media to pitch newsworthy stories

◆ Book media appearances for clients to appear on talk shows and radio programs, as well as to be featured in print publications

◆ Write talking points for clients who speak at press conferences and other media events

◆ Craft public personas and improve images for clients seeking to improve their public standing

◆ Act as a liaison between the client and organizations that may be interested in what the client has to say on relevant topics and issues

PR specialists can work in practically any industry or for any organization that wants to improve or maintain its public standing. The most common include businesses, nonprofit institutions, famous people, hospitals, government agencies, and interest groups. This is a fast-paced job in which you're often working on tight deadlines and handling PR emergencies on a moment's notice. Remember, in many cases, you're paid to help communicate and mitigate situations that arise out of nowhere. Night and weekend work is also very common as you'll often be attending events, conferences, and appearances. However, the fast pace and challenging work can be extremely rewarding if you enjoy the ever-changing nature of the job.

While there are no uniform requirements for entry into a PR specialist role, most firms seek candidates with a Bachelor's degree. You won't go wrong with a degree in communications, advertising, marketing, or journalism. If you're still in college, an internship in a PR firm won't hurt your chances either. If you have no experience in PR, another way to break into the field is to gain experience in an industry in another capacity. For example, experience in the health-care field could open the door to become a PR specialist for a hospital.

You can go the certification route to gain credentials in the PR industry and build

**Another Path**

We talked earlier in this book about recession-proof careers in the government. Here's a double recession-proof strategy—work as a PR specialist for the government. Roles such as press secretaries, communication specialists, and affairs specialists are all PR specialist roles within the government. You'll be applying your recession-proof PR skills to a recession-proof industry. Not a bad way to solidify your career prospects.

your resumé. The Universal Accreditation Board accredits PR specialists who are members of the Public Relations Society of America. To earn your credential, you'll need at least five years of work experience, a degree in a communications-related field, and passing grades on an exam. The International Association of Business Communicators (IABC) also offers accreditation for communications field professionals, including PR specialists. Earning your credential requires five years of relevant work experience, a Bachelor's degree in a communications field, and passing grades on both a written and oral examination. You'll also need to submit a portfolio of past work to demonstrate your command of key communications topics.

Beyond the academic requirements and credential opportunities, there are five qualities that make for a successful PR specialist:

1. **Performance under pressure**
   Imagine a company or individual turning to you in a time of need to put a positive spin on a misstep. You have one shot to get it right and change public perception. Now that's a lot of performance pressure.

2. **Written and oral communication skills**
   Whether writing press releases or speaking at press conferences on behalf of a client, you'll need expert written and oral communication skills. Remember, quotations are often widely distributed, so you have to get them right.

3. **Problem-solving skills**
   You'll be faced with companies and individuals who need help properly positioning their place in the public mind. You'll have to think through the options—and sometimes quickly—and find the best way to portray your client with the media.

4. **Research skills**
   This is a profession in which you need to know the industry you represent. You need to know the companies, individuals, and products that are important in your client's industry, and research is the best way to build your knowledge base.

5. **Outgoing nature**
   A PR career is not for folks who desire a day behind the computer. You're going to be interacting with people, building relationships, and meeting people like you and the clients you represent. Extroverts and those who like to mingle often do best in this career path.

How do you advance as a PR specialist? Taking on bigger and more challenging clients is the most typical advancement path. Your boss will see how effectively you handle simpler assignments and consider you for bigger projects. You can also get promoted to oversee a team of PR specialists who together handle a major client or a group of smaller clients.

One trend likely to help continued demand for PR specialists is the desire by many companies to hire contractors to handle public relations issues. This may mean fewer opportunities are available in-house for PR positions. However, the growing contractor opportunities should more than make up for it and keep PR specialists in a recession-proof position for years to come.

## The Least You Need to Know

- If you want to sell ad space on television, in print, or on the Internet, consider a recession-proof career as an advertising sales agent.

- If you enjoy helping clients protect their health and wealth, then working as an insurance sales agent might be the right path for you.

- You can help clients stabilize and grow their investment portfolios while stabilizing and growing your financial advisor career, too.

- In good times and bad, public relations specialists are needed to shape and manage the images of their clients.

# Chapter 23

# Get a Global Mind-Set

## In This Chapter

- ◆ How interpreters and translators smooth the way for people in court-rooms, in health care, and in business

- ◆ Why management analysts with international expertise will be in the highest demand

- ◆ How people who understand how consumers think always have a role with businesses

We've been hearing about globalization for years. We know the Internet has opened the door for anyone to sell a product to a consumer anywhere in the world. We understand that global commerce is helping companies that used to focus in one market to deliver goods and services to new and distant lands.

This chapter is all about the jobs that enable companies and people in one country to do business and make connections in other countries. We start with interpreters and translators. Before any deal is made or any political agreement is reached, people need to understand each other's written and spoken words. Interpreters and translators are vital in bridging communication, cultural, and language barriers. Next, we cover management analysts, particularly those who focus on international markets, products, and services. These are the people on the front lines of globalization—the ones helping international companies formulate new strategies to seize global opportunities and expand market share. Finally, we examine market and survey researchers. This is a job all about understanding how people think, act, and buy. The researchers are the ones who can analyze consumer behavior, make predictions about future buying decisions, and guide global companies in developing and marketing products that meet international demand.

By the end of this chapter, you'll see that interpreters, translators, management analysts, and market researchers with global expertise will be employed for years to come. Now let's get down to business!

# Interpreters and Translators

If only we could all agree on one global language. Life would be so easy. You could travel anywhere from China to South America and understand every street sign, restaurant menu, and conversation. Because a universal language doesn't appear to be coming anytime soon, interpreters and translators will be recession proof for years to come. Interpreters and translators convert the spoken and written word from one language to another to enable cross-cultural communication.

## Outlook for Interpreters and Translators

| | |
|---|---|
| Current Number of Employees | 41,000 |
| New Jobs Created by 2016 | 9,700 |
| Expected Job Growth by 2016 | 24% |
| Geographical Hotspots | Idaho, Nevada |
| Average Hourly Earnings | $13–$23 per hour |

*Sources: U.S. Bureau of Labor Statistics National Employment Matrix, State Occupational Projections*

Though interpreters and translators are often grouped together, they are actually two different professions. Interpreters work with spoken words while translators work with written words. Let's review them separately to get a clear picture of the nature of the work, training, and advancement opportunities for each.

# Interpreters

Interpreters translate spoken words from one language to another. The basic responsibilities of interpreters include the following:

◆ Travel to a conference or special event to translate spoken words for attendees from different nations

◆ Research the subject matter to be discussed to brush up on common terms likely to be discussed between parties

◆ Observe the tone of the speaker to appropriately translate the emotions behind the words

Two types of interpretation typically occur between languages. The first is called simultaneous interpreting. Here you'll start translating to the other person even before the speaker finishes each sentence. You'll need to be so familiar with the subject of discussion you can practically anticipate the end of each sentence. The second type is called consecutive interpretation. Here you wait until the end of each thought before translating. Taking notes is common to ensure that you fully grasp and translate everything mentioned.

> **Career Caveat** _____
>
> Interpreter careers are not for folks who don't like to travel. With the exception of a few jobs available in call centers for phone-based translation, you'll likely be traveling to conferences and events both nearby and around the world. Make sure extended time away from home is a plus in your mind before committing to this career choice.

Where might you find work as a translator? Your best bet is any environment where cross-cultural communication is required. The five most common interpreter jobs are these:

1. **Conference interpreters**
   This work is most common for events with attendees from multiple countries. Conference organizers may arrange interpreters for special guests or important attendees.

2. **Escort interpreters**
   Let's say a foreign dignitary is visiting the United States from Africa and she needs someone who speaks both English and her native tongue. You would stay by her side and translate between languages for the duration of her visit.

3. **Judiciary interpreters**

   If a defendant enters the courtroom and can't speak or understand English, someone has to make sure communication is not an obstacle. An interpreter would translate both what court officials say to the defendant and what the defendant says to the officials.

4. **Medical interpreters**

   Imagine a French-speaking patient suffering a life-threatening illness in an American hospital. Without a medical interpreter, the patient can't communicate symptoms, medication allergies, or any other pertinent information.

5. **Sign language interpreters**

   Sign language interpreters facilitate communication between people who are deaf or hard of hearing and those who can hear. For this job, you'll need to be fluent in both English and American Sign Language (ASL).

# Translators

Unlike interpreters, translators focus on the written word. Whereas interpreting spoken language involves getting the gist of the message, translating written words must duplicate the message flawlessly. That's because translations are often used in manuals, books, and official documents in which cultural precision is critical. Common responsibilities for a translator include the following:

◆ Rewrite text in a second language to ensure it has the same tone, flow, and content as the original language

◆ Interview the writer of the original language document to understand and capture the intent and themes of the document

◆ Use computer programs that can help translate documents, particularly slang words that may not have clear meanings in multiple languages

Though interpreters primarily work on site, many translators have the luxury of working from home and usually on a flexible schedule. The biggest challenge for translators is capturing and translating the emotions and meaning behind the written words. It's not enough to just do a word-for-word translation. If the original document is meant to convey humor, sadness, or surprise, then the translated document must do the same.

Similar to interpreters, there are distinct settings where translators typically find work. Here are the four most common:

1. **Judiciary translators**

   To land this role, you have to be extremely familiar with all the legal jargon in both English and the language into which you will be translating. The text may be technical, with terms specific to courtrooms only, so you must have that specialized knowledge.

2. **Literary translators**

   Here you're paid to translate text in books, pamphlets, and articles from one language to another. The big challenge here is to convey the same literary style as the original work to make sure the emotions and meanings are translated appropriately.

3. **Medical translators**

   Have you ever walked into a hospital and seen a patient brochure printed in both English and Spanish? This work was likely done by a medical translator.

4. **Localization translators**

   When a product crosses borders, the manufacturers want to make sure it "speaks" to the new region. Your job is to make it seem as if the product actually originated in the new country where it is now sold.

# Education and Advancement Opportunities

Though the responsibilities and job titles may differ for interpreters and translators, the educational requirements and advancement opportunities are somewhat similar. Regarding education, a Bachelor's degree is typical, although the most important qualification is fluency in two languages. The most qualified interpreters and translators typically grow up in a bilingual household. This background means you'll have the most in-depth cultural understanding of the two languages. You can, of course, still become an interpreter or translator without growing up bilingual. In this case, extensive time spent abroad or working with folks who speak the second language will be required to master the second language and be fully fluent.

While in college, you can major in the second language, but it's not required. At the end of the day, an ability to demonstrate fluency in two languages will be your biggest resumé builder. Through your college program, you can learn the ins and outs of the career beyond mastering two languages. You can even earn a degree in translation studies if you really want to target your academic studies.

**Another Path** _____

Mentor relationships are one of the most helpful ways for interpreters and translators to build confidence with experienced professionals. Both the American Translators Association and Registry of Interpreters for the Deaf offer formal mentoring programs. You'll get matched up with someone further along in his or her career who can show you the ropes.

After graduation it's all about building experience. Many top interpreting and translating agencies seek employees with a minimum of three to five years of experience. Volunteering and freelancing to build experience is a common path.

Interpreters and translators are not required to earn official certifications. However, several are offered for those who want to bolster their credentials. For example, the American Translators Association offers certification in more than 25 language combinations. If you want to go the court route with your career, then the National Association of Judiciary Interpreters and Translators offers certification for court-based interpretation and translation services.

The U.S. Department of State offers a three-test series for interpreters. The three tests prepare you for escort, court, or conference work. While you won't earn an official certification, passing grades on the tests typically demonstrate enough language proficiency to land gigs.

Of the more than 41,000 interpreters and translators working in the field, about 22 percent are self-employed. Many of these folks work part-time and take assignments as they come along through hiring agencies and repeat clients. Another 33 percent of interpreters and translators work in educational institutions such as colleges and universities. Approximately 12 percent work in health-care and social assistance settings, primarily in hospitals and health-care clinics. Another 10 percent of interpreters and translators work for the government, at the local, state, or federal level. Finally, the other 23 percent work for employers that fall into other, miscellaneous categories.

**Another Path** _____

Notice that one third of interpreters and translators work in educational institutions. This means your career is not limited to literally translating spoken and written words. You can in fact land a great job teaching foreign language skills to students of all ages. Choose an up-and-coming language and you'll recession proof your foreign language teaching career.

Two key trends are driving the continued need for interpreters and translators. First and foremost, the United States is increasingly becoming multicultural and multilingual. Companies based in the United States that want to reach non-English-speaking customers need interpreters and translators to make more sales. The second trend is the continued need by the Department of Homeland Security. So much of defense planning and information analysis requires people who can speak many languages and translate to English.

Ultimately, the expansion of global communications is the biggest driving factor in recession proofing careers in interpreting and translation. So if you're in school now, brush up on that second language. It just might land you in a stable career for years to come.

# Management Analysts

I know you're thinking that management analyst positions are often in jeopardy during a recession. That may be true for smaller firms focused only on the U.S. market. Remember, however, we're going global in this chapter. Solid job growth is expected for the largest management and consulting firms with international expertise. Smaller firms that focus on emerging areas such as biotechnology, health care, and information technology will also survive economic ups and downs.

Now that we've covered the recession-proof evidence for management analysts, let's dive into the nuts and bolts of the profession. Management analysts are responsible for helping organizations improve their profits, company structure, and operational efficiency.

## Outlook for Management Analysts

| | |
|---|---|
| Current Number of Employees | 678,000 |
| New Jobs Created by 2016 | 149,000 |
| Expected Job Growth by 2016 | 22% |
| Geographical Hotspots | Nevada, Virginia |
| Average Annual Earnings | $51,000–$92,000 |

*Sources: U.S. Bureau of Labor Statistics National Employment Matrix, State Occupational Projections*

Following are some common roles for management analysts:

◆ Help a fledgling company improve inventory control levels as supply and demand fluctuates

◆ Support a larger company through the acquisition of a smaller one, including organizational restructurings and redundancy eliminations

◆ Determine strategies to help one company gain a sustainable competitive edge over another company

◆ Interview employees involved in a procedure to identify bottlenecks and speed up the entire process

◆ Guide a company through identifying and building a new market or product

◆ Lead a department in outsourcing a particular function to reduce costs

**Another Path**

You can be a management analyst without working directly for large and small corporations. The government employs many management analysts to help guide the strategic decisions of various government agencies. If you like the work described in this section but feel a calling for the public sector, consider working as a management analyst for the U.S. government.

Most management analysts work for large and small consulting firms. After many years of experience, it's not uncommon to open a new firm as a single practitioner. Traditionally, management analysts will either specialize in a specific industry or particular business function. For example, you might specialize in the health-care or automotive industry. Or if you go the business function route, you might specialize in human resources or marketing.

Whether specializing by industry or by function, the primary job of a management analyst is to collect, examine, and analyze information to make strategic recommendations to the client. In many cases, the work goes beyond recommendations through to the implementation phase.

## Day-to-Day Duties

Why might a company turn to management analysts or consultants? One reason would be a company lacks the internal resources to accomplish a specific task. Sometimes it's simply easier to bring in management analysts without paying the overhead (i.e., benefits). Another reason is to assess a market opportunity before committing time and money. Bringing in an outside expert can help a company size up an opportunity and make an informed decision.

Let's take a brief look inside the life of a management analyst to see if the work would interest you. First, travel is common unless you land clients based in your immediate area. Otherwise, you'll spend some time in your home office, but much of your time on site with clients. The term "road warrior" is common in describing management analysts. There are three main responsibilities for management analysts:

1. Finding new clients

2. Doing great work

3. Managing client relationships

Depending on your level within the company, the emphasis on each of these three responsibilities varies. For example, less experienced management analysts tend to focus on doing the work. They are the ones cranking out the PowerPoint presentations, the initial recommendations, and the follow-up analyses. As you work your way up as a management analyst, the focus shifts to tracking down new business and managing client relationships. Rather than get assessed on the quality of your client work, the focus turns to attracting and retaining profitable clients. This is where the schmooze factor of the job comes into play. You have to be willing to take clients for dinner, meet them at conferences, and generally build positive working and personal relationships.

## Education and Training

What does it take to break into a management analyst career? You can likely score your first job with a Bachelor's degree. Though many areas of study lend themselves to this kind of work, degrees in economics, management, marketing, and engineering are very helpful in attracting suitable employers. At the outset, your job will likely focus on research and reporting to help more experienced management analysts get the job done. View your job as making their lives easier by providing the research and information to help your superiors make informed decisions and recommendations for the client.

If your goal is to work your way up the ladder, then at some point a Master's of Business Administration (MBA) is recommended, if not required, by your employer. MBA programs typically last two years. During the summer between years one and two, an internship in a specific industry or business function would be wise. For example, if you hope to be a management analyst in the health-care industry, land yourself an internship where you can gain some health-care experience.

**Career Caveat**

Long hours and tight deadlines are common for management analysts. Remember, companies are often reaching out when in crisis mode or acting from a sense of urgency. As a management analyst, you're going to take on the pressure and stress of your client. This is not the career for you if meeting tight deadlines and working under time constraints is not for you.

If you so choose, the Institute of Management Consultants offers a Certified Management Consultant (CMC) designation for management analysts who achieve a certain level of both academic achievement and work experience. Most employers do not require the designation, but it can give you a competitive edge.

People with certain personality characteristics tend to thrive in this field. For starters, you have to be self-motivated. You'll likely be on site with clients with minimal or no supervision. You still have to get the job done without someone looking over your shoulder. Analytical skills and the ability to synthesize large bits of information are also important. Often you'll be conducting interviews with several employees involved in a particular process. You need to be able to take in the information, identify themes, and convert all of the input into strategic recommendations and implementation suggestions.

Communication skills, both oral and written, are also a must. Clients will gain confidence in a management analyst after seeing and hearing clear and articulate recommendations. Finally, much of your work will be in teams, both teams of analysts and teams composed of your clients' employees. So you'll need the ability to work well with others.

Why is the outlook so favorable for management analysts, particularly the ones with global experience and clients? It comes down to three main factors:

1. **The need for lean**
   You might think that consultants would be the first to go in tough economic times. While some companies do eliminate all consulting expenses, others see management analysts as the way to get work done after layoffs.

2. **Growth of electronic commerce and information technology**
   The complex nature of running a global business requires experts who understand the international inner workings of e-commerce and information technology. Management analysts with these specialties will continue to be in high demand.

3. **The desire to penetrate emerging markets**
   We all know China and India continue to open doors for new business ventures. Companies based in the United States that see opportunities in emerging markets need management analysts who understand the regulations and trade rules in foreign markets.

One of the main advantages of working as a management analyst is getting to know clients who might then wish to make you an in-house employee. This becomes an especially powerful recession-proof strategy if you consult for one of the industries covered in this book. For example, work as a management analyst in the health-care industry. If the travel becomes too much for you, the opportunity may arise to work directly for a health-care company. Now you're jumping from one recession-proof job to another. That's what I call a stable and sound career strategy.

# Market and Survey Researchers

The last thing a company wants to do is spend gobs of money to create products nobody wants. It's this desire to meet consumer demand that keeps market and survey researchers in business. Their job is to help companies understand the products and services people want and what price they're willing to pay.

## Outlook for Market and Survey Researchers

| | |
|---|---|
| Current Number of Employees | 261,000 |
| New Jobs Created by 2016 | 51,000 |
| Expected Job Growth by 2016 | 20% |
| Geographical Hotspots | Arkansas, Nevada |
| Average Annual Earnings | $42,000–$84,000 |

*Sources: U.S. Bureau of Labor Statistics National Employment Matrix, State Occupational Projections*

Typically, responsibilities for market and survey researchers include the following:

◆ Gather data on competitive product and service offerings to help clients find niches and market opportunities

◆ Analyze data on past sales to help companies predict future product and service performance

◆ Design surveys, focus groups, and other market research techniques to gather data from consumers

◆ Help clients make decisions on the best promotion, distribution, and pricing strategies for products

◆ Guide client thinking on creating product extensions to capitalize on the popularity of existing merchandise

This is a job that's all about getting inside the head of the consumer, understanding what consumers want or need, and then translating that information into product creation and extension recommendations for clients. The better the information gathered and communicated, the more you're helping the bottom line of your client.

What makes this profession so recession proof? Well, in good times, companies want to put their abundant development dollars into worthwhile ventures. In bad times, this desire increases because development dollars become scarce. Companies can't afford to make wrong decisions in product development and marketing. Valuable research information becomes critical to maintaining a competitive edge in tough times.

There's a slight distinction between survey researchers and market researchers, and it's worth mentioning. Survey researchers gather information about consumer opinions, but their work focuses exclusively on creating and conducting surveys. Market researchers also conduct all kinds of surveys, but their responsibilities carry over into driving marketing decisions at companies. Market researchers are expected to weigh in on the "four *P*s" of marketing: pricing, promotion, product, and placement.

Both market and survey researchers use a variety of techniques to gather consumer opinions. The most common include Internet surveys, phone interviews, focus groups, face-to-face interviews, door-to-door data gathering, and even setting up booths in public places (i.e., shopping malls) to conduct surveys.

### Another Path

The analytical and quantitative skills used by market and survey researchers can transfer to other recession-proof careers as well. These same skills will serve you well as an urban or regional planner, an actuary, or even a management analyst. It's comforting to know you can always reinvent yourself if one career stagnates.

Breaking into a career as a market or survey researcher typically requires a Bachelor's degree. Majors in economics, psychology, statistics, marketing, and computer science are particularly helpful in getting that first job. In the early years of your career, you'll spend time designing surveys and doing the behind-the-scenes work. After all, someone has to do the detailed work to come up with recommendations that are eventually passed along to clients.

If you want to advance to more senior positions, a Master's degree may or may not be necessary. Often, your work performance is enough to advance your career within one company. However, if you're more of a job hopper, prospective employers may seek advanced degrees to pick you over the interview competition. If you want to go for a particularly technical or scientific research area, you may even need a Ph.D. to open doors to the most senior positions.

You can also go the certification route. The Marketing Research Association (MRA) offers a professional certification program for those who want to clearly demonstrate their expertise. Earning your certification requires the right mix of educational achievement and work experience, as well as the commitment to continuing education throughout your career.

Academic credentials and work experience are not the only important criteria for success as a market and survey researcher. In general, three personality characteristics and skills will help you excel:

1. **Attention to detail**
   Surveys are all about compiling and analyzing information. If you can't keep responses straight, lose track of information, and easily get distracted, this is not the career for you.

2. **Patience and persistence**
   Trends, insights, and findings are not always easy to come by. You must have the determination and wherewithal to comb through mountains of data looking for that nugget of key information. This requires an ability to stay focused as you work toward discovering themes in consumer survey responses.

3. **Social skills**
   Conducting interviews involves mingling with consumers via phone, the Internet, and in person. You have to be able to build camaraderie with folks quickly to gain their approval for survey participation. Social skills are therefore a must if you're on the front lines of data gathering.

Where are you likely to find work as a market and survey researcher? Jobs abound in companies, government agencies, and academia. Companies need researchers primarily in the development of new products and services. The government hires researchers for opinion polls on candidate positions and policy issues. University researchers conduct all kinds of surveys to back up or disqualify educational theories.

Ultimately, your compensation is based on experience and the industry you choose to work in for your career. Average earnings of $42,000 to $84,000 are a wide range. The highest salaries tend to go to researchers working in computer systems design industries and large private companies.

Regardless of where you end up, it's nice to know that your ability to collect and analyze data is going to keep you employed for years to come.

## The Least You Need to Know

- If you can write or speak more than one language, consider a recession-proof career as a translator or interpreter.

- The continued globalization of economies ensures a stable place for management analysts with international expertise.

- Market and survey researchers help companies figure out what consumers want to buy, thereby improving the bottom line.

# The Best Careers by Growth Prospects and Salary

With more than 100 recession-proof careers covered in this book, it can be hard to determine the best of the best. I've tried to make it easier for you with this appendix.

Here are the top 12 recession-proof careers by anticipated job growth and by income potential. The data presented here are based on U.S. Department of Labor statistics.

## Top 12 Recession-Proof Careers by Growth Potential

| Career | Growth by 2016 |
|---|---|
| 1. Personal and home-care aide | 51% |
| 2. Personal financial advisor | 41% |
| 3. Computer software engineer | 38% |
| 4. Computer scientist and database administrator | 37% |
| 5. Substance abuse and behavioral disorder counselor | 34% |
| 6. Social and human services assistant | 34% |
| 7. Gaming surveillance officer | 34% |
| 8. Dental hygienist | 30% |
| 9. Computer systems analyst | 29% |
| 10. Gaming and sports book writers and runners | 28% |
| 11. Physician assistant | 27% |
| 12. Physical therapist | 27% |

## Top 12 Recession-Proof Careers by Highest Annual Income

| Career | Average Annual Income |
|---|---|
| 1. Computer and information systems manager | $79,000–$129,000 |
| 2. Actuary | $59,000–$115,000 |
| 3. Personal financial advisor | $44,000–$114,000 |
| 4. Pharmacist | $83,000–$108,000 |
| 5. Geoscientist | $52,000–$101,000 |
| 6. Computer software engineer | $63,000–$98,000 |
| 7. Medical and health services manager | $57,000–$95,000 |
| 8. Atmospheric scientist | $56,000–$94,000 |
| 9. Management analyst | $51,000–$92,000 |
| 10. Physician assistant | $62,000–$89,000 |
| 11. Computer systems analyst | $54,000–$88,000 |
| 12. Medical scientist | $45,000–$88,000 |

# Appendix B

# Recommended Reading

I hope you've enjoyed *The Complete Idiot's Guide to Recession-Proof Careers*. May it be the start of your personal journey to finding and building a great career. If you're looking for even more reading material on this subject and related topics, I recommend the books listed in this appendix.

Bolles, Richard. *What Color Is Your Parachute? 2009: A Practical Manual for Job-Hunters and Career-Changers*. Berkeley, CA: Ten Speed Press, 2009.

Enelow, Wendy. *101 Ways to Recession Proof Your Career*. New York: McGraw-Hill, 2002.

Farr, Michael. *100 Fastest-Growing Careers: Your Complete Guidebook to Major Jobs with the Most Growth and Openings*. Indianapolis: JIST Publishing, 2009.

Field, Shelly. *Managing Your Career in the Health Care Industry*. New York: Checkmark Books, 2008.

Freiberg, Drs. Kevin and Jackie. *Boom! 7 Choices for Blowing the Doors Off Business-as-Usual*. Nashville, TN: Thomas Nelson, Inc., 2007.

Kaye, Beverly, and Sharon Jordan-Evans. *Love It, Don't Leave It: 26 Ways to Get What You Want at Work*. San Francisco: Berrett-Koehler Publishers, Inc., 2003.

Kessinger, Roger. *Recession- and Depression-Proof Careers and Businesses*. Whitefish, MT: Kessinger Publishing Co, 1989.

Lore, Nicholas. *The Pathfinder: How to Choose or Change Your Career for a Lifetime of Satisfaction and Success.* New York: Fireside, 1998.

Morgenstern, Julie. *Never Check E-Mail in the Morning: And Other Unexpected Strategies for Making Your Work Life Work.* New York: Fireside, 2005.

Pearson, Richard. *5 Necessary Skills to Keep Your Career on Track.* Parker, CO: Outskirts Press, Inc., 2009.

Quast, Lisa. *Your Career, Your Way.* Bothell, WA: Wingspan Press, 2007.

Richardson, Cheryl. *Life Makeovers: 52 Practical & Inspiring Ways to Improve Your Life One Week at a Time.* New York: Broadway Books, 2000.

Shatkin, Laurence. *150 Best Recession-Proof Jobs.* Indianapolis: JIST Publishing, 2009.

Tracy, Brian. *Reinvention: How to Make the Rest of Your Life the Best of Your Life.* New York: AMACOM, 2009.

U.S. Department of Labor. *Occupational Outlook Handbook, 2008–2009.* Indianapolis: JIST Publishing, 2008.

Weissman, Roger J. *Recession Proof Your Career.* Raleigh, NC: Lulu.com, 2009.

Zichy, Shoya. *Career Match: Connecting Who You Are with What You'll Love to Do.* New York: AMACOM, 2007.

# Top Search Firms by Industry

Building a recession-proof career is hard to do alone. Sometimes help from a credible search firm or headhunter can open the right doors for you.

Here are some of the best firms in the business for each of the industries covered in this book.

## Multi-Industry Global Executive Search Firms

- DHR International: www.dhrinternational.com
- Heidrick & Struggles: www.heidrick.com
- Korn/Ferry International: www.kornferry.com
- Russell Reynolds Associates: www.russelreynolds.com
- Spencer Stuart: www.spencerstuart.com

## Health Care

- B. E. Smith: www.besmith.com
- Cejka Search: www.cejkasearch.com
- HealthCare Recruiters International: www.hcrnetwork.com

◆ HealthCare Resource Solutions: www.healthcaresearchexperts.com

◆ Kraft Search Associates: www.kraftsearch.com

◆ Tyler & Company: www.tylerandco.com

# Education

◆ Ayers & Associates, Inc.: www.ayersandassociatesinc.com

◆ Boyden Global Executive Search: www.boyden.com

◆ Carney, Sandoe and Associates: www.carneysandoe.com

◆ Gary Kaplan and Associates: www.gkasearch.com

◆ Greenwood/Asher & Associates, Inc.: www.greenwoodsearch.com

◆ Performance Executive Search: www.performancesearch.com

# Environment

◆ The Avery Group, Inc.: www.theaverygroupinc.com

◆ Environmental Recruiting Services: www.environmentalrecruiting.com

◆ Life Science Recruiters: www.lifesciencerecruiters.com

◆ Management Recruiters of Lynnwood: www.mri-lynnwood.com

◆ On Demand Environmental: www.ondemandenv.com

◆ Renewable Search Group: www.renewablesearchgroup.com

# Government and Defense

◆ Defense Recruiters, LLC: www.defenserecruiters.com

◆ DRG: www.drgnyc.com

- Security Recruitment LTD: www.securityrecruitment.net
- Staff Pointe Federal Recruitment: www.staffpointe.com/federal-recruiting-services.asp
- USA Jobs: www.usajobs.gov

# Business

- A.E. Feldman: www.aefeldman.com
- American Association of Finance and Accounting: www.aafa.com
- CD Warner & Associates: www.cdwarner.com
- DW Simpson: www.dwsimpson.com
- HR Search Firm: www.hrsearchfirm.com
- Reaction Search International: www.reactionsearch.com
- Three Pillars Recruiting: www.threepillarsrecruiting.net

# Sites, Fairs, and Organizations

The Internet is a wonderful resource for helping you achieve recession-proof status. From job sites to fairs to career organizations, everything you need to learn about the best careers around is right here.

## Top Overall Job Search Sites

- www.beyond.com
- www.careerbuilder.com
- www.collegerecruiter.com
- www.execu-search.com
- www.hotjobs.yahoo.com
- www.hound.com
- www.indeed.com
- www.jobcentral.com
- www.jobserve.us
- www.momcorps.com

- www.monster.com

- www.simplyhired.com

- www.snagajob.com

- www.theladders.com

- www.truecareers.com

- www.usajobs.com

# Top Job Fairs

- www.careerconferences.com: Lists job fairs for college graduates, work-at-home opportunities, and international jobs.

- www.carouselexpo.com: Lists upcoming job fairs by state on an interactive, clickable map.

- www.diversityjobfairs.com: Conducts job fairs for diverse candidates to connect them with employment opportunities.

- www.expoexpertsllc.com: Hosts job fairs across diverse fields including aerospace, defense, security, health care, and advanced technology.

- www.idealist.org: Holds career fairs for people interested in nonprofit career opportunities.

- www.nationalcareerfairs.com: Holds more than 300 career fairs annually in more than 75 U.S. cities covering multiple career industries.

- www.peoplenotpaper.com: Conducts job fairs for sales and management, as well as general professional executives.

- www.psijobfair.com: Holds job fairs for diverse employees in multiple locations around the country.

- www.taonline.com/militaryjobfairs: Hosts job fairs for members of the armed forces looking to transition to civilian careers.

- www.targetedjobfairs.com/tjf: Conducts nearly 100 job fairs each year in multiple industries across many U.S. cities.

- www.womenforhire.com/career_expos: Holds job fairs to connect experienced women as well as female college seniors with job opportunities.

# Top Career and Industry Organizations

Many of the descriptions for the organizations listed below are taken directly from the "about us" sections of their websites. Who better than the organizations themselves to describe their mission and purpose for existence?

## Health Care

### American Academy of Physician Assistants
www.aapa.org
Represents physician assistants in all medical and surgical specialties.

### American Association of Pharmaceutical Scientists
www.aapspharmaceutica.org
Provides a dynamic international forum for the exchange of knowledge among scientists to enhance their contributions to health.

### American Dental Hygienists' Association
www.adha.org
Advances the art and science of dental hygiene, and promotes the highest standards of education and practice in the profession.

### American Occupational Therapy Association
www.aota.org
Represents the interests and concerns of occupational therapy practitioners and students of occupational therapy and strives to improve the quality of occupational therapy services.

### American Pharmacists Association
www.aphanet.org
An organization focused on optimal medication use that improves health, wellness, and quality of life.

### American Physical Therapy Association
www.apta.org
Goal is to foster advancements in physical therapy practice, research, and education.

### Association of Surgical Technologists
www.ast.org
A national organization representing surgical technologists and surgical assistants across the country.

**National League for Nursing**

www.nln.org

The preferred membership organization for nurse faculty and leaders in nursing education.

# Education

### Association for Career and Technical Education

www.acteonline.org

The largest national education association dedicated to the advancement of education that prepares youth and adults for careers.

### Council for Exceptional Children

www.cec.sped.org

The largest international professional organization dedicated to improving the educational success of individuals with disabilities and/or gifts and talents.

### Council of Graduate Schools

www.preparing-faculty.org

Provides opportunities to observe and experience faculty responsibilities at a variety of academic institutions.

### National Association for the Education of Young Children

www.naeyc.org

Dedicated to improving the well-being of all young children, with particular focus on the quality of educational and developmental services for all children from birth through age 8.

### National Council for Accreditation of Teacher Education

www.ncate.org

Works to improve the quality of teaching and teaching profession around the country.

### National Resource Center for Paraprofessionals

www.nrcpara.org

Serves teachers; policymakers and administrators; other education professionals; occupational, physical, and speech-language therapists; early childhood specialists; and personnel developers in colleges and universities.

# Environment

### American Academy of Environmental Engineers
www.aaee.net
Ensures public health, safety, and welfare to enable humankind to co-exist in harmony with nature.

### American Society of Agricultural and Biological Engineers
www.asabe.org
An educational and scientific organization dedicated to the advancement of engineering applicable to agricultural, food, and biological systems.

### American Solar Energy Society
www.ases.org
The nation's leading association of solar professionals and grassroots advocates.

### American Wind Energy Association
www.awea.org
Promotes wind power growth through advocacy, communication, and education.

### Environmental Protection Agency
www.epa.gov
Oversees environmental issues including water, air, climate, wastes, pollution, green living, human health, and ecosystems.

### Environmental Working Group
www.ewg.org
Works to protect children and kids from toxic chemicals in our food, water, air, and the products we use every day.

### National Science Foundation
www.nsf.gov
An independent government agency responsible for promoting science and engineering through research programs and education projects.

### U.S. Department of Energy
www.energy.gov
Governmental department whose mission is to advance energy technology and promote related innovation in the United States.

# Government and Defense

### American Arbitration Association

www.adr.org

Provides dispute resolution services worldwide.

### American Bar Association

www.abanet.org

Serves members, the profession, and the public as the national representative of the legal profession.

### American Correctional Association

www.aca.org

The authority in corrections providing training, certification, and networking for the industry.

### American Society for Industrial Security International

www.asisonline.org

Helps to increase the effectiveness and productivity of security professionals by developing educational programs and materials that address broad security interests.

### Armed Forces Careers

www.armedforcescareers.com

Explains the career prospects, nature of the job, and current openings among the Armed Forces: Army, Navy, Marine Corps, Air Force, and Coast Guard.

### Department of Homeland Security

www.dhs.gov

Leads the nationwide effort to protect U.S. borders from terrorist attacks and natural disasters.

### National Association of Legal Investigators

www.nalionline.org

Conducts investigations related to litigation.

### The White House

www.whitehouse.gov

U.S. government-sponsored site highlighting the departments and agencies that make up the federal government.

# Business

### American Institute of Certified Public Accountants

www.aicpa.org

Provides educational tools and networking opportunities for members of the accounting profession.

### Association for Computing Machinery

www.acm.org

The world's largest educational and scientific computing society that delivers resources that advance computing as a science and a profession.

### National Association of Schools of Art and Design

http://nasad.arts-accredit.org

An organization of schools, colleges, and universities with nearly 300 accredited institutions.

### National Institute for Automotive Service Excellence

www.ase.com

Official certification organization for the automotive industry.

### National Workforce Center for Emerging Technologies

www.nwcet.org

Provides state and national leadership to create innovative IT and IT-related educational programs through research, professional development, business partnerships, and curriculum development to meet the needs of the twenty-first-century workforce.

### Professional Landscape Network

www.landcarenetwork.org

An international association serving lawn care professionals, landscape management contractors, design/build/installation professionals, and interior plantscapers.

### Public Relations Society of America

www.prsa.org

The world's largest organization for public relations specialists.

### Society for Human Resource Management

www.shrm.org

The world's largest organization devoted to human resources management and development.

## Society of Actuaries

www.soa.org

Provides education and research to help actuaries in the measurement and management of risk.

## The League of Professional System Administrators

www.lopsa.org

Advances the practice of system administration and supports, recognizes, educates, and encourages its practitioners while serving the public through education and outreach on system administration issues.

# Index

## S

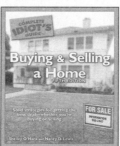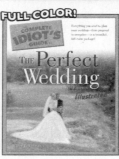

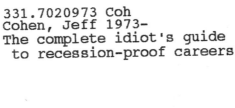

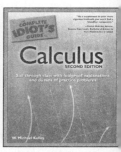